TUDOR ENGLAND OBSERVED

THE WORLD OF JOHN STOW

BARRETT L. BEER

SUTTON PUBLISHING

First published in the United Kingdom in 1998 by
Sutton Publishing Limited · Phoenix Mill
Thrupp · Stroud · Gloucestershire · GL5 2BU

British Library Cataloguing in Publication Data
A catalogue record for this book is available from the British Library

ISBN 0 7509 1943 4

 ™ ALAN SUTTON™ and SUTTON™ are the
trade marks of Sutton Publishing Limited

Typeset in 11/14pt Bembo
Typesetting and origination by
Sutton Publishing Limited
Printed in Great Britain by
WBC Limited, Bridgend.

CONTENTS

Memorial to John Stow, St Andrew's Church, City of London.

PREFACE

The discovery that the legends of iniquity surrounding John Dudley, Duke of Northumberland, originated with sixteenth-century historical writers first aroused my interest in early modern chroniclers. Similarly the marginalization of the mid-Tudor rebellions was initially the work of contemporary scholars committed to the ruling dynasty and a regime of law and order. The comments of G.R. Elton that modern editions of sixteenth-century chronicles were lacking and that we need to know more about the sources and materials used by these early historians also encouraged me to take a closer look at Tudor chronicles.[1] While John Stow is well known for *A Survey of London*, characterizations of him as an unlearned antiquarian and careless references to his chronicles based on the erroneous assumption that each edition told the same story convinced me that the most prolific of Elizabethan historians needed careful study and reassessment. In pursuing this task, the enduring scholarship of Charles L. Kingsford, who not only edited *A Survey of London* but provided a framework for further study of Stow, has been of great value.

I am pleased to acknowledge receipt of a semester research grant and a sabbatical leave from Kent State University that allowed me to work in England. I was also able to find time for Stow while preparing an edition of Sir John Hayward's *Life and Raigne of King Edward the Sixth* at the Newberry Library in Chicago. In 1997 the Folger Shakespeare Library in Washington, DC generously awarded a fellowship that helped me prepare the manuscript for publication. Over the years librarians and staff at the British Library, the Public Record Office and the Corporation of London Records Office have been very generous with their time.

Earlier versions of Chapters Three and Four were published as 'John Stow and Tudor Rebellions, 1549–1569', in *Journal of British Studies* 27: 4 (1988) and 'John Stow and the English Reformation, 1547–1559', in *Sixteenth Century Journal* 16: 2 (1985). Daniel Woolf, Roger Manning and Jerome Friedman were kind enough to read drafts of individual chapters and portions of chapters while conversations with Patrick Collinson, Charles Meyers and John Pocock proved helpful. Andrea Manchester convinced me that Stow should not be rehabilitated at the expense of Richard Grafton, and Sidney Reid supported my work at the Institute for Bibliography and Editing. My greatest debt is to my wife, Jill Parker Beer, who has assisted me in too many ways to enumerate.

BARRETT L. BEER
February 1998

1. G.R. Elton, *England 1200–1600* (London, 1969), 27.

LIST OF ILLUSTRATIONS

The author and publisher wish to thank the following for permission to reproduce illustrations:

Bodleian Library, 95 (GA Oxon. a. 73, p. 2, number 5), 131 (Gough Middl. 5, 2nd map), 138 (from Douce Prints a. 53); by permission of the British Library, 26, 27, 35, 37, 38, 44, 46, 48, 58, 87 (C18d.2), 116, 134, 145, 146, 156 (Geoffrey Drury), 157; © The British Museum, 71; by permission of the Syndics of Cambridge University Library, 98; Royal Albert Memorial Museum and Art Gallery, Exeter, 62; Folger Shakespeare Library: 19, 24, 30, 31, 32, 80, 105, 139; Guildhall Library, Corporation of London, 141; Hulton Getty, 41; Mansell Collection, 89, 148, 151; National Maritime Museum, London, 158; National Monuments Record: frontispiece; by courtesy of The National Portrait Gallery, London, 66, 78, 91, 107, 110, 111, 113, 115, 117, 123; New York Public Library, 79 (Rare Books Room), 161; Norwich Castle Museum, Norfolk Museums Service, 64.

CHAPTER ONE

CITIZEN AND HISTORIAN

'A citizen born of citizens of London,' John Strype

1. LIFE OF A LONDON CITIZEN

Born in 1525, John Stow was a product of Tudor London and, according to John Strype, a family 'of good substance and credit'. The Stow family was drawn from the ranks of the solid citizenry and had no ties to the commercial or governing elite of the city. His grandfather, Thomas, a prosperous tallow-chandler, died in 1527 leaving household goods worth £20 and plate valued at over £6. Thomas' son and namesake (d. 1559) followed the same trade. The younger Thomas and his wife, Elizabeth, had a large family of seven children of whom the historian was the eldest. Of John Stow's early life and education little is known, although he recalled a few experiences from his childhood in *A Survey of London*. He remembered living near Henry VIII's minister, Thomas Cromwell, who encroached on his father's garden but fed as many as two hundred hungry men and women in a single day. His youthful memories also included buying milk from a farmer's son, who later assumed the style of a gentleman, and a lusty chantry priest who was banished for his sexual indiscretions.[1]

There is no evidence that Stow attended a grammar school or indeed any educational institution, but he always spoke with respect and deference when writing of those who had the benefits of formal education. His education is clearly revealed in his writings and by his lifelong devotion to scholarship. Stow wrote English with fluency and clarity, had a good command of Latin, possessed an extraordinary knowledge of English history and literature, and became an enthusiastic collector of books and manuscripts. Stow's career must stand as a tribute to individual initiative and the education that might be obtained informally or in schools of little or no distinction.[2]

Unlike his father and grandfather, John Stow did not become a tallow-chandler but was apprenticed as a merchant tailor. While he was admitted to the freedom of the Merchant Taylors' Company in 1547, he remained for nearly thirty years a member of the subordinate Bachelors or Yeoman Company and was never admitted to the Livery or to any important office in the company. By 1549 he established himself in business at a house by the well within Aldgate between Leadenhall and Fenchurch Street. Business was good enough for him to take a younger brother, Thomas, as an apprentice. C.L. Kingsford determined that John married his wife, Elizabeth (who survived him according to the will), soon after establishing himself in business and noted that he had three marriageable daughters by about 1569.[3] In the 1570s he moved to a house in St Andrew's parish in Lime Street Ward where he lived for the rest of his life.

The quality of family life is always difficult to determine from written evidence inasmuch as intimate relationships are rarely expressed in written form. A few chance survivals such as personal letters or a documented legal controversy may offer valuable insights, but ones which are atypical of broader social relationships. Stow kept no personal journal or diary, and if he wrote letters to his wife and children, they have not survived. His will, unlike the will of Sir John Hayward, reveals no animosity towards his wife.[4] On the basis of a single undated letter from his married daughter, Joan, there is evidence of a good father/daughter relationship. Joan, who was living with her husband in Warwick, asked her father to obtain information about the foundation of a local hospital for a friend. The query shows very clearly that she understood her father's work; indeed, the tone of the letter tempts one to infer that Joan had more than a passing acquaintance with antiquarianism herself. 'It is supposed,' she said, 'that you shall find the foundation hereof in the Tower of London; therefore good father . . . I pray you take some pains therein.' Although Stow's reply has not survived, he made notes at the bottom of his daughter's letter with details of the hospital's founding and dissolution. It is not improbable that Stow actually sent the information requested by his daughter and that the correspondence typified family life at its best.[5]

A long and bitter quarrel between Stow and his younger brother, Thomas, offers a very different insight into early modern family life. A detailed but damaged manuscript has survived describing a feud over their mother's will.[6] In this account Stow relates that he feasted his mother with a cold leg of mutton, butter, and cheese as he persuaded her to recognize him as her principal heir. Later, when she returned to her home with his brother, Mrs Stow revealed that John had said that his brother was married to a harlot. Thomas, outraged at his brother's slanderous accusations, persuaded his mother to alter her will to give him the largest share of her estate. But Stow insisted that he had spoken the absolute truth and spoken it only to his mother:

> Thus was I condemned . . . for naming Thomas his wife a harlot, privily only to one body (who knew the same as well as I); but, if he could punish all men that will more openly say so much, he would soon be richer than any lord mayor of London.

Stow went on to say that his brother had himself denounced his wife as a whore, named a good number of her customers, and threw her out of his house. When she managed to return by climbing through a window, Thomas beat her and threw her into the street. Neighbours urged him to take her back, but Thomas replied that she would rob him to keep her bastard children and kill him with witchcraft and sorcery as she had her other husbands. The desperate woman returned yet again, and at ten o'clock one evening Thomas 'being bare legged, searched and found her "cropte" in the jakes [privy] entry and then fell again a beating her'.

Hearing the altercation from the upper floor where she lay sick on a pallet, the mother awakened, 'felt about the chamber for Thomas his hose and shoes, and crept down the stairs with them as well as she could, and prayed him to put them on lest he should catch cold'. She stood in her smock for more than an hour entreating her son to be more quiet. Then the unexpected happened: according to Stow's narrative, his brother and his wife 'went to bed and agreed well enough'. Subsequently, the mother 'drew near' her daughter-in-law and persuaded her to receive the Holy Communion with her husband.

At this point in his tale Stow got to the heart of the matter – the inheritance of his mother's estate. As the story unfolds, the clergy played a surprisingly large and positive role in attempting to resolve the family crisis. Stow says that the new minister of the parish asked to see his mother's will, and finding that he, the eldest son, was to receive only £5, the other children £10 each, except for Thomas, who was willed 'all her goods and houses' and named executor of the estate, asked the reason for the unusual arrangement. According to Stow, Thomas forced their mother to say that the historian was very rich and didn't need her goods.

She complained that her elder son had not visited her during six years of illness and had not asked her blessing in twenty years. It was alleged that he said

wherefore should I care for her, she had done nothing for me but only brought me into the world and for the pain she had at my birth she had pleasure at my begetting.[7]

Thomas, on the other hand, was a model son, who had kept her at great cost to himself and prevented her from starving. The minister doubted this incredible (and in Stow's view untrue) story and asked to see the younger brother. When Thomas and his wife refused, the minister denied them Communion.

New faces appeared as the controversy continued. Stow's brother-in-law, Master Rolfe, who was also a priest, tried to persuade his mother-in-law 'to set things in a better order'. Mrs Stow replied that she would have 'a life ten times worse than death' if either Thomas or his wife heard them speaking of the will, for 'I can nor do what I would, but as they will'. Rolfe told Stow that his mother wished to receive Holy

Communion after the meeting and sent for her daughter (Rolfe's wife) to join with her. Stow now sent his wife – with a pot of cream and strawberries – to visit his mother, but Thomas abused her, accusing her of witchcraft and Stow of conjuring. 'Get thee out of my doors,' he shouted at Stow's wife, 'or by Peter I will lay thee at my feet.' When Stow heard what had happened, he went to his mother's parish church to enlist the support of her minister.

Because of a break in the manuscript, the next stage of the controversy is unknown, but when the narrative resumes Stow and his brother have made their peace and are once again on good terms. Stow visited his mother and tried to persuade her to bequeath him an additional £5 so that his share would equal that of his brothers and sisters. He offered several ingenious arguments, including a text from Psalm 133: 'Behold how pleasant and how joyful a thing it is for brethren to dwell together and to be of one mind. . . .'[8] When a friend from outside the family attempted to argue on Stow's behalf, the brothers quarrelled again. But after Elizabeth Stow died a few months later, the brothers were not only reconciled but went to an inn where they 'drank a pint of wine or twayne'.

The strength of Thomas' claim to the larger share of the estate seems to have rested on his and his wife's devotion to the old woman, who was not only sick but incontinent. There is no evidence that John offered to care for his mother in his own house or contribute to her keep; his argument was based essentially on his status as the eldest son and his brother's manipulation and intimidation of their mother. Although the story ends abruptly, the will, proved 13 October 1568, indicates that John never received what he regarded as a fair share of her estate.[9] Frequent references in the chronicles to this unhappy quarrel leave no doubt that Stow never forgave his brother and carried a grudge against him for many years.[10]

If the controversy over his mother's will reveals a man with family problems, another episode at about the same time suggests that Stow also had difficulties with his neighbours. Around Christmas one year, after the Wardmote had forbidden William Ditcher to set a frame with 'fetharbends' [sic MS] in the street, he became incensed and accused Stow of making a complaint against him. Stow denied the allegation, but Ditcher and his wife 'railed at him, first as he passed by them, and after[wards] at his own door too shameful and slanderous to be spoken and heard'. When the Wardmote 'inquest had given up their indenture', Ditcher arrested Stow of a 'two hundred pound action' to which he had to put in sureties to answer.

The next morning the Ditchers came to Stow's stall and denounced him for 'a long hour'. According to Stow, he remained inside his house above the stall and carefully avoided a breach of the peace. Three days later Ditcher sent his landlord to Stow asking for forgiveness and permission to withdraw the legal action. Stow agreed to do so if Ditcher would pay the legal costs and admit that he had been procured by Stow's brother, Thomas, to initiate the feud.

Unfortunately, however, the matter was not so easily settled because William Ditcher completely denied asking his landlord to act as an honest broker and went on to commit new offences against Stow. Ditcher bragged that he would carry out 'such notable acts of displeasure' against Stow as 'the like hath never been done to any man and that all England shall speak of it'. To this end Ditcher informed a clergyman that only rogues and rascals who had been from alehouse to alehouse every night until two o'clock in the morning came to Stow's house. Ditcher slandered Stow's wife and three marriageable daughters by alleging that she had two illegitimate children before she was married. He also engaged in crude name-calling and denounced Stow as a 'prike louse', a common drunkard, and a lying knave who made a chronicle of lies.

The controversy with Ditcher was more than a war of words, because Stow's adversary

> one time suddenly leapt in his face, forced to have digged out his eyes, foully 'scrate' him by the face, drew blood on him, and was pulled off by the neighbours.

At the very moment that the feud turned violent, Stow's account ends, leaving the reader with more questions than answers. Without William Ditcher's side of the story we must trust Stow's reputation for historical accuracy although the controversy was anything but a debate over historical issues.[11]

William Ditcher was not the only neighbour with whom Stow quarrelled; in 1576 a seemingly trivial incident led to a summons to appear before the Court of Requests. Stow wrote:

> Somewhat before Christmas, Mister Crowche sent unto me a bill containing parcels to the sum of 5s 1d, 5s whereof I paid to Johan his maid on Christmas eve next following, and said I would be his debtor of the odd penny. Whereunto she answered and said, 'I pray you to be our debtor of goodwill and be not angry that I sent so small a sum, for otherwise you are even with my master and owe him nothing.'

Six months later Stow received another bill for 5s 1d, and when he asked the maid for an explanation, she said, 'Alas, Master Stow, you must make small account of my master's doings now, for his head is "intoxicate;" he has married a wife for riches, but he had done better to have married a poor wench.'

Later, when the two met face to face, Crowche insisted that he had no record of the payment in his account book and would charge Stow in the 'court of conscience'

[Court of Requests]. More time passed, but eventually Stow noted that 'I was warned to the courts, which I take to be no good dealing towards me.'[12]

Although a freeman of the city of London, Stow never served in the Common Council or the Court of Aldermen. He undoubtedly spent the bulk of his time collecting records and writing history but none the less served London in several capacities. In the 1570s he produced documents that were needed to resolve a dispute over ward boundaries and in 1584–5 he was apparently employed as a surveyor of alehouses. The latter year he was also appointed one of two collectors of the assessment in Lime Street Ward for a muster of 4,000 men to enter military service. These duties took Stow away from his books and gave him practical experience in local government.[13]

As a layman who held no important civic offices, Stow was not required to take a formal position on the religious changes that occurred during his lifetime, but he faced accusations of sympathizing with Roman Catholicism.[14] According to John Strype (1643–1737), a clerical apologist for the Church of England, Stow was popish during his early years and 'no great friend to the Reformation of religion'. Subsequently, historians have agreed with Strype that Stow either fell short of total commitment to the Protestant religion or was devoted to the 'old faith'.[15] That Stow was born before the Reformation is undeniable, and it is also quite likely that a full acceptance of Protestantism for him like most lay people came only after the accession of Queen Elizabeth.[16] Strype was probably less concerned about Stow's youthful religious orientation than his lack of zeal in defending the Church of England against its enemies. But neither Strype nor C.L. Kingsford was completely convinced that the charges of popery were true.[17]

Accusations against Stow's religious conformity date from 1569 when the Privy Council directed Edmund Grindal, Bishop of London, to have Stow's house searched for unlawful books. Among thirty-eight objectionable titles were an English translation (by Thomas Stapleton) of Bede, a manuscript of *Flores Historiarum*, a text that Archbishop Parker had published in 1567, and 'A Summary of the Chronicles, corrected by him'.[18] The list also included a number of Roman Catholic devotional works. Kingsford thought the devotional titles 'lent some colour to the charge of popish inclinations', but Sir William Cecil and the Council thought otherwise, and no action against Stow resulted.[19] As a historian and a collector of books and manuscripts, Stow undoubtedly used materials containing views with which he did not agree, and it is reassuring to find the queen's government rejecting the kind of argument that would hold that a person who owned a biography of Hitler was a Nazi sympathizer.

In 1570 Stow was brought before the Ecclesiastical Commissioners on serious charges contained in seventeen articles. A former servant who had allegedly defrauded Stow of goods turned government informer and sought, according to John Strype, to

A sixteenth-century engraving of Edmund Grindal, Archbishop of Canterbury from 1575 to 1583.

deprive him of his life. Moreover, witnesses procured to testify against him included perjurers and men burned in the hand for felony, but Stow successfully confounded his accusers before Archbishop Parker. Later, when he tried to prosecute the false accusers himself, he was told that there was no remedy against them. In his chronicles Stow blamed his brother for making these false charges against him.[20]

Against insubstantial charges of Roman Catholicism are impressive Protestant credentials. There are many examples of a Protestant piety in Stow's writings, such as the citation of psalms and other texts that demonstrate his familiarity with the English Bible. An examination of Stow's works – both published and manuscript – reveals no serious interest in the cult of saints or the sacrificial mass. While it is true that he never wrote as a defender of the Protestant faith, his approach to religion can be best

Portrait of John Stow, published by The Gentleman's Magazine *in 1837.*

described as conventional and conformist.[21] Stow's associations with prominent Protestants further support his conformity. Early in his career Stow received the patronage of Robert Dudley, Earl of Leicester, who persuaded him to begin his historical studies, and Matthew Parker, Archbishop of Canterbury.[22] He also praised both Grindal and his successor, John Whitgift, for their charity and good lordship in his chronicles and dedicated the *Annales of England* to the latter.

Neither *A Survey of London* nor the *Annales of England* could have been written by a Catholic, and the great success of these works indicates that Stow's readers were satisfied with his loyalty to the queen and her Church. His rival, Richard Grafton, a staunch Protestant, who would have benefited from Stow's disgrace, made many scurrilous charges but never accused him of popery.[23] Moreover, what is known of his family life suggests active participation in the parish life of the Church of England, and no evidence of Catholic sympathies can be found in the will that he signed in 1603 when he was seventy-eight years of age.[24]

2. FRIENDS, PATRONS, AND RICHARD GRAFTON

Although Stow encountered problems with his family and neighbours, he was a man with many devoted friends including university scholars, antiquarians, and persons of great influence. It is likely that friends intervened on his behalf when his house was searched for unlawful books. Records of the Merchant Taylors suggest that friends in the company assisted Stow when he was examined in February 1569 by the mayor, master, and wardens of the company for possession of an English translation of a Spanish manifesto against the queen's proclamation against the seizure of Spanish treasure in the straits of Dover. Stow admitted possessing the Spanish document and reading it to several persons, and others testified that they had read it, but no one challenged Stow's assertion that he had never given out a copy of the offensive document.[25]

Stow's friends and correspondents included the most famous men of learning in Elizabethan England. He enjoyed a long relationship with John Dee, the Elizabethan magus. Dee's biographer dates their association from at least 1574 and notes that they shared books and manuscripts.[26] Dee sent Stow information about the town of Dunwich and a list of burgesses who had represented the Cinque Ports. Dee also informed Stow that Sir Edward Dyer had delivered his books, probably the 1592 edition of the *Annales*, to two unnamed earls. Both Stow and Dee had close ties with William Camden, who asked Stow to lend him manuscripts concerning the foundation of abbeys in Lincolnshire, Warwickshire, and several other counties.[27] Included among Stow's manuscripts is a copy of Camden's translation of a text on the English conquest of Ireland,[28] while the

Survey of London generously acknowledged the contributions of Stow's 'loving friend', Camden.[29]

Stow praised William Lambarde, author of the *Perambulation of Kent*, for the 'sundry learned books that he hath published'.[30] It has been suggested that William Fleetwood, the recorder of London from 1571 to 1592, had access to Stow's manuscript of Leland's *Itinerary*. He kept a picture of Stow in his study and permitted him to use Guildhall muniments while he was recorder.[31] On a lighter note, Ben Jonson recalled an occasion when Stow and he were walking alone in London. As they passed two cripples begging in the street, Stow, who always exaggerated his poverty, asked them whether they would have him in their order.[32]

Stow maintained a correspondence with William Claxton (d. 1597) that lasted from 1582 until 1594. A Northerner, Claxton knew Camden and Lord William Howard and collected materials for a history of the bishopric of Durham, but according to May McKisack none of his work has survived.[33] His letters suggest that he lent books to Stow and encountered some difficulty in getting them returned. In April 1582 he sent his nephew to Stow's house to retrieve a book. After a visit to London in 1594, he asked for the return of three books that he had left in Stow's study, one of which dealt with Pepin, king of the Franks.[34] The latter volume reveals the broad scope of Stow's scholarly interests. Claxton also sent Stow notes on the bishopric of Durham and promised to send a parchment life of Edward the Confessor. The correspondence with Claxton also indicates that Stow was a lender of books as well as a borrower. Claxton was wholly devoted to Stow and assured him that as long as he lived 'you shall not want a friend to the uttermost of my power'. On one occasion Claxton sent Stow an English crown for a remembrance; later he assured Stow that his published work would bring him 'never dying fame'.[35]

Henry Savile (1549–1622), Warden of Merton, Oxford, a collector of medieval manuscripts, was a friend who relied on Stow's knowledge of the London book trade.[36] Writing from Halifax in May 1592, Savile remarked that he had made all of his acquaintances in London, including that of Robert Hare through Stow. He wanted to know about the work of Hare, who was collecting materials on the privileges of Oxford University, but the main point of the letter was to ask Stow about obtaining copies of the first edition of the *Annales of England* and Lord William Howard's edition of Florence of Worcester. Savile also wanted to know whether Howard intended to print the chronicles of Roger Howden, Henry of Huntingdon, and William of Malmesbury. Savile had a personal interest in the works because his own edition of these chroniclers was published in 1596. Stow replied to Savile within nine days of his writing; the delivery of the letter from Yorkshire to London was achieved through a courier who was instructed to wait for Stow's reply.[37]

After receiving the letter, Savile returned to Oxford where he again wrote to Stow making further enquiries about books. Savile complained that a book that Robert Hare was sending had not arrived and asked Stow

to go unto the good gentleman Mr. Hare in my name and request him to let me understand by whom and about what time he sent the book.

Savile also asked for information about printers and asked Stow to tell him who had printed the *Annales of England* and Florence of Worcester. To compensate Stow for his efforts Savile concluded, 'I have here sent you a mild sixpence to drink a quart of wine in your travail.'[38]

The theme of shared books and manuscripts occurs over and over again in Stow's correspondence. Lacking public archives and research libraries, scholars depended on personal networks of friends and acquaintances. Stow was unquestionably a pivotal figure in maintaining contacts between widely separated men of learning. In 1577 he lent Robert Glover, Somerset herald, a copy of *Marianus Scotus*, which was 'one of the best books' he had handled in a 'great while'.[39] Henry Ferrers, a Warwickshire antiquarian said to have Roman Catholic inclinations, apologized for his late return of a book and several pamphlets and asked Stow to lend him 'your Bede and your pedigree of kings', while Thomas Hatcher, fellow of King's College, Cambridge, returned a copy of 'John Blakeman's treatise of Henry VI' and encouraged Stow to publish whatever he had of Leland. He also asked Stow to speak to William Camden about publishing a book in Latin verse. In March 1586 the poet and physician Thomas Newton, writing from Little Ilford, Essex, where he was rector of the church, returned Stow's 'book of Mr Leland his poetries' and thanked him for courtesies and 'friendly amities many times showed unto me'.

One correspondent, Thomas Martyn, a civil lawyer and fellow of New College, Oxford, was bold enough to criticize Stow's treatment of Alice Perrers, mistress of Edward III, in the *Annales of England*. 'That tale of Alice Perrers is slanderous,' he wrote, 'and in my conscience most untrue.' Martyn's criticism was intended to be professional, not personal because he sent with his son, the bearer of the letter, 'a token to have me in remembrance' and asked his 'most assured friend' to arrange the delivery of a letter to another party.[40] With the exception of Martyn, Stow's friends lavished praise on him and encouraged him to publish his work as soon as possible. Working on his own, Stow undoubtedly needed the support of friends, and he seems always to have made himself useful to those who might benefit from his connections in London. Friends reciprocated by providing Stow with information that enlarged the scope of his chronicles. Henry Archer, described as a cousin, sent military news from the Netherlands,[41] Henry Docwra reported to Stow from Ireland, while William Segar provided details of the English embassy to Denmark in 1603.

Stow's literary executor and continuator of the *Annales*, Edmund Howes, knew him at the end of his life and wrote the following eloquent tribute:

He was tall of stature, lean of body and face, his eyes small and crystalline, of a pleasant and cheerful countenance; his sight and memory very good; very sober, mild, and courteous to any that required his instructions; and retained the true use of all his senses unto the day of his death, being of an excellent memory. He always protested never to have written anything either for malice, fear, or favour, nor to seek his own particular gain or vain-glory; and that his only pains and care was to write *truth*. He could never ride, but travelled on foot unto divers cathedral churches, and other chief places of the land to search records. . . . He was very careless of scoffers, back-biters, and detractors. He lived peacefully, and died of the stone colic, being four-score years of age.[42]

Another friend, Anthony Munday (1553–1633), poet and playwright, praised Stow, but unlike Howes found him 'weak and sickly' towards the end of his life.[43]

Stow's first patron was Robert Dudley, Earl of Leicester, who also patronized his rival, Richard Grafton. According to Stow, Leicester persuaded him to begin his historical studies after he gave Leicester a copy of the *Tree of Commonwealth*, written by his grandfather, Edmund Dudley.[44] In 1565 Stow dedicated the first edition of the *Summarie of Englyshe Chronicles* to Leicester. The dedication was a model of deference and humility that praised Leicester's 'good inclination to all sorts of good knowledges and especially the great love you bear to the old records of deeds done by famous and noble worthies. . . .' Two years later Stow dedicated the *Summarie Abridged* (1567) to the mayor of London rather than Leicester because of the controversy with Grafton, but later editions including the larger *Chronicles of England* (1580) were again dedicated to Leicester. While Stow certainly benefited from the use of Leicester's illustrious name, it is less clear whether Stow gained materially from Leicester's patronage although Eleanor Rosenberg concluded that Stow probably received some support.[45]

Stow never dedicated any of his books to Matthew Parker, the first Elizabethan archbishop of Canterbury, but the two scholars shared a strong commitment to preserving medieval manuscripts. Stow supplied manuscripts to Parker and assisted him in editing *Flores Historiarum* (1567), Matthew Paris (1571), and Walsingham (1574).[46] Stow thought of Parker as his 'especial benefactor', and it is likely that Parker protected him when he was accused of possessing popish books. Long after the archbishop's death, Stow recalled that he had encouraged him to publish his 'far larger volume' of history.[47] Parker and Leicester were both dead when Stow dedicated the first edition of *Annales of England* (1592) to another archbishop of Canterbury, John Whitgift. Here Stow reminded Whitgift of his many years of devotion to 'the study of histories and search of antiquities' and sought help in securing publication of his ill-fated larger historical work.[48]

Toward the end of his life Stow looked increasingly to the city of London for patronage. The last edition of the octavo *Summarie of the Chronicles* (1590) was dedicated to John Hart, lord mayor, the warden and assistants of the Merchant Taylors, and 'all the commons', while Stow's last revision of the shorter *Summarie Abridged* (1604) was dedicated to another mayor, Sir Thomas Bennet. Robert Lee, merchant tailor and lord mayor of London, the commonalty, and citizens received the dedication of *A Survey of London* (1603).[49] As early as 1579 the Merchant Taylors paid Stow an annuity of £4. From 1592 to 1605 Stow was a pensioner of the company receiving £4 annually, a sum personally underwritten by Robert Dowe, one of the masters, until 1600. After the company increased the pension to £6 annually in 1600, Stow's income reached a total of £10 per year. When Stow died, the two pensions were paid to Edmund Howes who published extended editions of the chronicles.[50]

While Stow enjoyed the support of friends and patrons, a bitter controversy with Richard Grafton reveals something of the darker side of his personality as he struggled to establish himself as a chronicler. Publisher of the English Bible under Henry VIII, printer to Edward VI, and a member of Parliament for London during the reign of Mary, Grafton towered over Stow at the accession of Elizabeth. Grafton printed a revised and enlarged edition of the chronicle of John Hardyng as early as 1543 and in 1563 produced a chronicle based on Thomas Lanquet to compete with previous editions of Robert Crowley and Thomas Cooper. Controversy between Crowley and Cooper created an opportunity for Stow to publish the first edition of the *Summarie* in 1565, a venture that led directly to conflict with Grafton that ended only with the latter's death in 1573.

To secure his share of the market Stow had to overcome Grafton's established position with the Protestant establishment in London. This he did with passion as he denounced Grafton as a mere plagiarist who was incapable of making accurate copies of the work he used. Grafton's scholarship proved an easy target, but despite Stow's harsh charges, both men borrowed from Cooper and other chroniclers. Stow's attack on Grafton was similar to behaviour in conflicts with his brother and neighbours. He was petulant, self-righteous, and boastful about his devotion to accuracy and historical truth and exaggerated the failings of his adversary. Stow's behaviour may be interpreted as evidence of paranoia or alternatively nothing more than fighting words from an underdog trying to make good in a competitive publishing world. While no one has yet defended the reputation of the hapless Grafton, Stow always showed his worst qualities when proclaiming his personal integrity.[51]

3. VISION OF THE PAST

Stow loved the past, and his historical vision extended to virtually everything that was old. In dedicating the *Annales of England* to Archbishop Whitgift, he explained that it had been more than thirty years since 'I first addressed all my cares and cogitations to the study of Histories and search of Antiquities. . . .'[52] It is likely that Stow's difficulties with religious authorities resulted from his passion for the past. The past – or the pre-Reformation past – was Roman Catholic, and it was easy for contemporaries to confuse his antiquarianism with popery. But Stow's vision of the past was broadly based as he was a lover of all kinds of artefacts, including manuscripts, books, monuments, and buildings. When writing of his own times, Stow grieved at the destructive aspects of the Reformation and the impact of population expansion on the citizens of London. Like other contemporary antiquarians, Stow thought that life in the past was better than the present, views that by the end of the sixteenth century reflected more realism and historical consciousness than romantic escapism. He was always loyal to the Tudor regime but cannot be counted as an apologist for the dynasty, the government, or the state church.[53]

Unfortunately, Stow's passion for the medieval past was not accompanied by a critical understanding acceptable to modern scholars. May McKisack observes that for a diligent searcher in the public records, Stow 'swallowed Geoffrey of Monmouth whole, and offers us Brutus, Joseph of Arimathaea, Arthur and the rest as sober history'. In fact, Stow revealed some scepticism about the historical Arthur and cited numerous authorities including Gildas, Nennius, and William of Malmesbury.[54] 'He gives us', McKisack continues, 'human and animal monstrosities, comets, floods, and pillars of fire in generous measure.' While Stow stands convicted of these accusations, it is anachronistic for McKisack to condemn Stow for writing 'with complete detachment of such controversial figures as [Thomas] Becket, King John, and John Wyclif' since his scholarly agenda was not determined by interests of modern historians.[55]

Stow was a zealous collector whose interests included not only manuscript texts of chronicles but also charters, ecclesiastical and municipal records, wills, literary works and learned treatises. May McKisack concludes that 'it is doubtful if any historian of his day knew more about records than Stow'.[56] C.L. Kingsford compiled a long list of manuscripts that 'belonged to or were used by Stow'. These include the *Chronica Majora* by Matthew Paris, *Gesta Regum* by William of Malmesbury, and the cartulary of the Hospital of St John at Clerkenwell. The manuscripts are found today in several collections including the British Library, the Bodleian Library at Oxford, the Lambeth Library, and the library of Trinity College, Cambridge.[57] To Kingsford's lists may be added a volume at the Folger Shakespeare Library, *The Arms of the Nobility . . .*, containing the coats of arms of English nobles in colour.[58] Stow used the manuscripts in his own work and lent them to other scholars. Archbishop Parker borrowed a copy of Matthew Paris' *Chronica Majora* while the Welsh historian Dr David Powel, a fellow of All Souls, Oxford, obtained several manuscript chronicles from Stow.[59]

Stow was an equally enthusiastic collector of printed books, which he also made available to others. In *Divers Voyages Touching the Discovery of America* (1582), Richard Hakluyt mentioned that the copy of the chronicle of Robert Fabyan from which he quoted was in 'the custody of John Stow, citizen'. There appears, however, to be no complete compilation of his collection; the list of books compiled in 1568 is limited to 'unlawful works' and includes manuscripts as well as printed books. Stow never prepared an inventory of either his printed books or manuscripts, and the whole collection was dispersed after his death in 1605.[60]

But Stow was more than a record searcher and a collector of books and manuscripts because what C.L. Kingsford called his 'own collections' include the fruits of his labour as a copyist and editor.[61] His deep interest in the middle ages is further revealed by the time devoted to copying medieval texts. Harl. MS 545 includes a copy in Stow's hand of the chronicle of Robert of Avesbury (d. before 1359) for the years 1322–56 as well as the chronicle of Adam Murimuth (d. 1347).[62] Using English translations supplied by Raphael Holinshed, Stow copied forty-nine folios of Florence of Worcester (d. 1118) in February 1572 and a portion of Asser, the biographer of Alfred the Great, the following September.[63] He transcribed the 'History of the Arrival of King Edward IV in England and the Final Recovery of His Kingdoms from Henry VI, A.D. 1471' in Harl. MS 543, a work subsequently published in several editions.[64] He also compiled extensive lists of medieval historical data including the bishops of London and Exeter, benevolences demanded of churches and religious houses by Edward III and burials at St Paul's Cathedral from 1264 to 1525.[65]

During the 1570s Stow made copies of contemporary English topographical works that acquainted him with scholarship very different from chronicles and prepared him for his most famous work, *A Survey of London*. He copied the manuscript of Lambarde's *Perambulation of Kent* in 1575, the year before it was first published.[66] About the same time he transcribed John Leland, 'Six Books of Collections', now Tanner MS 464 at the Bodleian Library in Oxford. According to Lucy Toulmin Smith, editor of *The Itinerary of John Leland*, Stow copied the manuscript in 1576 and altered the spelling.[67] Subsequently, the Welsh scholar, Robert Vaughan, borrowed Stow's copy of Leland's autograph and copied it for himself.[68]

Stow's interest in British as opposed to English medieval history and topography anticipated modern scholarship that looks beyond a single dominant kingdom. Working from unidentified translations, Stow copied a medieval commendation of Gerald [Giraldus] of Wales (c. 1146–1223) by Master John Price and the *Description of Wales* (c. 1194).[69] He transcribed Gerald's *Itinerary through Wales* (1188) with the intriguing notation, 'here begins the itinerary and description as well of Wales as Britain' and in another hand 'written in Latin and then in English by John Stow, merchant taylor in 1575'.[70] The phrasing raises the possibility that Stow may have translated the work himself. Gerald of Wales' Irish writings also attracted Stow's attention as he copied his topography or history of Ireland and followed it with a transcript of the *History and Conquest of Ireland*, based on an English translation by William Camden.[71]

His vision of the past extended beyond history and topography to a wide range of literary works. Stow had great interest in John Lydgate (c. 1370–1450), a major poet of the fifteenth century. A monk of Bury St Edmunds, the prolific Lydgate was patronized by Henry VI and the Lancastrian court. Stow copied his poems and a ballad of London, 'London Lickpenny', that he believed to be the work of Lydgate but is no longer ascribed to him.[72] Stow may have been attracted to the ballad by its refrain, 'For lack of money I may not speed'. He also transcribed Lydgate's translation of 'Pilgrimage of the Life of Man' by Guillaume de Deguilleville, another work incorrectly ascribed to Lydgate. An early fourteenth-century Cistercian, Deguilleville remained popular during the fifteenth century.[73] Stow copied some twenty folios of the poetry of another fifteenth-century writer, George Ripley (d. 1490), whose best known work is 'Compound of Alchemy'.[74] Among the sixteenth-century works copied was Edmund Dudley's *The Tree of Commonwealth*, which was presented to his grandson, Robert, Earl of Leicester.[75] A contemporary copy of 'Vox Populi', a popular Tudor ballad protesting oppression of the commons included among Stow's manuscripts, provides evidence of his sympathy for commonwealth issues and the poor.[76]

Stow's devotion to literature is best illustrated in his editorial work. His first publication, *The Workes of Geffrey Chaucer, newly printed with diuers addicions whiche were neuer in printe before* (1561), reveals his profound love of poetry.[77] Stow explained in *A Survey of England* that 'the most famous poet of England' had been 'partly published in print' by William Caxton during the reign of Henry VI and 'increased' by William Thynne under Henry VIII. But Stow was not self-effacing about his own contribution. The works of Chaucer, he wrote, had been 'corrected and twice increased through mine own painful labours', first in 1561 and in 1597 when Chaucer was 'beautified with notes by me collected out of divers records and monuments'. Modern students of Chaucer have been less complimentary but acknowledge the influence of Stow's edition on Edmund Spenser.[78]

As a literary scholar, Stow found a kindred spirit in John Shirley (1366–1456), who served a growing reading public a century earlier. To Stow he was

a great traveller in divers countries, amongst other his labours, painfully collected the works of Geoffrey Chaucer, John Lydgate, and other learned writers which works he wrote in sundry volumes to remain for posterity. I have seen them and partly do possess them.[79]

In later years literary work continued along side of Stow's historical studies. He edited *Pithy Pleasaunt and Profitable Workes of Maister Skelton*, a collection of thirty-three works printed by Thomas Marshe in 1568.[80] Stow pursued literary interests until late in life when he published *Certaine Worthy Manuscript Poems of Great Antiquity Preserved Long in the Studie of a Northfolke Gentleman* (1597). The book was dedicated to Edmund Spenser and included the 'Statelie Tragedy of Guistard and Sismond', 'The Northern Mother's Blessing', and 'The Way to Thrift'.

Although Stow was not a lawyer, he had a serious interest in Sir John Fortescue that developed from his study of the fifteenth-century conflict between the Lancastrians and Yorkists. Educated at Lincoln's Inn, Fortescue served in Parliament and was made chief justice of the King's Bench in 1442.[81] Stow copied texts of Fortescue that were of importance to constitutional and legal historians, especially *The Governance of England*, the earliest constitutional treatise in English, a work that analyses the failures of the Lancastrian kings and proposes a bold but realistic programme of financial and institutional reform.[82] He had enough interest in one of Fortescue's shorter works, 'A Defence of the Title of the House of Lancaster', to make two copies that are included in separate volumes of the Harleian manuscripts.[83] While it is doubtful whether Stow understood the significance of Fortescue, modern legal scholars have benefited from the survival of his manuscripts.[84]

4. CITIZEN HISTORIAN

With his love of the past and passion for books and manuscripts, Stow fits the definition of an antiquarian, but he is of greater importance as a citizen historian. He was a direct descendant of early sixteenth-century London chroniclers such as Richard Arnold and Robert Fabyan, but lacked the education of Edward Hall, who was educated at Eton and Cambridge and sat in Parliament. Stow's great rival, Richard Grafton, made a small fortune publishing bibles and prayer books during the reign of Edward VI and also sat in Parliament. John Speed, like Stow, was a merchant taylor, but his influential patron, Fulke Greville, secured him a waiter's room in the customs house and the lease of a prebendal estate held of the chapter of St Paul's by the Merchant Taylors' Company.[85] Another contemporary, Raphael Holinshed was, according to Annabel Patterson, 'university educated, probably at Cambridge, and had taken clerical orders'.[86] The political and social world of the next generation of historians – Francis Bacon, William Camden, Samuel Daniel, John Hayward, and Walter Ralegh – included active association with the court and the aristocracy. As a citizen historian, who never styled himself as a gentleman, Stow stood apart from most of his contemporaries: he was not university educated, he did not study law at the inns of court, he never travelled abroad, he did not receive a humanistic education. He neither sat in the House of Commons nor danced attendance at court.

Stow's status as a citizen historian makes his perception of the past particularly valuable. As a historian of English society, he offers a perspective different from most of his contemporaries because his social status placed him closer to the ordinary men and women of Tudor England than to the political elite. Having worked as a tailor, Stow understood the values and the culture of the common people. His London included the small crowded houses found in narrow streets and alleys as well as the fine homes of aldermen, bishops, and nobility. The contempt of the educated elite for a citizen historian appears in the writings of Thomas Fuller, who belittled Stow when he compared him with the learned William Lambarde whose 'labours are feasts for scholars, not (like Stow's works) daily fare for common people'.[87]

Although modern scholars praised Stow's enthusiasm for research and his commitment to the truth, some severely criticized his chronicles and questioned whether he really was a historian. Sir John Neale drew attention to Stow's lack of sophistication and his interest in the commonplace, but Neale thought history was an academic pursuit that should concentrate on Parliament and the politics of the governing elite.[88] Despite his admiration for Stow, C.L. Kingsford conceded that he 'suffered from the limitations which no self-taught man can escape entirely'.[89] May McKisack wrote that while Stow was dull and 'much less readable than [Edward] Hall', he was 'unquestionably a better historian . . . '. McKisack thought that Stow's material overwhelmed him and deprived him of all power of discrimination. She argued that he demonstrated 'little sense of language' in the chronicles and wrote 'less lucidly than Polydore and less rhythmically than Hall'. Stow's talents, according to McKisack, found full scope only in *A Survey of London*.[90]

As a citizen historian, Stow addressed religious controversies arising from the Reformation differently from clerical writers such as John Foxe and John Knox and other apologists who used history as a vehicle for promoting the Protestant religion. During the seventeenth century, Peter Heylyn, John Strype, and Gilbert Burnet developed a vigorous clerical historiography that enthusiastically defended and promoted the Church of England. Clerical scholarship representing a broad spectrum of Anglican and non-conformist thinking came to dominate the Reformation studies in England and retained its influence until the mid-twentieth century.[91] In contrast to the learned priests and pastors, Stow's interests were those of a literate citizen with a small appetite for theology, doctrinal controversy, and apologetics. While it would be incorrect to characterize Stow as an anticlerical writer, his outlook was secular, and he had no vested interest in protecting clerical privileges.

Recent studies have demonstrated the growth of lay power in the Church during the early modern period. Before the Reformation, a variety of anticlerical protests challenged the authority of the clergy to govern the Church. After the break with Rome, many of the laity continued to struggle against the clergy and worked to reshape the Church through control of patronage and by promoting teaching and

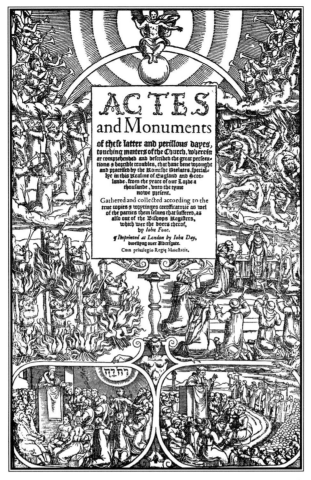

The title page of John Foxe's Actes and Monuments, *first published in London in 1563.*

preaching that reflected their understanding of Biblical Christianity. But other lay people responded to religious change with a sense of detachment and indifference. Stow was a spokesman for those of the laity who simply refused to be drawn into the Reformation debate. His chronicles and *A Survey of London* recount the important events of the Reformation, but while accepting the overall framework of reform, Stow declined to engage in polemics. While no one can say with confidence what the ordinary man or woman thought of the Reformation, Stow is a better representative of the silent majority of lay people than clerical scholars whose historical writings reflect a readily identifiable vested interest.[92]

The neglect of Stow resulted not only from his detachment from the great Reformation debate but also because his writing was not influenced by the Renaissance. Since Stow lacked the benefits of a humanistic education, he was not inspired by the new

John Knox, the Scottish Protestant reformer, c. 1513–72.

Italian historiography; and as twentieth-century historians praised the achievements of the new history, they inherited the disdain of Stow's contemporaries for his work. Polydore Vergil, whose *Anglica Historica* was known to Stow, introduced Italian historical scholarship to England and received severe criticism, but he offered the programme of the future. Camden, Hayward, and a host of seventeenth-century English historians followed in his footsteps with the result that historiographers dismissed Stow, the citizen historian, as a relic of the medieval past.[93]

Following a traditional format, Stow published his first chronicle in 1565 and followed with historical works in every subsequent decade of the reign of Elizabeth. In all a total of twenty-one editions and issues of chronicles and *A Survey of London* appeared during his lifetime. In terms of sheer volume Stow was the dominant historian of his era.

Stow's historical publications over five decades: Chronicles and A Survey of London[94]

> 1560s – 1565, 1566, 1567
> 1570s – 1570, 1573, 1574, 1575, 1579
> 1580s – 1580, 1584, 1587
> 1590s – 1590, 1592, 1598, 1598L, 1599L
> 1600s – 1600, 1601, 1603L, 1604, 1605

L=Editions of *A Survey of London*

The early chronicles or *Summaries* drew on various medieval chronicles as well as sixteenth-century writers such as Edward Hall, Richard Grafton, and Thomas Cooper for the contemporary period. These octavo works were enlarged in successive editions but superseded in 1580 with the publication of the quarto *Chronicles of England*. Shorter chronicles or abridgements appeared as early as 1566 and continued until 1604, only a year before Stow's death. He unquestionably understood the advantages of a chronicle that was small in size and cheap when he wrote in 1567 that he had put his work in 'a new form such as may both ease the purse and the carrying and yet nothing omitted convenient to be known'.[95] The abridgements recognized readers' interest in contemporary history and placed heavy emphasis on the Tudor century. The Anglo-Saxon period down to 1066, for example, was covered in 40 folios out of 197 in the first edition that appeared in 1566. The abridgements included additional non-historical information that made them resemble an almanac.[96] The buyer received a calendar, rules for determining law terms, and a table entitled 'How a man may journey from any notable town in England to the city of London'. By 1587 a description of the universities of Oxford and Cambridge had been added, suggesting perhaps that students were buying this work. Stow needed support from the mayor and aldermen to whom he dedicated the chronicles to meet the challenge of his rival, Richard Grafton. To promote sales he praised Thomas Cooper, who enjoyed the favour of Archbishop Parker and the queen, and boasted enthusiastically of the accuracy and truth of his own work.

The *Annales of England*, Stow's largest chronicle, followed the *Chronicles of England* which appeared in only one edition. Beginning with the first edition in 1592 and ending with an edition of 1605, published in the year of Stow's death, the *Annales* covered the entire reign of Elizabeth as well as the accession and coronation of James I. Although continued by Edmund Howes, the *Annales* has never appeared in a modern edition and has suffered in comparison with Holinshed and *A Survey of London*. In C.L. Kingsford's opinion, the *Survey* was a vastly superior work. Stow, he said

> has an indisputable right to our regard for the amount of information, which he collected and preserved. Yet when this is admitted, the *Annales* entitle him to little other distinction than that which belongs to a painstaking seeker after truth, who brought the results of his toil into a chronologically exact narrative, without the power to impress them with any great vitality.[97] [sic]

Contemporaries who bought successive editions of the *Annales* would have rejected this harsh condemnation, and modern scholarship must also challenge it because this richly detailed work is the only Tudor chronicle that covers the sixteenth century including the reign of Elizabeth from beginning to end.

Stow made significant contributions to the famous second edition of Holinshed's chronicle published in 1587.[98] He regularly laid claim to Holinshed calling it his larger chronicle in the *Annales of England*, and he incorporated many of his manuscript notes into it.[99] *A Survey of London*, Stow's most famous work, is examined in a separate chapter. May McKisack conceded that Stow's reputation as a general historian of England was a great advantage that allowed him to set the history of London in a 'national framework' and added

Neither his long searches in the records, nor his extensive knowledge of chronicles misled Stow into presenting his readers with a mass of ill-digested and unexplained transcripts. The material is under control, subordinated to the demands of the author's plan, and allowing full scope for the exercise of his skill and the display of his qualities as historian.

McKisack concluded that Stow, 'the surveyor of England's greatest city, must rank as one of her greatest local historians'.[100]

John Stow, the quintessential Londoner, remained a citizen historian throughout his long life. Although untouched by Renaissance humanism, he was always a critical scholar. A meticulous collector of evidence, he gave his sources when reporting strange and dubious occurrences as well as when describing overseas voyages, foreign embassies, and military campaigns in Ireland. He preserved the traditional chronological format in his chronicles but demonstrated greater organizational skill in *A Survey of London* and in his popular abridgements where he emphasized the recent past, presumably on the modern assumption that the ordinary reader lived in the present and therefore had less interest in remote periods of history. Never satisfied with his work, Stow corrected, extended, and improved the chronicles as well as *A Survey of London*. He worked hard and possessed a strong commitment to getting it right. Stow was an articulate observer of his own world who reported on a wide range of current events, but his work is not introspective or autobiographical.[101] If one avoids dogmatism in defining history, Stow easily qualifies as a significant practitioner of the historian's craft. The acid test for any historical scholar is whether he actually writes history, and not even Stow's most severe critic could deny that he was the most prolific historian of his day.

CHAPTER TWO

TUDOR SOCIETY

'All of them [were] gentlemen, except their honoured colleague,
John Stow.'

When writing of John Stow in the *Worthies of England*, Thomas Fuller observed, 'So hard it is for a citizen to write a history, but that the fur of his gown will be felt therein.'[1] Fuller, a Cambridge educated clergyman, the son of a fellow of Trinity, Cambridge, and the nephew of a bishop, understood the significant connection between the social status of a historian and the history that he wrote. As a mere citizen, Stow was identified as a man whose inferior social status separated him from contemporary chroniclers and historians who were recruited primarily from the court and the university-educated elite. Francis Bacon, William Camden, and John Hayward were gentlemen and scholars, but Stow was only a merchant tailor and citizen of London. Stow's status followed him wherever he went, and nowhere was it more evident than when he was among the Society of Antiquaries where many of the members were knights and 'all of them gentlemen, except their honoured colleague, John Stow'.[2]

Stow's social status created financial needs that help explain why he was obliged to write history for a wide audience and produce more editions of his work than his contemporaries. It also influenced the way that he wrote about his own social environment. A citizen historian of the sixteenth century such as Stow could neither conceal his identity nor directly criticize accepted social values. It was also essential for him to identify with other contemporary writers and the literate audience that must inevitably be the buyers of his books. Therefore it would be unrealistic to expect Stow to present a bold critique of Tudor society, but at the same time his writings reveal the mentality of a London citizen.

Stow's social philosophy was shaped by his own experience in London and his study of the past. Although he owned a large number of books and manuscripts, his writings suggest that no single learned author or seminal work determined his social values. It would appear, however, that his attitude toward society was similar to that of Edmund Dudley in *The Tree of Commonwealth*.[3] Stow knew this work as he presented a manuscript copy to Dudley's grandson, the Earl of Leicester. Like Dudley, Stow accepted an ordered, organic society held together by bonds of custom, religion, deferential behaviour, and law. In *A Survey of London* he used something as basic as water to explain his thinking. For him water was a commodity that contributed to the good of the whole realm because it was available 'for the poor to drink and the rich to dress their meat'. Even prisoners

An illustration from the ballad 'The famous Ratketcher with his travels into France, and his return to London'. Rat-catching was a poorly-paid employment, but it allowed the catcher to avoid the harsh Elizabethan penalties for vagrancy.

benefited from the 'sweet water' that was piped to the gates of Newgate and Ludgate for their benefit.[4] At the end of *A Survey of London* Stow appended an anonymous discourse defending the city.[5] Among many persuasive arguments offered in behalf of London, the learned author emphasized its role as 'the hive of this commonwealth' where merchants, handicraftsmen, and labourers worked together in harmony and praised the distribution of wealth in London arguing that the 'greatest part of them' were neither too rich nor too poor. The city's commitment to the commonwealth ideal was especially notable in its response to poverty. As he explained, 'It relieveth plentifully, and with good policy, not only her own poor people, a thing which scarcely any other town or shire doth, but also the poor that from each quarter of the realm do flock unto it.'[6] We must assume that Stow rescued the discourse from oblivion and included it in his most important work because he approved of the social philosophy that it contained.

The world of John Stow was one of a divinely ordained hierarchy in which men and women accepted without question the right of monarchs, nobles, and gentry to govern. Wherever Stow's historical enquiries led him, he found that past generations agreed about the legitimacy of the established order. The king and governing elite, working in accordance with custom and within the framework of traditional institutions, might initiate lawful change, but popular challenges to the social order were an abomination to be condemned by all God-fearing people. As Stow described his world, he wrote as a conservative who looked to the past for wisdom, not an advocate of a better tomorrow. Looking back to the London of the middle ages, he noted with regret changes that had occurred since William Fitzstephen wrote during the reign of Henry II:

> In those days (and till of late time) every man lived by his professed trade, not any one interrupting another: the cooks dressed meat, and sold no wine, and the taverner sold wine, but dressed no meat for sale.[7]

In an age when Renaissance scholars drew inspiration from classical antiquity, Stow's social ideals were deeply rooted in the middle ages.

1. GOOD LORDSHIP AND GOOD WORKS

Good lordship contributed to harmony in a society in which wealth and power were concentrated in the hands of a privileged few. Derived from concepts of Christian charity, it included a variety of personalized obligations owed to inferiors based on faithful service and need. Stow remembered the good lordship of a London merchant tailor and alderman and his widow who repaired their property, took no fines, and did not increase rents during the inflationary mid-Tudor decades.[8] By the end of the sixteenth century Stow longed for the better times of the past. Rich merchants who lived in fine houses in Bread Street built elaborate summer houses in the suburbs, but they did not provide for the poor as their fathers and grandfathers had done. These 'ancient citizens', Stow remembered, had built the hospitals and almshouses that served the poor.[9] It was perhaps as a spokesman for a passing generation that he added a page at the end of the *Summarie Abridged* of 1604, published only a year before his death, praising the charitable bequests of Sir Wolstane Dixie, a former mayor, whose 'good deeds [were] forgotten until the book was printed'.[10]

As Stow clearly understood the meaning and importance of good lordship, it is appropriate to ask how much of this socially correct behaviour he recorded in his historical writings. The crown, by exercising the greatest authority in the realm and possessing the most wealth, had the greatest opportunity to practise good lordship. Yet Stow's *Annales of England* is remarkably thin on examples of good lordship by Tudor monarchs between 1547 and 1603. An objective reading of his account of the reigns of

Edward VI and Mary leaves serious doubts whether the country derived significant benefits from their reigns. Queen Elizabeth – despite her long reign – does not fare any better. In the 1605 edition Stow proudly declared that the queen's accession contributed to the 'great comfort of England' thereby creating a legitimate expectation that the ensuing account would illustrate these comforts in detail. But Stow failed to deliver. Aside from anecdotal references to gifts such as one thousand marks in gold for the repair of the steeple of St Paul's Cathedral, Stow was unable to show that the reign of Elizabeth was much of an improvement on the record of her predecessors.[11] It must be emphasized that Stow never directly or indirectly criticized the crown for failing to practise good lordship, but his eloquent silence may be interpreted to mean that while loyal subjects reaffirmed their devotion to the crown over and over again, the sovereign reciprocated only with fair words and tokens of appreciation.

While Stow wrote little of the good lordship of the Tudor monarchs, the same is not true of the political and social elite. In *A Survey of London*, he compiled a list of citizens, including sixty-seven men and five women, who demonstrated their devotion to the

A rich man ignores the pleas of a beggar, from Bateman's Chrystal Glass of Christian Reformation *(1569).*

city and the country. These worthies included Walter Brune and his wife Rosia, who founded a hospital for the care of the needy in 1197, William Sevenoke, the founder of a school for children of the poor in Kent in 1419 as well as thirteen almshouses, and the famous mayor, Richard Whittington.[12] He remembered seeing two hundred persons served 'twice every day with bread, meat and drink' at the gate of Thomas Cromwell's house.[13] Although Stow emphasized the contributions of men, he compiled a select listing of women, 'citizens' wives, deserving memory for example to posterity'. One of the women, Margaret Danne, left £2,000 to be lent to young men of the company of ironmongers, 'paying after the rate of five pounds in the year for every hundred; which one hundred pounds so rising yearly, to be employed on charitable actions'.[14]

Stow's praise of good lordship reached beyond the lists of worthy Londoners found in *A Survey of London* and included peers whose deaths were noted in the *Annales*. When he recorded the death of Edward Stanley, 3rd Earl of Derby, at Latham, Lancashire in 1572, he remembered a life and death 'deserving commendation and craving memory to be imitated'. Derby had served two kings and two queens 'in dangerous times and great rebellions'; he practised a 'godly disposition' to his tenants, never forcing any service from them and requiring only payment of their rents; and he was known for his liberality to strangers.

But Derby was especially famous for his 'house-keeping' which maintained:

two hundred twenty in checkroll never discontinuing the space of forty-two years; his feeding especially of aged persons twice a day sixty and odd, besides all comers, thrice a week appointed for his dealing days, and every Good Friday these thirty-five years one with another, 2700 with meat, drink, money, and money worth. There was never gentleman or other that waited in his service but had allowance from him to have as well wages as otherwise for horse and man. His yearly portion for the dispenses of his house 4000 pounds; his cunning in setting bones disjointed or broke [and] his delivery of his George and seal to the Lord Strange with exhortation that he might keep it so unspotted in fidelity to his prince as he had. . . .[15]

An aged woman (Roxburghe Ballads).

Stow's enthusiastic regard for the Earl of Derby was far from typical of his usual way of recording the deaths of peers. Although the Earl of Sussex, like Stow, was a merchant tailor, no bequests or acts of good lordship were mentioned when he died in 1583. The same treatment was accorded Lord Howard of Effingham, the Earl of Arundel, the Earl of Warwick, and most surprisingly Lord Burghley.[16] The venerable William Paulet, Marquess of Winchester, lived ninety-seven years before his death in 1572 and served each of the Tudor sovereigns, but Stow wrote only of his worthiness and faithful service.[17] While Stow received no favours from Derby, his favourable attitude toward the Earl of Leicester was undoubtedly the result of literary patronage. Stow described Leicester's creation as an earl in great detail and after his death in 1588 wrote a modest obituary, remembering his foundation of a hospital in Warwick for twelve poor men.[18]

Although Stow revealed a layman's detachment from the doctrinal aspects of the Reformation, he did not hesitate to praise the good works of the three Elizabethan archbishops of Canterbury, Matthew Parker, Edmund Grindal, and John Whitgift. Parker (d. 1575) was remembered for his learning and patronage of scholarship, a subject close to Stow's heart, but he also emphasized Parker's generosity to Corpus Christi College, Cambridge, and to its library and two other colleges of the university. Stow further noted Parker's personal expenditure for the rebuilding of the archepiscopal palace at Canterbury and his provision for the poor in Norfolk.[19] Parker's successor, Edmund Grindal (d. 1583), a former bishop of London, had stronger ties with the city than Parker yet his good works also benefited other parts of the country. Grindal founded a school in his native Cumberland and left money to colleges at both Oxford and Cambridge. Like Parker, Grindal remembered the needy, leaving £50 for 'the eight little poor' almshouses at Croydon, and £100 to Canterbury 'to be employed upon a stock to set the poor on work'. But Stow hastened to add that the stock, 'as I am informed, was never put to so good a use'.[20] The death of the third Elizabethan archbishop of Canterbury, John Whitgift, occurred in 1604, only a year before Stow's own death. To Stow he was a 'notable and memorable monument of our time', who founded a school and hospital in Croydon where he was buried.[21] Stow remembered Parker, Grindal, and Whitgift for their secular accomplishments and chose to offer no opinion on the religious controversies that formed an important part of the life of each man.

Robert Johnson, 'a zealous minister' in Rutland, was another clergyman whose good works Stow praised. Before his death in 1590, Johnson founded free grammar schools at Okeham and Uppingham as well as a hospital for twenty-four poor persons. For many years he had also provided for the education of the children of forty poor men at his expense. For Stow, Johnson was an exemplary figure who represented the highest ideals of the Church of England; for 'he preached both by word and life, not to enrich himself, but was bountiful to the poor'.[22]

In assessing the good lordship of the gentry, Stow used an approach very similar to that employed for the peerage and clergy. His historical writings say very little about the great county families of the period and practically nothing about the lesser gentry. The gentry who attracted his attention were learned, prominent in government, or part of the ruling elite in London. Stow remembered Sir William Petre (d. 1572), who had been secretary and privy councillor to four monarchs and 'seven times lord ambassador abroad in foreign lands', for his 'judgment and pregnant wit'. Whereas Petre's modern biographer, F.G. Emmison, made an extensive analysis of Petre's good lordship, Stow was more selective and referred only to his gifts to Exeter College, Oxford, and his construction of ten almshouses for the poor at Ingatestone, Essex.[23] Two other prominent officials, Sir Nicholas Bacon (d. 1578), lord keeper of the great seal, and Sir Walter Mildmay (d. 1585), chancellor of the exchequer, were remembered for their generosity to Cambridge University. Although Sir Francis Walsingham was perhaps more influential in government than Petre, Bacon, or Mildmay, Stow noted his death, like that of Lord Burghley, without comment or reference to good works.[24]

Sir Thomas Gresham was a special case because he was not only prominent in national affairs but arguably the most famous Londoner of his generation. Described as a knight and 'agent' to the queen at the time of his death in 1579, Gresham legitimately received substantial notice from Stow in both the *Annales of England* and *A Survey of London*. Gresham's bequests were extremely generous and extensive, because he gave the Royal Exchange to the city of London and the company of mercers, established Gresham College by endowing lectures to be given in his house in Bishopsgate Street, and made generous provision for prisoners and the poor.[25]

It was also easy to celebrate the life of Sir Philip Sidney, the Protestant knight and poet, who died heroically fighting in the Netherlands. Stow praised his wisdom, goodness, and valiant courage, and said that Sidney 'so behaved himself that it was [a] wonder to see'. After his death in October 1586, Stow described the return of his body to England and the funeral the following February.[26] Wishing to honour the memory of the fallen Sidney, his father-in-law, Sir Francis Walsingham, spared no cost in arranging what has been called the most magnificent funeral ever given to an English subject.[27] As Sidney's life began to be commemorated at the annual celebrations of the accession of Queen Elizabeth, Stow contributed to the legend in his chronicles.[28] While Stow never questioned the fallen hero's greatness, the account of his death, unlike that of Sir Thomas Gresham, mentioned no good works that would have benefited less fortunate subjects of the crown.

2. THE POOR

Stow's interest in good lordship is fundamental to his view of Tudor society, but it represented only half of an equation based on supply and demand. Persons of status, wealth, and power supplied the charitable needs of the poor because there was a demand for it. The need for good lordship was created by the weak, the poor, the sick,

A page from A book of divers devices, *illustrating the month of February, shows the obvious importance of the fire during the winter months in the sixteenth century.*

children and the aged, persons for whom Tudor central government assumed no direct responsibility. Moreover, Stow clearly understood that many of the citizens of London – the group to which he belonged – could never be wholly free from the fear that they might become dependent on their betters. Stow's chronicles and *A Survey of London* reveal his identification with the common sort of people and a keen understanding of the world in which they lived.[29]

Concern for the poor is a theme that recurs frequently in *A Survey of London*. When the lodgings of choir men were given to the poor, Stow referred to this as 'blessed work of harbouring the harbour less'.[30] In his youth he remembered that devout people walked to the cottages of the sick to bestow their alms, but by 1547 new houses replaced the cottages.[31] He noted that after a merchant demolished Suffolk House in Southwark, new cottages of 'great rents' were built on the site thereby increasing the number of beggars living in the district. In contrast, St Bartholomew's Hospital was founded to bring the poor 'from out of their streets, lanes, and alleys . . .'.[32] Stow's compassion reached down to the level of prisoners as he criticized bad conditions at the privately owned Compter in Bread Street, where jailers, who bought their offices, dealt harshly with the 'pitiful prisoners'.[33]

In his chronicles Stow repeatedly drew attention to the plight of the poor and called for efforts to improve the conditions under which they lived. On one occasion he used a rather far-fetched anecdote to make his point. William Lumney, a poor

Elizabethan men enjoying making music in the open air. The instrument being played by the man on the right is a lute, while the horn-like instrument held by the man in the tree may be intended to represent a cornett, a forerunner of the oboe. ('May', from A book of divers devices*)*

man from Worcestershire, was kept in prison by a rich widow for reasons that are not given. During the time of incarceration, his 22-year-old mare foaled a mare colt with an udder that produced a pint of milk immediately following its birth. Later the young mare produced three pints of milk a day which sustained the man's wife and children 'for long time after'. Although Stow gives no authority for this strange tale, he assured his readers that the extraordinary mare had been seen by 'many thousands' of people. The tale of the mare undoubtedly amused credulous and critical readers alike, but its moral suggests that Stow had more in mind than amusement.[34]

Stow's use of a strict chronological format in the chronicles precludes broad assessments or generalizations about the magnitude of poverty during the later sixteenth century. The frequency of references leaves little doubt that Stow understood that poverty was a persistent and chronic problem while individual incidents mentioned in the chronicles illustrate its dimensions. In September 1600 three hundred and fifty masterless men were rounded up for military service in Ireland; when some deserted and fled for their lives, a number were hanged as an example to others.[35] Here Stow characteristically does not say how many vagrants roamed through the countryside in 1600, but the actual number available for military service in a single month provides at least limited quantitative evidence. A gruesome tragedy about a year later provides another example of how many lived in poverty. The burial of Lady Mary Ramsey,

This hurtlesse beast with meeke moode yelds his woll
And skin. to clothour naked clotte of claye
He giues his flesh to feede our bellies full
Nought for him selfe he bringe but for our staye

June
Cancer

mayd milke cleane

The page illustrating June from A book of divers devices *shows, in the background, a maid milking a cow, and, in the foreground, the dipping of sheep to guard against infectious diseases.*

widow of a former mayor of London, in November 1601 at the parish church of Christ Church by Newgate market was followed by a charitable dole distributed in her memory at Leadenhall. Because the needy were so desperate, mayhem resulted, and no fewer than seventeen poor and weak people were among the uncounted sturdy beggars crushed and trodden to death.[36]

By the 1590s growing economic difficulties and perhaps the financial insecurity of his own old age caused Stow to give greater attention to the plight of the poor and also prompted an outburst of righteous indignation more characteristic of Commonwealth writers of the mid-sixteenth century or radical Puritan preachers. It accompanies an account of a fire at Tiverton, Devon. According to Stow, this thriving clothing town 'maintained' 9,000 people in Devon, Cornwall, and Somerset and had a market where £2,000 were spent each week. As Tiverton lay far outside the area of which Stow had direct, personal knowledge, information may have been supplied by his collaborator, John Hooker of Exeter. On 3 April 1598 fire broke out in a cottage where a woman was frying pancakes on a fire of straw. The conflagration lasted for an hour and a half, consumed 409 houses, destroyed money, plate, and merchandise worth £150,000, and killed fifty people. In the *Annales of England* Stow wrote angrily that the fire was God's punishment of the unmerciful rich. Their offence was a 'small regard of the poor' who were seen daily to 'perish in the streets of that town for lack of relief'.[37]

Although Stow was obviously capable of moral outrage and a willingness to condemn the wealthy without presenting convincing historical evidence of culpability, such outbursts were uncharacteristic of his writing. He clearly understood that human suffering was usually caused by complex social and economic problems. For example, he attributed 'the dearth of corn' in 1587 to three causes, none of which invoked providence: the weather, the 'unlawful and overmuch' exporting of grain to foreign countries, and the 'uncharitable greediness' of great corn masters. The government issued a royal proclamation to fix prices and relieve the poor, but Stow noted with regret that prices continued to rise.[38]

3. SOCIAL INSTABILITY

As Stow wrote compassionately about the effects of poverty on the common people of Tudor England, he also witnessed the social instability that was a consequence of poverty, rapid population growth, and warfare. Like all traditionalists, Stow was not altogether comfortable or conformable with his own times. For him life had been better in the medieval past when virtue was more abundant. Unfortunately, Stow did not always appreciate that many of the social problems of his own time had also existed in the past. In fact, the lawlessness and violence of the middle ages posed a continuing challenge to the Tudor monarchs as Stow's chronicles unwittingly reveal. He wrote at great length about an incident in 1571 in which two men from Kent wanted to settle by personal combat a minor dispute over the ownership of lands. Champions were appointed who ceremoniously appeared in the rich trappings of medieval splendour, before the lord chief justice intervened and called a halt to the nonsense.[39]

Since Stow failed to understand the historical significance of issues such as personal combat, he understood social stability in purely contemporary terms and certainly was not alone among sixteenth-century writers in arguing that strict maintenance of law and order was necessary to preserve the heritage of the past. Like all right-thinking Tudors, Stow abhorred rebellions, riots, and all forms of popular protest. He condemned the Peasants' Revolt of 1381 for its destructiveness and denounced Wat Tyler as a 'presumptuous rebel'.[40] The major Tudor rebels – Robert Kett, Sir Thomas Wyatt, the Northern earls, and the Earl of Essex – violated the laws of both God and man and deserved no mercy. Neither did Stow show remorse for the long list of traitors whose executions he recorded. These included the dukes of Somerset, Northumberland, Suffolk and Norfolk as well as Lady Jane Grey and Mary, Queen of Scots. Their unfortunate followers may have been poor and deluded, but Stow fully accepted that they too must bear the full weight of the law for their crimes.

While Stow supported the punishment of every rebel and traitor, his reporting of individual episodes was not always consistent from one edition of a chronicle to another. For example, the reader of the *Annales of England* in the 1605 edition, the last edition published before the author's death, learned that in June 1581 Thomas Butchar, a brewer, and a few followers 'congregated themselves in West Smithfield of London and in other places in manner of rebellion'. For this offence Butchar was whipped from Newgate to West Smithfield and 'there relieved, taken from the beadles, and sent away to shift for himself'. Later four others, another brewer and three shoemakers, were also whipped and set on the pillory for two hours.[41] From this account of 1605 one might readily conclude that Thomas Butchar was a small-time rogue and troublemaker who probably imbibed too deeply of his own wares.

The shorter *Summarye of the Chronicles*, published fifteen years earlier, tells a different story. In this version Butchar's supporters numbered no fewer than 1,000 persons. He was sentenced to execution – not merely whipping – but was rescued by his friends before the sentence could be carried out. The narrative ends in an extremely unsatisfying way because Stow never says what happened to the culprit. The second edition of Holinshed's chronicle agrees with Stow on the number of persons involved but also fails to explain what happened to Butchar.[42] In addition to Thomas Butchar and his followers, unruly youths – the ancestors of modern street gangs – disturbed the peace of London. During a period of high prices in 1595, Stow noted that groups of apprentices and other young people 'being pinched of their victuals' took butter from market people in Southwark paying only 3*d* per pound when the going price was 5*d*. The culprits were whipped, set on a pillory, and given what Stow termed 'long imprisonment'. Despite severe punishment, young people continued to cause trouble. On a Sunday afternoon at the end of June, youths threw stones at warders of Tower Street ward. To restore order the mayor, Sir John Spencer, rode to Tower Hill attended by his officers 'to see the hill cleared of all tumultuous persons'. A scuffle ensued, and the mayor's sword bearer and several others were injured. In Stow's judgement order was restored through Spencer's wisdom and discretion. Afterwards at Guildhall, five of the ringleaders were convicted of treason. They were subsequently drawn from Newgate to Tower Hill where they were hanged, drawn, and quartered.[43] Harsh justice was the law of the land, and John Stow was not a crusader for the reform of criminal law.

Beginning in the 1580s Stow began to record the impact of war on the common people, especially in London. Although he did not see the connection between warfare and social instability, several entries in the chronicles allow glimpses of a society at war. In July 1585 Stow briefly noted that 'certain soldiers' had been impressed for the defence of the Low Countries with the cost paid by the companies and citizens of London. Although his main interest was in the triumphs of English arms and the heroism of the commanders, a few revealing details about ordinary persons may be found. On Good Friday in 1596 the mayor and aldermen, after hearing a sermon at St Paul's, were suddenly summoned to appear before the queen and privy council, who ordered them to impress 1,000 men to assist the French against Spain at Calais. If Stow is to be believed, the whole process of enlistment was completed by eight o'clock the very same evening. The men were to leave the following day, but before their departure the orders were changed, and everyone was discharged. The next day, Easter Sunday, word arrived at ten in the morning that the recruits really were required. At this hour most citizens were in church preparing to receive the Holy Communion, but services were abruptly halted when the aldermen and other authorities closed the church doors so that the men in attendance might again be pressed. By noon the numbers reached 1,000, and the new recruits were duly equipped and marched off to Dover to await embarkation for Calais. A week later everyone returned to London because France had lost Calais to the Spanish.[44] Since Stow gives only the bare facts of this outrageous episode, it is impossible to determine his own attitude. For the unfortunate victims of these Tudor recruiting officers, however, the experience was not only socially disruptive, but one that may have eroded the integrity of the government in the eyes of ordinary citizens.

In the years that followed, repeated references to impressment reveal the growing burden of war on English society. In May 1597, 550 were pressed in London, equipped at the expense of the citizens, and trained in open fields surrounding the city. On this occasion only 400 were ultimately chosen to serve. These men joined an army of 6,000 who were recruited to accompany Essex to the Azores.[45] Early in 1599 more men were pressed from London, Essex, and other counties for service in Ireland and the Low Countries. For the first time Stow gives an indication of exactly how much the wars were costing the citizens of London. The 'subsidy men' were assessed at the rate of 8d in the pound on either land or goods, and loans were also demanded.[46] In July 1600, 500 went to Ireland and these were followed the next summer by 1,000 more who were part of a larger contingent of 8,000. Men were impressed twice in 1602: in May for the Low Countries and in August 200 men for Ireland. The citizens of London were assessed £6,000 in 1603 to provide two ships and a pinnace 'to lie before Dunkirk'.[47]

Stow's treatment of war and its impact on society implies that he approved of recruitment procedures and that he fully supported government policy toward Spain and Ireland. Whatever Stow's personal views may have been, it is

A beggar, illustrated in the Roxburghe Ballads.

anachronistic to think of an anti-war historian getting his writings published in Elizabethan England. Patriotism and sound politics were as important for a Tudor chronicler as they were for the eighteenth-century dramatist, George Farquhar, whose play *The Recruiting Officer* delighted London audiences with its uninhibited jingoism. On the other hand, the recruits of Stow's day were a rougher lot than the Shropshire country bumpkins in Farquhar's play. A few defiant men among the 350 vagrants pressed for Ireland in 1600 deserted although their punishment was an appointment with the hangman. Whether the thirty men who broke out of the prison at King's Bench in Southwark in 1603 included men destined for military service is uncertain, but two years later others impressed for the wars ran from their captains and colours only to suffer hanging as an example to their comrades.[48] The different responses of the recruits may be explained in terms of the authors' perceptions and literary forms, but another possibility lies in the relative social stability of the early eighteenth century compared with the turbulence that prevailed a hundred years earlier in the world of John Stow.

4. CRIME AND PUNISHMENT

Although Stow was an assiduous reporter of popular discontent, the chronicles are filled with more examples of serious crime, especially murder, and capital punishment. Stow obviously saw crime from the perspective of his own times, and the attitudes of his age toward crime and punishment differed significantly from later periods. Offences such as wife-beating, corporal punishment of children and servants, and various forms of sexual and verbal abuse are examples of acts that are criminalized today but were not usually regarded as crimes in the sixteenth century. In contrast, the law of Tudor England punished Roman Catholic clergy and radical Protestants for offences that are unique to the early modern period. The question of what is appropriate punishment for a particular crime is another issue where the values of one era differ from another. Stow recorded brutal whippings as routine matters without comment and never questioned the imposition of capital punishment.

Since historians of crime during the early modern period concentrate on recorded crimes, our knowledge of criminal activity is dependent on reporting, enforcement, and prosecution. Punishment of convicted criminals was indeed severe, but it must be understood that many offenders of Stow's era committed crimes that were never reported or prosecuted. Consequently historians who study crime encounter formidable obstacles in determining its impact on early modern society.[49]

What Stow offers to the history of crime are his own records and perceptions. Unlike many nineteenth- and early twentieth-century historians, Stow regarded crime as a legitimate part of the history of Tudor England. He was not only well positioned to observe and record crime in London, but he also took great interest in crimes that occurred in other parts of the country. His record of a crime might be a very brief entry that omitted the name of the perpetrator and victim or it might include fascinating details. Stow's attitude toward crime was not influenced by his limited wealth and modest social status, and there is no evidence that he thought of crime as the exclusive concern of the gentry and aristocracy. His chronicles show very clearly that crime was no respecter of wealth or status. Stow's approach was very simple: all he did was describe criminal activity that came to his attention and that he thought would be of interest to the readers of his chronicles. The result is a series of anecdotes which appear in sufficient

A prisoner carries the chain that binds his ankles together (Roxburghe Ballads).

detail and with such frequency that one can only conclude that Stow thought that crime constituted a serious threat to the social order.

On one occasion Stow attempted unsuccessfully to charge a man with making false accusations against him. The story is found in a description of the punishment of another man who falsely accused 'one of the court of common place [i.e. pleas] in Westminster of treason'. For his offence the culprit was pilloried and burned with a hot iron on both cheeks with the letters F and A. 'The like justice', Stow wrote, 'I once wished to the like accuser of his master and eldest brother, but it was answered that in such case could be no remedy though the accuser himself were in the same fact found the principal offender.' The man was not only unrepentant but swore blasphemously that he never committed any such offence and threatened to murder Stow. His response was uncharacteristically detached and philosophical, for he comforted himself with the 37th Psalm: 'Fret not thyself with these cursed harmful men, neither envy angrily these workers of wickedness, for like grass anon shall they be cut down.'[50] The unnamed man in this curiously cryptic account was undoubtedly Stow's brother, Thomas, with whom he had quarrelled about their mother's will.[51]

When dealing with issues that did not involve his family, such as street crime, Stow abandoned philosophical detachment. In *A Survey of London*, he learned from a contemporary authority that it was 'common practice' in London during the twelfth century for a hundred or more men of all ages to make 'nightly invasions upon the houses of the wealthy' for the purpose of robbery. If these mobs found anyone in the

An illustration from The Life apprehension, arraignement, and execution of Charles Courtney *(1612). Two prisoners attempt to escape from jail. As re-offenders were always hanged, their fate was to be the same as the two unfortunates who flank the scene.*

streets at night, they would simply murder them. Stow condemned such 'enormities' and noted with approval the establishment of regular night watches during the reign of Henry III.[52] In the chronicles it is murder that attracted Stow's interest and, of course, his unequivocal censure. Details of the most notorious killings are presented in a manner that even today makes compelling reading. It is tempting to think that Stow's readers delighted in these stories as much as readers of a modern newspaper relish lurid accounts of sensational crimes.

Stow begins one of these stories in a matter of fact way by saying that Martin Bullocke was hanged on 24 May 1572 for robbing and murdering a merchant named Arthur Hall. The circumstances of the homicide followed. Bullocke enticed his victim to meet him at a parsonage to buy a quantity of (silver) plate. After viewing the goods, Hall exclaimed, 'This is none of your plate; it hath Dr. Gardener's mark, and I know it to be his.' Bullocke did not deny that the plate was Gardener's but explained that he had been appointed to sell it. While Hall was weighing the plate, Bullocke fetched out of the kitchen a thick washing beetle, and coming behind him, struck the said Arthur on the head, that he felled him with the first stroke, and then struck him again, and after took the said Arthur's dagger and stuck him and with his knife cut his throat.

Problems developed as Bullocke attempted to dispose of the body. First he tried to place Hall in a Danske chest, but the corpse was too long to fit. Next he tried to drag the body down a flight of stairs in order to bury it in the cellar. But as the legs stiffened, the body wedged in the circular staircase and could not be moved further. Bullocke then chopped off Hall's legs with a hatchet and packed the pieces into a 'dry fat' – or cask – and saying that it contained his own books and apparel had it shipped by water to 'Rie' (?Rye). Although Bullocke was immediately suspected of the murder, he initially escaped from London only to return a few days later to the scene of his crime. His fate was sealed when the dry fat was opened and found to contain the mangled corpse of Arthur Hall.[53]

Peter Burchet, gentleman of the Middle Temple, was another dangerous criminal whose misdeeds were recorded by Stow. In October 1573 Burchet 'suddenly assailed, cruelly wounded and meant to have killed' John Hawkins with a dagger as he walked with two friends near the Strand. After being apprehended and committed to the Tower of London, Burchet curiously protested that his attack on Hawkins was a case of mistaken identity as he had intended to kill Sir Christopher Hatton. During the course of further examination, Burchet was also found to hold 'erroneous opinions' for which he was sent to the Lollards' Tower. He was called before Edwin Sandys, Bishop of London, to answer charges of heresy, but just before the death sentence was pronounced he 'foreswore and abjured his opinions [as] erroneous and damnable'.

Burchet remained in confinement after promising to do the penance required of him. He was imprisoned with two men who 'had by appointment kept him company'. One of these was called away leaving Burchet in a locked room with the other, Hugh Longworth. As this man stood in a window reading the Bible, Burchet

took a billets end [a thick piece of wood] out of the fire and knocked the said Longworth on the head and left not till he had stricken him stark dead.

He intended to murder the other companion as he returned to the room, but the intended victim saw the body lying behind the door and ran for help. On the following day Burchet was tried and condemned to death. A gibbet was set up near the place where his first victim, John Hawkins, had been wounded. Stow recounted that Burchet showed no sign of repentance and had to be drawn by brute force up to the gibbet where his right hand was cut off and nailed to the gibbet before he was hanged.[54]

Although most of the crimes reported by Stow occurred in London or involved Londoners, he had sources of information in distant parts of the country. An example of this may be seen in his account of a murder that took place at Worcester in November 1576. Stow's report is extremely brief and gives neither the names of the persons involved nor any indication about how Stow learned of the crime. In this instance 'a cruel and unnatural brother (as another Cain) murdered his own natural and loving brother'. The killer first 'smote out' his brother's brains with an axe and afterwards cut his throat. He subsequently buried the body under the hearth of a chimney, hoping to have enjoyed his brother's goods 'long before in his possession'. Of course, news of the murder and secret burial came to light, and Stow was able to conclude with satisfaction that the murderer was 'rewarded according to his deserts'.[55]

Without question the most fascinating murder described in Stow's works is that of Thomas Arden of Faversham, Kent in 1551. The circumstances of the murder are meticulously recorded in Stow's own hand in Harleian MS 542 at the British Library.[56] It is likely that Stow's manuscript notes are based on a transcript of the trial that took place in Faversham. The manuscript dates from 1554 or later because Sir Edward North, who was raised to the peerage in that year, is referred to as Lord North. Stow's narrative forms the basis of a short account in the *Annales of England* (1605) as well as longer versions in both editions of Holinshed's chronicle. Raphael Holinshed explained his interest in the murder as follows:

> The which murder for the horribleness thereof, although otherwise it may seem to be but a private matter, and therefore as it were impertinent to this history, I have thought good to set it forth somewhat at large, having the instructions delivered to me by them that have used some diligence to gather the true understanding of the circumstances.

The link between Stow's manuscript notes and Holinshed is an interesting example of the way in which sixteenth-century historians utilized contemporary evidence. Stow, who had a manuscript text, chose to make little use of it while Holinshed, as well as the editors of the second edition of his chronicle, printed an extended account. The murder of Thomas Arden is significant for the history of the theatre as well as the history of crime because it inspired the play *Arden of Feversham* (1592) which is included among the Shakespeare apocrypha.[57]

The murder of Thomas Arden was of political importance in Kent and played a role in the struggle between Protestant reformers and conservatives in Faversham. As the son-in-law of Sir Edward North,[58] chancellor of the court of augmentations and privy councillor, Thomas Arden was well connected to the political elite that governed the country during the reign of Edward VI. Mayor of Faversham in 1549, Arden was in Stow's eyes 'a full gentleman' as well as 'a comely personage'. He had a successful

A harvest scene from Holinshed's Chronicles *(1577). On the right men are reaping while in the centre men and women are gathering the crop into sheaves. The operation is being watched over by the bailiff, with his dog, on the left.*

career as a London merchant and became one of the leading landowners in the Faversham area. After playing an active role in the downfall of Clement Norton, the leading Henrician conservative in the town, Arden acted as the principal representative of the government. Although his death was the direct consequence of a lovers' quarrel, Arden has been portrayed as little more than a 'pious crook', whose murder may have been related to disputes between him, Sir Anthony Aucher, another prominent local political figure, and others in the community.[59]

The conspiracy that led to Arden's death began with an affair of over two years' duration between his wife, Alice, and a tailor named Thomas Mosby, 'a black, swart man', who was one of the chief gentlemen around Sir Edward North. The relationship had its ups and downs, and at one point Mrs Arden sent Mosby a pair of silver dice to regain his favour. Subsequently 'he resorted to her again and would very often times lie at Arden's house'. Arden determined that 'their mutual familiarity' was much greater than their honesty but continued to cultivate Mosby for political advantage with North.

As time passed Mrs Arden's passion for Mosby increased, and she decided that her husband must be killed. She first conspired with a local painter who was skilled in the preparation of poisons. 'I would have such a one made', she said, 'as should most speedily dispatch the eater thereof.' The painter concocted an appropriate poison and advised her to put it at the bottom of a porringer before the milk was added. As Mrs

Arden served a deadly breakfast to her husband, she failed to follow the painter's instructions and poured the milk first and then added the poison. After eating a spoonful or two, her husband, noticing the unusual colour and taste, said to his wife, 'Mistress, alas, what milk have you given me here?' She looked at it and retorted, 'I wene [think] nothing can please you.' Arden left the house and rode toward Canterbury, but *en route* he fell into 'a great vomiting and a lask and so purged upwards and downwards that he was preserved for that time'.

After failing in the attempt to poison her husband, Mrs Arden turned for assistance to another local man, John Grene, who was a servant of Sir Anthony Aucher. Grene and her husband were avowed enemies because of a dispute over monastic land that had led to threats and blows.[60] Grene therefore accepted her offer to pay £10 to anyone that he could find to kill her husband. An opportunity presented itself while Grene was travelling to London on business for Sir Anthony Aucher. Because Grene had 'some charge' with George Bradshaw, a goldsmith, he asked him to accompany him as far as Gravesend. As the two approached Rainham Downs, they saw three or four serving men coming from Leeds and Black Will, 'a terrible ruffian with a sword and a buckler', with a companion coming up the hill from Rochester. Bradshaw exclaimed to Grene, 'We are happy that here cometh some company from Leeds, for here cometh as murdering a knave as any is in England, and it had not been for them we might have chanced to have escaped hardly of our money and lives.' Bradshaw went on to explain that he and Black Will had been soldiers together at Boulogne and that the latter had murdered many people travelling between Boulogne and France.

The vicious Black Will was exactly the kind of man John Grene was hoping to find. At the invitation of the men from Leeds, Black Will agreed to join the travellers and accompany them to Gravesend where they offered him supper. After the meal Grene met secretly with Black Will and offered him £10 to kill Thomas Arden. Black Will accepted the contract to commit murder but said that he did not know the intended victim. Grene arranged for Black Will to meet Arden the following day in St Paul's Cathedral. Before proceeding on to London, Grene gave his companion, Bradshaw – who was returning to Faversham – a letter for Mrs Arden which said that thanks to Bradshaw plans for her husband's murder were complete.

From Gravesend Grene and Black Will went by water to London where they found Arden walking with a friend in St Paul's. An attempt was made to kill Arden outside the cathedral, but the effort had to be abandoned because too many gentlemen were present. Another attempt was arranged for that night while Arden was sleeping at a parsonage of his in London. With the connivance of Michael Maston, a servant who wanted to marry a kinswoman of Mosby, the doors of the house were to be unlocked so that Black Will could gain entry. At the last minute Maston got cold feet and decided to lock up. Black Will became so angry that he offered to kill both Arden and the servant in order to finish the job quickly.

Grene managed to calm the hired killer and arranged for another attempt to be made at Rainham Downs as Arden returned to Faversham. This effort was also foiled as Arden was protected by several gentlemen travelling with him. At this point Mrs Arden's lover, Mosby, tried to provoke Arden into a fight. Although Stow tells us that Mosby had a certain reluctance to kill a gentleman, the real obstacle was Arden, who refused to be drawn by verbal taunts of 'knave, villain, and cuckold'.

It was perhaps with a sense of desperation that the conspirators finally decided to kill Thomas Arden in his own house at Faversham on St Valentine's Day. Black Will concealed himself in a closet at the end of the parlour, and servants who were not privy to the plot were sent away. Arden arrived home at about six o'clock in the evening and found Mosby standing at the door wearing a silk nightgown. When Mosby told Arden that the supper was not yet ready, Arden replied, 'Then let us go and play a game at tables.' At this moment Black Will emerged from hiding and strangled Arden with a towel. Mosby then struck him on the head with a pressing iron that weighed 14 pounds. Arden fell and was carried to the counting house. When he groaned showing signs of life, Black Will finished him off with his dagger and also took the victim's money and rings. Mrs Arden paid the killer the £10 fee that he had been promised, and Black Will rode away on a horse supplied by another conspirator. To guarantee that Arden was truly dead, the wife stuck him seven or eight times in the chest.

As Thomas Arden's body was carried into a nearby field, it began to snow. The murderers, hoping that a heavy snowfall would cover their tracks, returned to the house to dine with guests who had arrived from London. During the meal Mrs Arden inquired about her husband's absence. Later the guests 'played at the tables' and were entertained by Arden's daughter who played the virginals and danced. After everyone had gone to their lodgings. Mrs Arden asked the neighbours about her husband and began to cry. The mayor of Faversham organized a search party and quickly found the body. Because the snow had stopped falling, the footsteps from Arden's body were easily followed to his house. Mrs Arden and a servant confessed when the knife, blood, and hair were discovered. The officials went on to the house of Mosby where he also confessed after blood was found on his hose and purse.

During the trial at Faversham all of the conspirators were implicated and convicted of the crime. Executions were carried out at several different places. Mrs Arden, who was charged with petty treason, was burned at Canterbury. A female servant was burned at Faversham, and the male servant Michael Maston was hanged in chains in the same town. Thomas Mosby and a sister, Elizabeth, who was privy to the conspiracy, were hanged at Smithfield, London. Grene initially escaped but was hanged in chains 'in the highway against Faversham' when he reappeared a few years later.[61] Black Will was also captured eventually and burned on a scaffold at Flushing in the Netherlands. The murder claimed the life of at least one innocent person. The unfortunate Bradshaw, who had only delivered a letter to Alice Arden, was condemned to die despite protests from the other prisoners that he was not one of the conspirators.

Tudor justice required the lives of eight persons for the murder of Thomas Arden. Stow accepted the punishment as the law of God and man.[62] He condemned Thomas Arden for acquiring land illegitimately but believed that he had loved his wife faithfully all of his life. On the basis of the information provided by Stow, it would be virtually impossible to argue that Alice Arden, Mosby, or Black Will were innocent victims of an unjust society or a prejudicial legal system. Stow certainly entertained no such thoughts and probably repeated local gossip when he wrote that for a period of two years no grass grew in the place where Arden's body had lain. As a citizen historian, Stow would not have understood the efforts of modern scholars to see the murder as a cultural phenomenon, and if he knew about allegations that Alice Arden was a rape victim, evidence has not survived.[63]

The historical tragedy *Arden of Feversham* (1592) differs from Stow's manuscript account and the printed version in Holinshed's chronicle. The play follows the

An innkeeper and her customer having a disagreement over the extent of the bill! (Roxburghe Ballads).

historical narrative rather closely, but it exaggerates the villainy of Arden's wife, who has been seen as a forerunner of Lady Macbeth, and offers a fascinating cast of dishonest and sinister characters including a few created for theatrical effect. A higher payment for the contract killing – a total of £30 – may reflect the inflation of prices at the end of the sixteenth century. The effectiveness of the play is marred by a level of intrigue and human duplicity that is scarcely credible. Although a number of influential critics including Algernon Swinburne once attributed the work to a youthful Shakespeare, the weight of modern opinion has assigned it to the apocrypha.[64]

Murder was unquestionably the crime receiving the most attention from Stow, but his chronicles demonstrate that criminal activity was extremely diverse. Prostitution, theft, counterfeiting, and piracy all have a place in his writings. Early in 1573 a large-scale naval operation against pirates led to the capture of twenty ships and nine hundred men of 'all nations', but Stow mentions the execution of only three individuals. The three pirates had robbed the Earl of Worcester of a gold font weighing 326 ounces as he sailed to France to present the queen's christening gift to the daughter of the king of France.[65] Occasionally Stow recorded the punishment without explaining clearly what the crime was. For example, in August 1589 eight soldiers and sailors were hanged at Kingston, Westminster, and London presumably because they behaved rudely and 'many men misliked their doings'. Their deaths, Stow asserted confidently, were of benefit to society because they served to terrorize others who might behave in the same way.[66] Since crime in Tudor England included political and religious offences, Stow's chronicles include accounts of persons charged with treason such as the Duke of Northumberland and the Earl of Essex as well as references to Roman Catholics and radical Protestants who violated parliamentary statutes protecting the royal supremacy.

Stow's interest in crime included lurid descriptions of the punishments inflicted for specific offences. From the data compiled by Stow and later historical research it is clear that Sir Thomas Smith's pronouncements on the humaneness and rationality of the 'punishment of malefactors' in *De Republica Anglorum* were exaggerated and outdated by the end of the sixteenth century if not earlier.[67] The chronicles offer many examples of corporal punishment including the pillory, whipping, and mutilation. In 1581 three men were condemned to lose their right hands for writing, printing, and distributing a libel. Stow recorded without comment that one was pardoned while the other two 'lost their hands by chopping off'.[68] The exact offence of another man, described as 'gentleman in countenance, but a cozener in quality', somehow escaped Stow's attention, but he found space to record that the unfortunate individual was set on the pillory twice and lost an ear.[69]

For many offences the death penalty was the accepted punishment. Convicted felons were hanged although persons of high rank such as the Duke of Somerset were beheaded as a special favour bestowed by the crown. According to Sir Thomas Smith,

In this illustration from Holinshed's Chronicles *a criminal is led through the streets to the gallows. The man at his rear is whipping him with a cat o' nine tails as he walks.*

traitors were hanged, cut down alive, drawn, and quartered, while heretics and wives who murdered their husbands were burned. Exceptions to these rules may be easily found. Traitors such as Lady Jane Grey, the Duke of Norfolk, and Mary, Queen of Scots died on the chopping block while Thomas Arden's female servant as well as his wife were burned. It was customary for the nobility and persons of royalty who were convicted of high crimes to receive privileges denied to the common people at the time of execution. If hanging, beheading, and burning were not severe enough forms of capital punishment, one was even worse – pressing, the punishment reserved for persons who refused to enter a plea when charged in court. Stow recorded one occasion in 1589 when this punishment was invoked. Lodowike Griuell, Esq, from Ridcote [sic], Warwickshire, was found guilty of being an accessory to murder, but 'standing mute, had judgment to be pressed to death'. Stow spared his readers the details of the execution but noted that the pressing was administered at the King's Bench jail in Southwark.[70]

The chronicles record the death of virtually every important person who was executed for treason or felony. Stow's coverage of the Marian martyrs was inadequate, but he did a better job with religious persecution during the reign of Elizabeth.[71] Although Stow mentioned his own presence at the execution of the Duke of Somerset in 1552, he does not appear to have attended public executions on a regular basis. In the case of the eight persons executed for the murder of Thomas Arden, Stow's fascinating narrative of the complex conspiracy is not matched by comparable coverage of the executions. Many other examples could be cited where his account of an execution is extremely superficial. An entry in the *Summarie Abridged* of 1604 indicates that on 17 February 1579, 'a young man was hanged on the miles end [Mile End Road] for murdering a man in a garden of Stepenheath [Stepney] parish'. An earlier chronicle, the *Summarye* of 1590, adds that the killer was hanged in chains, but the larger *Annales of England* (1605) omits the incident altogether.[72]

Between 1580 and 1603 the *Annales of England* (1605) records no fewer than 194 executions for all types of crime. The peak years were 1583, 1586, and 1598 when 26, 23, and 24 persons, respectively, died. For the whole period Stow listed in one way or another the execution of an average of over eight persons per year. Of these the great majority were males; in fact, only nine women are mentioned, one of whom was Mary, Queen of Scots. Although Stow did not always indicate whether the person executed was clerical or lay, about 50 priests are included among the total of 194 executions. The statistics not only testify to Stow's interest in crime and punishment, but they also demonstrate that criminal activity was a regular and accepted part of the social fabric of early modern England. It has been suggested that elaborate public executions were a sixteenth-century innovation developed by the government to achieve ideological control over an unruly populace. At these savage, but realistic educational exhibitions ordinary citizens might learn firsthand the high price paid by convicted criminals. Whether the ceremonial executions achieved this goal or whether they merely provided grisly outdoor spectacles is a question that Stow did not address.[73]

5. WOMEN

The writings of John Stow like those of his contemporaries record primarily the deeds and misdeeds of men. In central government the only office open to a woman was that of monarch, and while Stow often refers to the two queens, Mary and Elizabeth, his lack of contact with the court precludes anything like an intimate glimpse of the women who wore the crown. Outside the court, politics, religion, and society were male-dominated, and in London, the world that Stow knew best, men not only governed but created and controlled most of the wealth that lay at the heart of the city's prosperity.

Whenever women appear in the chronicles of Stow they are more often than not malcontents threatening the social order or outright criminals.[74] A butcher's daughter from East Cheap, posing as a gentlewoman, endangered political stability in 1592 by pretending to be the daughter of Philip, King of Spain. Not astute enough to plan and execute her own mischief, the nameless woman had been duped by 'accompted soothsayers after proved liars' and received a whipping as her reward.[75] More severe

A dairymaid churning butter (Roxburghe Ballads).

punishment awaited a woman whose actions undermined religious stability, because in 1588 Margaret Warde, an authentic gentlewoman, was hanged at Tyburn for helping a Catholic priest escape from Bridewell. Her crime was passing a cord with which the priest lowered himself to the ground.[76]

While no woman could challenge Alice Arden for criminality and sheer wickedness, only the lack of sordid details may separate her from several potential rivals who also committed murder. The wife of Thomas Arden failed in her attempt to poison her husband, but other women succeeded; in fact, a woman was burned for this crime at Tonbridge, Kent, in 1576, and two days later her male accomplice –

perhaps a latter day Mosby – was hanged.[77] In 1571 another poisoner, Rebecca Chamber, was 'found culpable' of poisoning her husband, Thomas, of Harrietsham, Kent, at the Maidstone assizes. When she was burned the very next day, Stow, who was ignorant of the plight of the modern battered wife, observed confidently that the punishment was 'well deserved'.[78] On at least three other occasions Stow referred to women being burned for the same offence.[79] Either women of the Tudor period found poisoning a practicable way of eliminating their husbands, or Stow had an unusual interest in the practice.

Traditional early modern prejudices about the wickedness of women appear in a variety of guises. Unsubstantiated accusations of witchcraft were made against Stow's wife and sister-in-law while he compared with his estranged brother a dishonest widow who died after cheating a shopkeeper. Stow boldly proclaimed that this woman through the judgement of God fell down speechless 'casting up at her mouth in great abundance and with horrible stink, the same matter which by nature's course should have been voided downwards, until she died'.[80] Two young women, Agnes Bridges, aged about twenty, and Rachel Pinter, 'a wench about the age of eleven or twelve years', pretending to be possessed by the devil, 'marvellously deluded' many people in 1574 and were required to submit to a humiliating penance.[81] Stow's views about the regulation of prostitution and the punishment of prostitutes indicate that he subscribed to the conventional wisdom that women's sinful and uncontrollable sexual desires drove them into crime.[82]

The trussed and charred body of William Bruister, a sixty-year-old haberdasher, symbolized the fate that befell men who consorted with wicked women. In February 1583 the odour of burning flesh drew parishioners of St Bride's, Fleet Street, to rooms over the porch of the church where Bruister lodged. Finding the door locked from the inside, they forced their way in and found the burned corpses of Bruister and Mary Breame, whom he had bailed out of Bridewell. Both died of suffocation, but the story suggests that the woman murdered her victim before committing suicide. Stow added that Mary's husband had accused her of being 'a nice woman of her body', but 'being a bad man and having spent fair and large possessions' hanged himself many years later. While Stow leaves the moral to the reader, it is tempting to conclude that the unfortunate Bruister had attempted to befriend an evil woman who was beyond human redemption.[83]

6. EPIDEMICS AND PLAGUE

John Stow was an important eye-witness to the epidemics that swept through Tudor England, and his chronicles record the response of a literate citizen of London. Today a large scholarly literature has analysed the character of the plague and other epidemic diseases, charted the demographic effects, and examined the response of government and society. The world of Stow, like that of antiquity and the middle ages, did not understand the causes of epidemics and was powerless to prevent their outbreak or treat the victims. His chronicles give merely the grim details of the occurrence of an epidemic, describe its effects, and offer basic data about the people who died.

Stow asked no profound questions about why both the good and the bad must suffer or why one area was infected and another spared. According to Paul Slack, an average of three or four medical books came out during each year of Elizabeth's reign, but Stow's writings give no indication of familiarity with this literature. Despite living through repeated outbreaks of the plague, he showed no interest in survival techniques that involved the use of a variety of improbable medical treatments including drinking urine, bleeding, and taking rigorous religious exercises. Stow shared a sense of helplessness with contemporary Londoners and did not expect the government to prevent disease or relieve the suffering of the victims. While modern society demands unapologetically that the state and medical science actively protect public health, the world of Stow could only accept what could not be changed.[84]

Stow's treatment of individual epidemics varies considerably. In 1548, for example, he says that 'a great mortality by the pestilence was in London', but there is no indication when it occurred, how long it lasted, or how many people were affected. It was forbidden to bury the dead before six o'clock in the morning or after six o'clock in the evening. Numbers of dead may have been small since a bell was to be rung for three-quarters of an hour at each burial although burial records from eighteen parishes suggest a mortality rate of 8 per cent.[85] Three years later the sweating sickness evoked a larger response. The exact nature of this disease, which struck a community quickly and usually killed its victims within twenty-four hours, remains unknown although it may have been an arbovirus infection.[86] Stow noted that the infection began in April 1551 at Shrewsbury, spread throughout the northern part of the country, and lasted until September. Within a few days of the sickness reaching London on 9 July, as many as 960 'gave up the ghost'. The infection was highly selective, attacking men in their thirties and forties but few women and children. Stow describes a household of seven that ate together one evening, and before eight o'clock the following morning, six were dead. People began 'to repent and remember God, but as the disease relented', he noted that 'the devotion decayed'.[87]

Unlike the sweating sickness, epidemics in 1555–6 and 1558 were seen by Stow as affecting older people. 'Hot burning fevers' took the lives of seven aldermen of London between December 1555 and October 1556. Stow gives the name of each victim and notes that five of the seven had served as lord mayor. By limiting his coverage of these fevers to aldermen, he presented what is really a list of notables and ignored large numbers of ordinary men and women who were also afflicted.[88] A 'quartaine ague' began in 1557 and continued until 1558, the year in which Queen Mary died. It too attacked the aged, especially priests. As a result, wrote Stow, 'a great number of parishes were unserved and no curates to be gotten'. The most notable clerical victim was Reginald, Cardinal Pole, Archbishop of Canterbury, and it is possible that the fever that fatally weakened the queen may have had the same cause. As this infection also struck down young people, 'much corn was lost in the field for lack of workmen and labourers'. The epidemics of these years constituted the greatest mortality crisis of the century and included outbreaks of typhus and influenza. Recent estimates indicate that the population of England declined by at least 6 per cent between 1556 and 1560.[89]

A deadly epidemic of short duration described by Stow as a 'dampe' appeared in Oxford at the time of the assizes in July 1577. The sick were 'smothered', and very few survived who 'were not taken at that instant [sic]'. Stow reported that the victims did not infect each other and that no women or children died. The infection began on 6 July and ended on 12 August, 'after which day died not one of that sickness'. Victims included jurors at the assizes, Sir Robert Bell, lord chief baron, Sir Robert de Olie, and others persons of rank. A total of 300 persons died at Oxford, and some 200 in other places.[90]

Although Stow does not give the source of his information about the epidemic at Oxford, another historian, John Hooker (alias Vowell), is cited as the authority for an outbreak of 'jail fever' at Exeter in 1586, that first infected Portuguese (Portingals) fishermen. A group of thirty-eight who were returning with their catch from Newfoundland were captured as 'a good prize' by Sir Bernard Drake and imprisoned at Exeter Castle. Confined to a 'deep pit and stinking dungeon', the unfortunate Portuguese were forced to lie on the bare ground 'without succour or relief'. Some of them became ill and died, while others had to be carried to their appearance before the court of assizes. The sickness spread quickly, claiming the lives of Drake, eleven of a jury of twelve men, as well as other local dignitaries, and many of the common people of Exeter. Stow's sympathies, however, were with the Portuguese fishermen. 'The sight of these men's pitiful cases,' he wrote, 'being thought to be hunger starved, rather than otherwise diseased, moved many to pity them.'[91]

Frequent epidemics as well as a whole range of debilitating illnesses encouraged 'counterfeit physicians' to exploit a helpless and credulous public. In 1550 a poulterer from Surrey named Grig was regarded by many people as a prophet because he could cure a variety of diseases by words and prayer. Unlike the modern faith healer, the honest Grig took no money for his services; yet he was pilloried in Croydon and Southwark on the order of the king's council. Stow was unequivocally hostile to phony healers who, 'never trained up in reading, or practice of physicke and chirurgerie', took advantage of women.[92]

Stow described three major epidemics – in 1563, 1593, and 1602–3 – and compiled statistics about the number of fatalities that offer a basis for comparison. Soldiers returning from Newhaven brought the 'plague of pestilence' to England at the end of July 1563. Sadly, acts of mercy that evacuated the sick from France began an epidemic that was especially severe in London. The infection became 'so hot' by September that the law courts suspended their regular term; the following January the situation had improved so little that Hilary term was kept well outside London at Hertford Castle. Stow noted that this plague affected the poor more severely than the rich. Poor citizens, he said, were stricken by a three-fold plague: 'pestilence, scarcity of money, and dearth of victuals, the misery whereof were too long here to write'. In contrast, the rich, making shift for themselves, fled into the countryside leaving the capital to those lacking the wealth to leave.

The plague of 1563 caused international repercussions when Philip II of Spain ordered a temporary embargo against English cloth coming into the Low Countries because of the fear of contamination. Although other issues also interfered with the trade, London merchants were outraged by what they regarded as a discriminatory policy. In the spring the cloth fleet was sent to Emden in East Friesland rather than the Netherlands. When the plague ended, Stow compiled statistics documenting the demographic impact. His data are based on bills of mortality that were compiled from records that parish clerks prepared on a weekly basis and certified to the crown. During the twelve months from January to December 1563, fatalities were as follows:[93]

Table 1: Epidemic of 1563

	All Diseases	**Plague**
London and its liberties (108 parishes)	20,372	17,400
11 adjoining parishes	3,283	2,732
Totals	23,655	20,132

[note that Stow gives different totals]

Thirty years later, in 1593, plague struck again. The Surrey court of assize, held at St George's Field, Southwark, completed its work in a single day rather than three. Stow noted with almost a touch of regret that while nineteen prisoners were burned in the hand by way of punishment, none was executed, perhaps because of the urgent need to wind up the assize quickly. The plague also caused the cancellation of the annual St Bartholomew's fair, and by October it had claimed the life of Sir William Roe, the lord mayor, and several aldermen. On this occasion Stow's statistics distinguished between deaths in the city within the walls, and deaths in the liberties and outside the walls:

Table 2: Epidemic of 1592–3

	All Diseases	**Plague**
London within the walls	8,598	5,390
In the liberties and outside the walls	9,295	5,385
Totals	17,893	10,775

These statistics, covering the period from 29 December 1592 to 20 December 1593, clearly indicate the impact of the plague on suburban areas of London. As population moved in larger numbers outside the historic walls of the city, the poorer suburban parishes became more susceptible to epidemic disease.[94]

The last plague of pestilence described by Stow in the *Annales of England* was brought into the country at the end of 1602 by soldiers returning from the Low Countries. After giving a lengthy account of the joyous accession of King James the next year, Stow was either too old and tired or at least disinclined to write at length about yet another epidemic. He offered neither colourful anecdotes, nor lists of worthy men who perished, but the vital statistics tell a grim tale of human suffering. Deaths for the period from 23 December 1602 to 22 December 1603 for the city of London and its liberties numbered 30,578 from the plague and 38,244 from the plague and all other diseases.[95]

Modern works analysing the demographic impact of epidemics in London during these years rely on the same data as Stow and arrive at very similar conclusions. Population estimates showing the growth of London from 85,000 in 1563 to 141,000 in 1603 were not available when Stow wrote. Using these estimates it is possible to conclude that while the total number of deaths was greater during the epidemic of 1602–3, the earlier epidemic of 1563 claimed a slightly higher percentage of lives, about 24 per cent of the population.[96]

7. POPULAR SOCIAL HISTORY

The chronicles as well as *A Survey of London* include a considerable amount of popular social history or what traditional historians deplore as trivia. As a historian of popular culture, Stow included sensational events such as severe weather, earthquakes, the birth of deformed children, and various bizarre happenings. These are survivals from the medieval chronicle tradition but also the forerunners of the cheap popular literature that attracted a growing market in the seventeenth and eighteenth centuries.[97] Over the years the demand for sensationalism has grown with the result that from the end of the nineteenth century the popular press, radio, and television marketed gossip, rumours, and the 'man bites dog' story to a rapidly expanding public. The sensationalism of Stow's historical writings not only reaffirms and strengthens a centuries–old literary tradition, but also links him with a powerful strain of modern popular culture.

Many historians would agree with Sir John Neale's characterization of Stow as 'a naive, unsophisticated mind', whose fascination with trivia offended the adult intellect and filled many pages with details 'of little or no significance in a national history'.[98] Modern social historians, on the other hand, are eager to understand how popular culture is created and consumed. As a mere citizen of London without a university education, Stow can lay claim to being a popular writer when compared with the likes of John Foxe, William Camden, or Sir John Hayward. The consumers of Stow's work were primarily literate although his publication of three different types of chronicles reveals a shrewd appreciation of a diverse audience for historical writing. The authors of the broadsides and chap-books studied by Tessa Watt targeted a more limited audience of readers who could afford only the cheapest available printed work, although, as Watt clearly shows, the audience for print included hearers as well as readers. Expensive books such as Stow's *Annales of England* that were purchased by the gentry might be read aloud on winter nights to carpenters, butchers, graziers, and certainly household servants while the cheaper abridgements enjoyed wider sales.[99]

The character of Stow's chronicles suggests that he was writing for a single culture, not one that was polarized.[100] Sensational stories appeared in virtually the same form in each of the three chronicle formats. In other words, Stow assumed that the audience for the cheaper abridgements was about as much interested in trivia as the wealthy buyer of the *Annales*. The shorter versions of the chronicles offer abbreviated accounts of the medieval centuries, but the level of sophistication in terms of the writing or credibility of the reader hardly varies. The continuing demand for Stow's chronicles, especially the shorter and cheaper ones, leaves little doubt that few, if any contemporary writers understood the taste and the buying habits of the reading public better than he.

While a constitutional or political historian might dismiss chronicle entries dealing with the weather, fires, unusual mechanical contraptions, and hungry mice with contempt, the reader of such accounts could legitimately counter that these subjects were of greater interest to the general public than incomprehensible parliamentary statutes or the subtle intrigues of court politicians. Men and women living in the sixteenth century certainly suffered more from adverse weather and fire than persons of more recent times. The severe cold that caused the Thames to freeze in 1564, the heavy snowfall of 1590, and the hailstones 9 inches in circumference that fell in June 1602 had significant human consequences.

A fire at Nantwich, Cheshire, in 1583 was not only a dramatic spectacle, but a social and economic catastrophe as well. On 13 December

> Through negligence of indiscreet persons brewing in the town of Nantwich, the fire being carelessly left, upon some light matter and so burst forth to the roofs of the house and in short time increased, that from the west end of the town the flame was dispersed so furiously into the town that in short space a great part of the town was burned down to the ground, and there was consumed about the number of 200 houses, besides brew houses, barns, stables, etc., in all about 600 houses.[101]

From the perspective of these townspeople, real trivia would have been tales from the south relating to the queen or the machinations of her privy councillors.

Part of Stow's journalistic genius was the ability to seize the attention of his readers with a story that was almost incredible. Such a bizarre incident occurred in 1580 in marshland near Southminster, Essex, where 'an infinite multitude of mice' overwhelmed the marshes, and then sheared, and gnawed the grass by the roots, spoiling and tainting it with their 'venomous' teeth. Cattle grazing in the marsh became ill and died, and everything appeared hopeless until the miraculous appearance of a multitude of owls – of such number that 'all the shire was not able to yield'. These wonderful birds quickly devoured the mice and saved the local community from total ruin.[102] While it may be doubted that Stow's better educated readers swallowed this tale, it successfully combined a memorable story with an account of economic misfortune caused by the death of the cattle.

Anecdotes that were of little or no social or economic significance were sometimes included for moralistic purposes or to reveal God's presence in human affairs.[103] A story included in the *Summarie Abridged* of 1604, but omitted from the longer chronicles, told of William Withers, an eleven-year-old boy from Sussex, who

> lay in a trance and then coming to himself again, uttered to the standers by many strange speeches against pride, covetousness, and coldness of charity.[104]

Stow the moralist and animal lover was visible as he reported the collapse of a scaffold at the bear garden south of the Thames in 1583. Although eight men and women died and many others were injured, Stow saw the accident as a 'friendly warning to such as more delight themselves in the cruelty of beasts than in works of mercy, the fruits of a true professed faith, which ought to be the Sabbath day's exercise'.[105] Stow was either too cautious or too sceptical to allow a large role for providence in his historical writings. During the summer of 1552, he noted without comment the birth of Siamese twins near Oxford and the appearance of unusually large fish. The same incidents were used later in Sir John Hayward's *Life and Raigne of King Edward the Sixth* (1630) as prodigies foretelling 'some imminent and eminent evil', namely the approaching death of King Edward.[106]

The reader of Stow's historical works found not only anecdotes that offered social insights and moralistic guidance but also trivia included simply because they were fascinating. We must assume that Stow enjoyed entertaining and occasionally shocking his audience with a good story. An example suggesting that popular interest has changed very little over the centuries is the incredible tale of William Foxley, a potmaker employed at the Mint in the Tower of London, who fell asleep on 27 April 1546 and did not awaken for fourteen days. Henry VIII, his physicians, and learned men examined Foxley, but the sleeper could not be aroused with 'pricking, cramping, or otherwise burning'. After he awakened, it was 'as if he had slept but one night'. The good news was that Foxley lived for forty years after the long sleep and enjoyed a normal life.[107]

Stow's account of the strange illness of Ferdinando Stanley, 5th Earl of Derby, in April 1594 unfortunately had a tragic ending. As Lord Strange, he has attracted attention as a patron of Christopher Marlowe and Thomas Nashe. With a claim to the throne, he also had a following among Catholic conspirators to whom he may or may not have given encouragement.[108] Ferdinando Stanley died at the age of thirty-five after sixteen days of intense suffering despite receiving treatment from 'a doctor of physicke'. Morbid details obviously fascinated Stow as he meticulously recorded the stricken man's final agony day by day. Derby was afflicted with uncontrollable episodes of vomiting which Stow numbered at fifty-two. In a single day Derby vomited seven times; 'the colour of his vomits was like to soutie [sic ?sooty] or rusty iron, the substance very gross and fatty, the quantity above seven pints'. The earl's medical treatment included enemas, infusions of rhubarb and manna, and external applications of oils and plasters to 'stay and comfort his stomach'. When he could no longer pass urine, the physicians inserted a catheter into his bladder.[109]

After treating his reader to a long list of gruesome symptoms, Stow disappointed anyone who was anticipating profound medical insights. He offered two possible diagnoses, neither of which will stand scientific scrutiny: according to his physicians, Derby died partly of a surfeit and partly of 'a most violent distempering himself with vehement exercise, taken four days together in the Easter week'. Nevertheless, Stow reported that 'many learned men' thought Derby was bewitched and included 'a true report of such reasons and conjectures' supporting this conclusion. He was troubled with bad dreams after he denied the supplication of an unidentified woman; later a witch named Jane asked 'whether he made water as yet or no and at that very time, notwithstanding all helps, his waters utterly stopped'. Derby's suffering mercifully ended, and he died a pious death at Lathom House, Lancashire, after being ministered to by his chaplain and the bishop of Chester.[110]

Stow may have been attracted to Derby's story less by the qualities of the victim than by the bizarre circumstances. In relating the anecdote, Stow relied on information given to him by a trusted informant. He explained that the details had been 'gathered by those who were present with him [Derby]' and added that he had often been asked to publish the narrative, 'but I could never get the particulars authentically'.[111] Stow always found space in his chronicles for tales of unusual interest that stretched the readers' credibility, and this episode combining gruesome details of human suffering with allegations of witchcraft was certain to delight readers and promote the sale of his books.

During the summer of 1581 Stow watched and described a public spectacle that entertained contemporaries but would be regarded with disgust in an age of greater social sensitivity. Two Dutchmen of 'strange statures', a giant and a dwarf, performed before crowds of amused Londoners. The larger man stood 7 feet 7 inches tall and was a 'comely man' except for his legs which had been broken while lifting a barrel of beer. His companion

was in height but three foot, had never a good foot, nor any knee at all, and yet could he dance a galliard; he had no arm but a stump to the elbow or little more on the right side.

The severely handicapped man was an accomplished street busker who juggled a cup on his stump of an arm, played a trumpet, and sang. Stow noted that he could drink

10 quarts of beer every day 'if he could get it'. Stow was also amused to see the giant seated on a bench bareheaded next to the dwarf who stood at full height on the same bench wearing a hat with a feather and was still lower than his companion.[112]

Another unedifying, but sensational story was an account of an autopsy performed on a horse that died suddenly at Spaldwick, Huntingdonshire, in 1588. As the body was examined, a strange worm was found imbedded within the heart, 'the like whereof before hath not been heard of in our time'. The length of the worm divided into fifty 'greines' (forks or prongs) which spread from the body of the worm like the branches of a tree and dripped a reddish fluid. The worm measured 17 inches from the snout to the end of the longest 'greine', while its circumference was 3½ inches. Readers eager for indications of scientific curiosity came away empty-handed because Stow merely ended by saying that the worm was stabbed with a dagger as it crawled away.[113]

Wells Cathedral, like rural Huntingdonshire, was located far from Stow's own world of London, yet he managed to learn of strange happenings there on the morning of Sunday 5 December 1596:

> In the sermon time before noon a sudden darkness fell among them, a storm and tempest followed with lightning and thunder such as overthrew to the ground them that were in the body of the church, all which church seemed to be on a light fire, a loathsome stench following some stones were stricken out of the bell tower, and wires and irons of the horologe were molten, and no timber burnt, which tempest being ceased, and the people came to themselves, some of them were found to be marked with sundry figures in their bodies, and their garments not perished.[114]

A second version of this story appears in Edmund Howes' edition of the *Annales* published after Stow's death. The place and date are identical, but Howes had additional details and told a different tale. When a newly ordained priest, preaching his first sermon before a large congregation in the presence of the bishop, began to discourse on 'spirits and their properties',

> there entered in the west window of the church a dark and unproportionable thing of the bigness of a football and went along the wall on the pulpit side and suddenly it seemed to break but with no 'leue' sound and terror, then if an hundred double cannons had been discharged at once, and therewithal came a most violent storm and tempest of lightning and thunder as if the church had been full of fire; in this strange tempest all the people were sore amazed and many of them stricken down to the ground; the preacher himself was struck down in his pulpit and many in the body of the church were marked in their garments, arms and bodies with the figures of stars or crosses. . . .

Published in a work called Groundeworke of Conycatching, *this picture shows the same person, Nicholas Jennings, as gentleman and 'counterfeit Cranke', a sham beggar.*

When the storm ended, the resourceful bishop spoke to the terrified congregation and invited them to a sermon in the afternoon in which, according to Howes, he comforted them all.[115] The two narratives offer compatible perspectives on the same incident, but it is not easy to explain why Howes rewrote Stow's account or exactly why it was included in the first place.

Stow was a citizen historian whose works were aimed at all levels of society. Although a political narrative lay at the heart of his chronicles and provided a common core of history for the nation, his readers could also feel the heartbeat of English society. From Stow one could learn about the stewardship of eminent Tudors and understand how the poor struggled to survive. Every reader of his writings was reminded that social instability, crime, and epidemic disease were part of daily life in the sixteenth century. Women were either exemplified by grotesque characters such as Alice Arden or existed only in the margins of his writings. Stow's attitude toward gender issues mirrored the prejudice of his age; nevertheless, he remembered a few especially worthy women for their acts of charity. Stow's anecdotes were for men and women of all ranks and degrees. These sensational morsels of popular history not only provided healthy doses of moral suasion and amusement, but also improved the sale of his chronicles.

Christopher Hill identified many writers during the century before 1640 who saw the common people as fickle and unstable, a many-headed monster threatening an ordered society, but Stow belonged to a different tradition.[116] The learned Revd Thomas Fuller was correct when he said that the fur of Stow's gown shaped his attitude to the past, because he retained something of a 'commonwealth' mentality throughout his long and productive life. Although Stow never defined who the 'people' were, they were always human beings with the potential for decency, and his history was inclusive, not limited to the crown, court, and nobility.[117]

CHAPTER THREE

POPULAR AND UNPOPULAR REBELLIONS

In recent years historians have brought the role of rebellion in the political, social, and religious life of sixteenth-century England into sharper focus. Indeed, the Tudor dynasty established itself on the throne in 1485 as a result of a successful baronial rebellion, and each succeeding generation experienced a major rebellion as well as numerous lesser stirs and riots. Before the revival of interest in Tudor rebellions, the majority of historians preferred to portray the century as an era of law and order in which a strong but popular monarchy ruled over grateful and largely obedient subjects.[1] Although contemporaries living in the sixteenth century knew of rebellion and popular disorder, often through direct personal experience, the government understandably opposed anything resembling impartial and disinterested discussion of the rebellions. Government propagandists denounced rebellion vigorously in royal proclamations and manifestos, while the clergy echoed similar themes from the pulpit.[2] Of the two histories of rebellion published during the sixteenth century, the first, John Proctor's history of Wyatt's Rebellion, was unadulterated government propaganda, and the other, Alexander Neville's history of Kett's Rebellion, was a polemic written in Latin to guarantee a select readership.[3] Without specialized books on rebellions, the literate public had one primary source of historical information, the chronicles that appeared with greater frequency and variety as the century progressed.

Stow was the only Tudor historian who experienced and wrote about every rebellion from the death of Henry VIII to the accession of James I. The period included the rebellions of 1549 that affected half the counties of England, Wyatt's Rebellion of 1554, the Northern Rebellion of 1569, and the rising of the Earl of Essex in 1601. As a Londoner Stow was well placed to witness the popular discontent of 1548–9 firsthand and to see the military failures of Wyatt and Essex. The location of the Northern Rebellion required him to rely on outside sources of information as did conspiracies and risings in Norfolk and Devon. In 1549 Stow's career as a chronicler lay in the future as his first published work, an edition of Chaucer, did not appear until 1561. When the desperate revolt of Essex ended with the execution of the queen's favourite, Stow was an old man whose chronicles and *Survey of London* enjoyed a wide readership.

John Stow recognized the wide geographical scope of the rebellions of 1549 when he observed in his earliest chronicle, *A Summarie of Englyshe Chronicles* (1565), that 'the commons in most part of this realm made sundry insurrections and commotions'. The largest risings occurred in the West of England, where there was violent resistance to Protestant reforms, and in East Anglia, where Robert Kett called for sweeping social reforms. Before Stow published his first chronicle, several accounts of the rebellions had already appeared. *An Epitome of Chronicles . . .*, by Thomas Cooper, an Oxford scholar with connections at the court of Edward VI, was published in 1549 with an enthusiastic dedication to Protector Somerset as a champion of the poor, but its narrative ended at Michaelmas 1547. *The Thre Bokes of Cronicles* by John Carion and Gwalter Lynne, published in 1550, may be the earliest printed account of the rebellions.[4] John Mychell's *A Breuiat Cronicle Contaynynge All the Kinges from Brute to This Day*, first published at Canterbury in 1552, included a short account of the rebellions.[5] Thomas Crowley's enlarged version of Cooper's chronicle (1559) also touched on the rebellions, but Cooper's own revision of 1560, with its bitter denunciation of Crowley, carried a better narrative of the events of 1549. Other sixteenth-century writers whose chronicles were published before Stow include Robert Fabyan (1559) and Stow's great rival, Richard Grafton (1562).[6]

The text of Stow's *Summarie* of 1565 gives no indication of his sources for the rebellions of 1549, but the list of sources at the beginning of the chronicle includes two of the earlier accounts, Robert Fabyan and Thomas Cooper. While Stow drew quite heavily on Cooper, it does not appear that he used Fabyan or any other previously published historical narrative. Nor is there any indication that he had access to official sources or state papers. If Stow consulted any of the unpublished historical accounts such as the Grey Friars' chronicle or the chronicle of Charles Wriothesley, he made no use of them in 1565. The same may be said of Nicholas Sotherton's history of the rebellion in Norfolk.[7] As for personal recollections, the chronicles offer nothing. Stow's only personal anecdote is found in *A Survey of London* and is the tale of the bailiff of Romford, Essex, 'a man very well beloved', who came to London during the rebellions and was executed. As he climbed the ladder to the gibbet, he accused Sir Stephen, curate of St Katherine Christ's church, of having informed on him. The bailiff's offence was to have reported that 'many men be up in Essex'. Popular reaction against the curate was such that to avoid reproach he left London and was never seen again. Stow heard the unfortunate bailiff's last words 'for he was executed upon the pavement of my door where I then kept house'.[8]

The more substantial *Chronicles of England* (1580) provided additional information about the rebellions, including references to risings in Somerset, Lincolnshire, Essex, Kent, and Yorkshire. Twenty-five years later, in the *Annales of England* (1605), Stow was able to add only a few minor details to his narrative of the rebellions. By 1580, the first edition (1577) of Holinshed's chronicles was available, and this work drew on

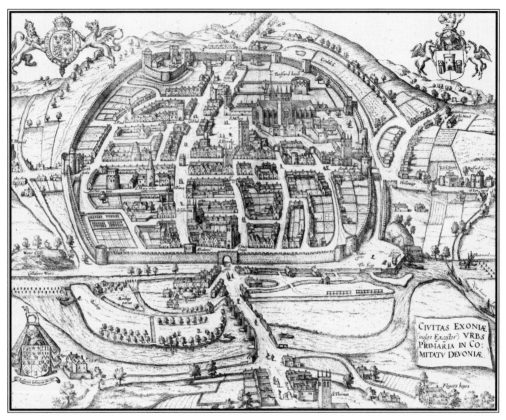

A town plan of the city of Exeter, drawn in 1583 and published in 1618. The coat of arms of Stow's collaborator, John Hooker, appears in the bottom left-hand corner.

sources that were available to Stow but for some reason were not consulted by him. For an account of the Norfolk rebellion, Holinshed used the important Latin narrative of Alexander Neville that was published in 1575. Holinshed's account of the rebellions in the West of England and in Yorkshire was based on John Foxe, a writer who was consistently neglected by Stow. Among the works consulted by Holinshed were Stow's *Summarie* and numerous unnamed books belonging to Stow, yet three years later, when completing the *Chronicles of England*, Stow chose simply to ignore Holinshed's excellent account. By the time the *Annales of England* first appeared in 1592, Stow had available not only the first edition of Holinshed but also the second to which he had himself made a major contribution, but none of Holinshed's material was incorporated in Stow's own work. Consequently, the second edition of Holinshed, containing the detailed account of the Norfolk rebellion based on Neville, John Hooker's valuable description of Exeter, and John Cheke's *Hurt of Sedition*, stands in a class by itself as the best Tudor account of the rebellions of 1549.

In explaining the causes of the rebellions, Stow followed Thomas Cooper by emphasizing the importance of grievances connected with 'parks, pastures, and enclosures made by gentlemen'. No one has ever doubted that enclosures were critical in the East Anglian risings, but little evidence to corroborate enclosure risings in the West survives. Both Cooper and Stow stated unequivocally that enclosures were a cause of unrest in Devon and added the rebels' demand for the restoration of the 'old religion'.[9] Stow's interpretation of the causes of the risings, based on Cooper, is continued into the *Chronicles* of 1580 and the *Annales of England*. Further insight into Stow's thinking may be found in a manuscript note that argues for the broad territorial scope of the rebellions and their popular character:

> This year [1549] the commons in all parts of England made sundry insurrections and commotions about Whitsuntide and so forth until September among whom divers of commons of Cornwall and Devonshire in sundry camps besieged Exeter.[10]

The *Summarie* of 1565 identifies Robert Kett, leader of the Norfolk rebellion, only as a tanner, but from 1580 Stow notes that Kett was a relatively wealthy man with land worth £50 per year and movable property valued at more than 1,000 marks or £667.[11] In each of the chronicles, Stow portrayed John Dudley, Earl of Warwick, as a heroic figure who, facing great danger, successfully pacified the rebels. Stow's partiality for Warwick might be explained by the fact that his early historical writings were dedicated to Warwick's son, Robert Dudley, Earl of Leicester, but on closer examination it is clear that Stow's assessment of Warwick is taken from Thomas Cooper, who also enjoyed the patronage of Leicester.[12]

No Tudor chronicler could write sympathetically about rebels or popular protest and expect to have his work published. Accordingly, Stow assured his readers that God in his wisdom worked to confound those who defied royal authority but avoided the polemics found in Alexander Neville's history of the Norfolk rebellion. While Stow wrote with compassion about the bailiff of Romford and may have known other examples of injustice, he included the anecdote as a digression in *A Survey of London*, not as a historical event in the chronicles.[13] Stow's restraint may also be seen in his approach to the consequences of the rebellions. Cooper argued that Protector Somerset had been held responsible for the rebellions and the heavy loss of life because 'it was thought that he minded a redress of the great enclosing that many gentlemen before that time had used and that the common people, upon occasion thereof, was stomached to be the bolder in this attempt'.[14] Stow did not follow Cooper's line of argument in the *Summarie* of 1565. Instead, Stow cited losses to the French outside Boulogne and wrote that Warwick, with the consent of other nobles, openly accused Somerset of misgovernment 'as well in this as in divers other matters'.[15]

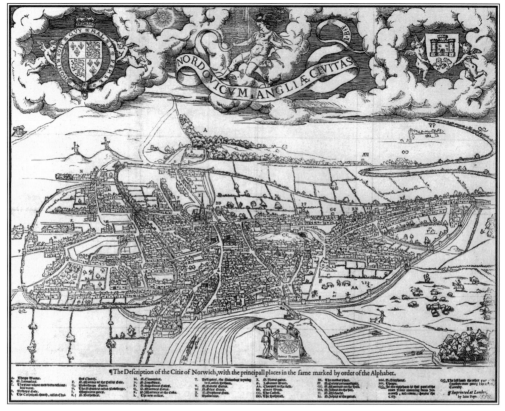

Cunningham's map of Norwich, published in 1558, the year of the accession of Elizabeth I.

The *Annales of England* (1605) offers a much longer account of the fall of Somerset, including letters and a list of charges against him; however, Stow did not argue that the failure of Somerset's leadership during the rebellions led to his fall from power. After a short imprisonment in the Tower of London, Somerset was released and restored to the king's council, but following a second fall, he was executed in 1552. When the duke was beheaded, Stow's manuscript notes state that the execution was to the 'great discontent of the Protestants', but this comment was not included in the *Annales*.[16] Although Stow's narratives of the rebellions of 1549 are weak on analysis and less detailed than the second edition of Holinshed, his work offers sound accounts of varying lengths with an interpretive commentary that is consistent with the best historical writing of the sixteenth century.

As a resident of London, Stow was ideally situated to witness and report on Wyatt's Rebellion of 1554. The first major challenge to the regime of Mary Tudor, the rebellion culminated in Sir Thomas Wyatt's march on the capital from Kent. The role of London was critical because he expected the city to support him, and its failure to do so led directly to his humiliating surrender to the queen's forces. After the rebellion ended, Stow would have had access to persons who were eyewitnesses and also to those who had been participants. It was eleven years later – 1565 – when he published his first chronicle account, but by then several narratives of the rebellion had already appeared.

The earliest published account of Wyatt's Rebellion is contained in the 1554 edition of *A Breuiat Cronicle* by the Canterbury printer John Mychell, printed between 25 February and 25 March. His narrative of Wyatt's Rebellion is very short and confined to events in Kent. By emphasizing that the revolt began at Maidstone and boasting that his city of Canterbury remained loyal to the queen, Mychell revealed a narrow, provincial historical perspective:

> At which commotion and stir, although there came to them divers out of great places of Kent, goodness of God and the circumspect provision and diligent attendance of John Twyne, mayor, and his brethren the aldermen, with the faithful assistance of other, the city was defended from foreign rebels and not so much as one known of the said city to have fled to Wyatt or to any of his adherents.[17]

It was to remedy the deficiencies in Mychell's chronicle and to provide a better narrative of the rebellion that John Proctor published *The Historie of Wyates Rebellion* in December 1554. A Tonbridge schoolmaster, who had written against an alleged Arian heretic during the reign of Edward VI, Proctor presented the official view of Mary's government that Wyatt's Rebellion was the work of seditious heretics whose objective was to uphold Protestant doctrines. Proctor's history is the fullest contemporary narrative of the rebellion and has been reprinted and widely cited by historians.[18]

Several other accounts of the rebellion were published before the appearance of Stow's earliest chronicle. In 1559 John Kyngston printed a continuation of *The Chronicle of Fabian* that drew on Mychell, and Robert Crowley published what was denounced as a plagiarized edition of Thomas Cooper under the title *An Epitome of Chronicles*. Cooper produced a new edition of his chronicle the following year in which he repudiated Crowley. Richard Grafton published his first *Abridgement of the English Chronicles* in 1562 and followed with new editions in 1563 and 1564; the next year he published another work, *A Manuell of the Chronicles of England*, which also included an account of Wyatt's Rebellion. None of these chroniclers has been studied as a historian of his own era, but modern historiographers have given each of them consistently low marks for learning and originality.[19]

The early chronicle accounts, as well as Proctor's narrative, were in print and presumably available when Stow prepared his first chronicle for publication. In addition to the printed books, several contemporary narratives survive today that were not published during the sixteenth century. The most important of these for Wyatt's

Rebellion is a pocket diary covering the period from July 1553 to October 1554 that was edited by J.G. Nichols and published by the Camden Society in 1850 as *The Chronicle of Queen Jane and of Two Years of Queen Mary*. The manuscript diary (British Library, Harleian MS 194) came into Stow's possession and was used in his chronicles, but its author, 'Row. Lea', has never been satisfactorily identified.[20] Also published for the first time during the nineteenth century were *The Chronicle of the Grey Friars of London*, *The Diary of Henry Machyn*, and Charles Wriothesley's *Chronicle*, which was likely to have been available to Stow in manuscript.[21] Another important personal narrative for Wyatt's Rebellion is that of Edward Underhill, a member of the gentlemen pensioners and a supporter of the Duke of Northumberland, who was known as the 'hot gospeller'.[22] As this survey of surviving sources shows, the events of Wyatt's Rebellion were recorded in various accounts before Stow published his first chronicle, and when later works such as the two editions of Holinshed and Stow's *Annales* appeared, the printed and manuscript sources could be described best as part of the historical tradition of the previous generation.

Sir Thomas Wyatt, the instigator of the 1554 rebellion that bears his name, by an unknown artist.

In the first edition of his *Summarie*, Stow offered a short account of the events of Wyatt's Rebellion, one that was appropriate to the scope of this chronicle. In neither the text nor the margins are there any indications of his sources. However, if Stow is compared with Cooper's chronicle of 1560, the accounts are virtually identical. In other words, John Stow seems to have lifted his narrative of Wyatt's Rebellion from Thomas Cooper. There is full agreement on the question of causation, as each attributed the revolt to opposition to the queen's marriage to Philip of Spain and to religious change: 'The purpose of this marriage was so grievously taken of divers noble men, and a great number of gentlemen and commons, that for this, and religion, they in such sort conspired against the queen.'[23] Each writer accepts the initial popularity of Wyatt's cause in Kent and London and records the desertions from the Duke of Norfolk's hastily recruited army. There is a brief account of the Duke of Suffolk's abortive rising, and both Stow and Cooper state categorically that he proclaimed his daughter, Lady Jane, queen, an event that remains highly controversial.

The differences in the two narratives are more curious than historically significant. For example, Stow uses spellings of certain words that are closer to the modern usage:[24]

Stow	**Cooper**
Charing crosse	Charyne crosse
returned	retourned
defeated	defeited

Whereas Cooper says only that a great number were hanged after the revolt ended, Stow is more specific, saying that 'about the number of 50' were hanged; but Cooper informs the reader that the gallows 'remained there a good part of the summer following to the terror and fear of other'. Moreover, only Cooper recorded the flight of Sir Peter Carew, the Devonshire conspirator, to France.[25]

It is unlikely that we shall ever know why Stow chose simply to lift his account of Wyatt's Rebellion from a previously published work. We might speculate that Mychell's chronicle was rejected because London readers were not interested in the reputation of Canterbury, and that Proctor was ignored as the mouthpiece of the discredited Marian regime. Whether Stow possessed the invaluable source material contained in Harleian MS 194 as early as 1565 is another question that cannot be answered. Whatever his reasons for not drawing on the best available printed sources, as well as on an important manuscript narrative – if it was, in fact, in his possession – his *Summarie* of 1565 was a poorer work because of these omissions. Certainly the most puzzling of all the unanswerable questions is why Stow failed to include personal recollections of a rebellion that aroused strong feelings in London and concluded with a rebel march to the very gates of the city.

After 1565, when Stow published enlarged and revised chronicles, the earlier versions inevitably became sources for the later works. In the *Annales of England* of 1605, Stow refers the reader to the second edition of Holinshed for a full account of the arraignment of Sir Thomas Wyatt.[26] The only other source for Wyatt's Rebellion cited by Stow in the *Annales* is 'Row. Lea', the author of the *Chronicle of Queen Jane* – Harleian MS 194.[27] There is no indication that Stow consulted Mychell's chronicle during the forty years that had elapsed since the first edition of the *Summarie*, and a few details from Proctor probably came from Holinshed, whose authors acknowledged use of the former's narrative. The *Annales* contains a few passages similar to Wriothesley's chronicle, but nothing to suggest that Stow worked with either Machyn's diary or the *Chronicle of the Grey Friars*.[28]

The various editions of Stow's chronicles do not give a single, consistent interpretation of Wyatt's Rebellion. One finds, on careful examination, subtle and not so subtle differences in emphases and also unexplained deletion of important historical events. The question of the causes of the rebellion has been studied by David M. Loades, who rejected John Proctor's notion that Wyatt's Rebellion was the work of a nasty band of Protestant heretics. By analysing the background of the leaders of the rebellion, Loades showed that all of them had been 'prominent supporters of one or other of the Edwardian regimes', and that opposition to Queen Mary's marriage to Philip of Spain and the anticipated impact of the marriage on foreign policy were the major causes of the rebellion.[29] From the appearance of Stow's first chronicle in 1565 to the *Annales* of 1605, he, unlike Loades, argued that the rebellion had multiple causes – religion *and* the marriage. In 1565 Stow also reported that Wyatt spoke to a company of rebels and denounced the queen's religious policies. He said that she and the council 'intended not only by the alteration of religion to bring in the pope, but also by marriage to a stranger to bring the realm into miserable servitude and bondage'.[30] Five years later the enlarged 1570 edition of the *Summarie* did not include the above criticism of the queen's religious policy; the same omission occurs in the *Chronicles* of 1580 and the *Annales of England*. Therefore, only the earliest edition does anything to spell out the exact nature of Wyatt's religious motivation with the result that the later editions of Stow moved very slightly, but perceptibly, closer to the position of Loades with regard to the causes of Wyatt's Rebellion.

Although Stow occasionally deleted details from later editions, he more often added information, which, of course, contributed to the greater length of the *Chronicles* of 1580 and the *Annales of England*. One example of the lengthening process concerns Wyatt's activities in Southwark. Advancing toward London from Kent, Wyatt arrived in Southwark hoping that his supporters in the city would assist him in crossing London Bridge. The mayor and sheriffs learned of Wyatt's approach and 'forthwith the draw bridge was cut down and the bridge gates shut'.[31] While Wyatt decided what his next move should be, some of his men began looting. The *Summaries* of 1565 and 1570 say nothing of the looting, only that Wyatt left Southwark for Kingston after two days. In the *Chronicles* of 1580 Stow mentions only Wyatt's proclamation against soldiers taking anything without paying for it.

The *Annales*, however, contains a detailed account of the looting of Winchester Place, the house of Stephen Gardiner, the lord chancellor:

> Divers of his company being gentlemen (as they said) went to Winchester Place, made havoc of the bishop's goods (he being lord chancellor) not only of his victuals, whereof there was plenty, but whatsoever else, not leaving so much as one lock of a door, but the same was taken off and carried away, nor a book in his gallery or library uncut or rent into pieces so that men might have gone up to the knees in leaves of books cut out and thrown under feet.[32]

Here we feel the passion of Stow the manuscript collector and bibliophile. Wyatt's men – claiming to be gentlemen – took not only food but also maliciously sacked Gardiner's house. Although Stow never denounced Wyatt's Rebellion directly, his account of the events at Southwark discredits Wyatt's claim to be fighting against the Spanish marriage and Roman Catholicism.[33]

Stow is the principal authority for the participation of John Ponet, the Edwardian Bishop of Rochester and Winchester, in the rebellion. Best known as the author of *The Short Treatise of Politike Power*, Ponet left only vague traces of his activities between the death of Edward VI and his exile to Germany.[34] He does not appear in Proctor's history of the rebellion, although as Bishop of Rochester and a close associate of Archbishop Cranmer, he must have had connections in Kent. Stow says nothing of Ponet in the chronicles of 1565, 1570, and 1580, but the *Annales of England* reveals him as an important advisor of Wyatt who lost confidence in his leadership and abandoned the rebel army as it advanced from Kingston toward London. According to Stow, Ponet advised Wyatt not to waste valuable time trying to move a broken gun carriage because the rebels would lose all advantage of a surprise attack on the queen's army in London. John Ponet's appearance in Stow's narrative is limited to a single episode; the chronicler does not say when Ponet joined the rebels, what his motives were, or where he went immediately following the break with Wyatt. On the other hand, the very presence of a Protestant leader of Ponet's stature among Wyatt's supporters gives support for the view that religious motivation was an important ingredient in the rebellion.[35]

Beginning with the *Chronicles* of 1580 and continuing in the *Annales*, Stow described the rebel attack on Whitehall Palace. It is surprising that the attack has never received the attention of modern historians, inasmuch as Queen Mary was at the time in residence there. Stow's account is borrowed completely from the anonymous author of the *Chronicle of Queen Jane*:

At Charing Cross there stood Sir John Gage, lord chamberlain, with the guard and a number of other being almost a thousand; the which upon Wyatt's coming shot at his company, but at the last fled to the court gates against them. At this repulse the said lord chamberlain and others were so amazed that many cried treason in the court and had thought that the Earl of Pembroke, who was assaulting the tail of his enemies had gone to Wyatt, taking his part against the queen; there was running and crying out of ladies and gentlewomen, shutting of doors and windows and such a shrieking and noise as was wonderful to hear.[36]

Whereas Stow indicated that Sir John Gage withdrew from Charing Cross and retreated southward toward Whitehall, Edward Underhill, an eyewitness, says that a rebel force, led by Anthony Knevett and Thomas Cobham, came 'through the Gatehouse from Westminster'. Neither Stow nor Underhill says whether the attack was part of a plan to capture the queen, but each leaves little doubt that there was panic and disorder. Underhill inserted a humorous note when he observed that the aged Gage was so frightened by the approaching rebels that he fell into the dirt. 'Master Gage came in amongst us all dirt,' Underhill continued, 'and so frighted that he could not speak to us.'[37] Fortunately for the queen, leaders, who retained their composure, determined that Pembroke had not gone over to Wyatt and took steps necessary to protect the court.

Wyatt's Rebellion was intended to be only one of three regional risings against Queen Mary. The two others, planned for the West and the Midlands, fizzled out hopelessly, but the Midlands fiasco is of considerable importance because of the alleged proclamation of Lady Jane by her father, the Duke of Suffolk. Although Lady Jane remained in the Tower of London under a sentence of death following the Northumberland conspiracy, her father was released. He joined Wyatt's conspiracy and made his way to Coventry. That Suffolk, the rebel, achieved as little in 1554 as he had the previous year has never been disputed; however, a cloud of uncertainty has surrounded his intentions. Loades approached the question cautiously, showing the disagreement between government attitudes and Cooper's chronicle (1565) on the one hand and Holinshed on the other.[38] Unfortunately, an investigation of Stow's views only adds to the existing uncertainty. Since Stow's *Summarie* of 1565 is almost identical to Cooper's edition of 1560, it is easy enough to identify the authority behind Stow's assertion that Suffolk proclaimed Jane queen.[39] In the 1570 edition of the *Summarie*, Stow tells a different story: Suffolk made a proclamation against the queen's marriage with Philip of Spain; Jane is not mentioned. Stow maintains the latter position in both the *Chronicles* of 1580 and the *Annales*.[40]

The Duke of Suffolk was obviously guilty of treason against Queen Mary whether or not he proclaimed his daughter queen, and no one has ever argued that he was unjustly executed. The execution of Lady Jane and her husband, Lord Guildford Dudley, is an entirely different question. If Lady Jane was not proclaimed queen by her

Contemporary woodcuts showing Lady Jane Grey proclaimed as queen, and executed.

father or connected in any way with the rebellion, why did the government decide to execute her at the same time as her father and Wyatt? Loades' response would seem to be that the government wanted to associate Jane, Suffolk, and perhaps even Wyatt with the 'odious' reputation of Northumberland.[41] It could further be argued that the queen had been lenient with Jane and her father in 1553 and was repaid with a rebellion. Stow's position on Jane's execution is consistently presented beginning with the *Summarie* of 1565 through the *Chronicles* of 1580 and the *Annales of England*. Her death and that of her husband 'were the more hastened for fear of further troubles and stir for her title, like her father had attempted'.[42] Regrettably, Stow's explanation still leaves important questions unanswered. Did he continue to believe that Jane was proclaimed queen or did he merely report official thinking? He also sidestepped the ethical question of whether Jane's execution in February 1554 was in any way a just sentence by the standards of his age.

Princess Elizabeth, like Lady Jane, was suspected of complicity in Wyatt's Rebellion. If the rebels intended to depose Queen Mary, rather than prevent the Spanish marriage, Elizabeth had significant advantages over Jane because the queen's half-sister had a better claim to the throne and no connections with the Greys or Dudleys. Over the years, modern historians have engaged in a good deal of second-guessing about Elizabeth's role in the rebellion, but the subject was hardly one that a contemporary chronicler like Stow could address with candour. In the *Summarie* of 1565, he stated what appears to be the bald facts, that is that Elizabeth and the Earl of Devon 'were both in suspicion to have consented to Wyatt's conspiracy and for the same were apprehended and committed to the Tower'.[43] In the edition of 1570, Stow omitted the cause of Elizabeth's imprisonment, and he maintained his silence in the *Chronicles* and *Annales of England*. Stow may have removed what he regarded as doubtful passages from his later work as he freed himself from dependence on Cooper's chronicle, but he may have wanted also to dissociate Queen Elizabeth from any hint of treasonous activity in the aftermath of the Northern Rebellion of 1569. In 1554 Protestants such as Elizabeth and Lady Jane were vulnerable to charges of disloyalty, but after 1569, Stow, who was suspected of Roman Catholic sympathies, could scarcely afford to remind readers that the Protestant queen had once been imprisoned for supporting Wyatt's Rebellion.

In contrast to Stow's later chronicles, the second edition of Holinshed offers a detailed account of Elizabeth's precarious situation after Wyatt's surrender, based on John Foxe's *Book of Martyrs*. Here Foxe's villain, Stephen Gardiner, Bishop of Winchester – 'always a capital enemy to the Lady Elizabeth' – declared that he had evidence of her complicity in the rebellion and impugned Wyatt's declaration that she was innocent of any wrongdoing.[44] The lengthy treatment of Wyatt's Rebellion in Holinshed, which cites not only Foxe and Stow but also Richard Grafton and includes a complex dialogue based on the arraignment of Sir Edward Throckmorton for treason, none the less fails to note the participation of John Ponet and barely mentions the looting of Winchester Place and the attack on the court at Whitehall. If Stow was obliged to remove references to Elizabeth's alleged association with Wyatt in the 1570 edition because of the Northern Rebellion, it is not easy to explain why in 1587 the editors of Holinshed felt free to devote considerable space to the same subject. Problems such as this suggest that it is unwise to link editorial changes in Tudor chronicles too closely with historical events.

Stow's interest in Wyatt's Rebellion with its focus on London and the court is readily understandable, but he also recorded lesser disturbances far from the capital. Cleber's attempted rising at Yaxley in July 1556 was merely a failed conspiracy in a remote part of Norfolk, but it was not too obscure for Stow to notice. Cleber, who 'sometime kept a school' at Diss, conspired with the brothers named Lincoln to organize a rising during a wedding service. The Lincoln brothers were to bring 'one hundred horse with men' while Cleber would initiate the revolt by reading a proclamation in the church. Upon receiving incorrect information about the approach of his confederates, Cleber stood up in the Yaxley parish church and proclaimed Princess Elizabeth queen and 'her bedfellow' Lord Edward Courtenay king. When his supporters failed to appear in sufficient numbers, the hapless Cleber fled, only to be captured at Eye in Suffolk. The story ends predictably with Cleber and the Lincoln brothers being tried at quarter sessions at Bury St Edmunds and then hanged, drawn, and quartered.

Identical narratives of the Cleber rising appear in the second edition of Holinshed and the *Annales of England* (1605). Both are based on an undated manuscript note in the Harleian manuscripts which included more information than actually appeared in print. Neither the manuscript nor the printed texts give the exact date. According to the manuscript, the affair took place 'on a Sunday in the forenoon in summer time, 1556', while Stow and Holinshed indicate that it occurred about 8 July. The most important difference, however, between the manuscript and the printed versions is that only the manuscript gives Cleber's ultimate political objective. The vague traitorous proclamation of Holinshed and the *Annales* was nothing less than the proclamation of Elizabeth and Lord Edward Courtenay as the successors to Queen Mary. As late as 1605, two years after the death of Elizabeth, there was a need to conceal this fact from the reading public.[45]

While Stow was an eyewitness to many of the events of Wyatt's Rebellion, the location of the Northern Rebellion of 1569 made him dependent on information that was available in London. The rising of the earls of Northumberland and Westmorland was a direct challenge to the leadership of Sir William Cecil and to the restored Protestant church. The Northern earls and their allies not only threatened the peace of the realm but also endangered the throne of Elizabeth as a consequence of their support for Mary, Queen of Scots. Wallace MacCaffrey saw the Northern Rebellion as an important episode in what he called the testing time of the Elizabethan regime, but Stow was content merely to chronicle events as they unfolded and to ignore the complex question of causation and the significance of the rising for the crown, court, and country.[46]

Stow's first opportunity to describe the Northern Rebellion came in the 1570 edition of the *Summarie*, but he brought his narrative to the beginning of that year without mentioning it. His first account of the rebellion appeared in the 1573 edition of the abridged *Summarie*, and the same material was included in the 1574 edition. A second, more detailed version of the rebellion may be found in the *Chronicles* of 1580 and with slight variations in the *Annales of England*. Each account begins with the Earl of Northumberland being awakened at night by a servant who warned that a group of enemies would place him under arrest. The second version gives a better narrative of the rebels' advance southward to Wetherby and Tadcaster and includes a fuller account of the role of the Earl of Westmorland and a reference to a skirmish between the rebels and loyal forces led by Sir John Foster and Sir Henry Percy. In the chronicles of 1573 and 1574, Stow gives no information about his sources. The absence of letters or documents precludes comparison with surviving manuscripts or with Sir Cuthbert Sharpe's *Memorials of the Rebellion of 1569*. Although the rebellion inspired a large polemical literature, the authors of these works did not produce the kind of material that could be incorporated easily into general chronicles.[47] Stow's rival, Richard Grafton, published a new edition of his *Abridgement* in 1572, but there is no indication that this work influenced Stow. The only acknowledgement of his sources appears in the 1605 edition of the *Annales* where Stow wrote that Sir George Bowes ordered the execution of rebels 'in every market town and other places betwixt Newcastle and Wetherby, about 60 miles in length and 40 miles in breadth *as himself reported unto me*'.[48] Since Bowes died in 1580, conversations between the two concerning the Northern Rebellion would have taken place sometime before that date.

One of the most striking differences between the chronicles of 1573 and 1574 and the *Annales* of 1605 concerns the dating of important events during the rebellion. In the former, the Earl of Northumberland received a summons to court on 9 November; in the *Annales* he received the summons on 14 November. Letters from the Earl of Sussex, Lord President of the North, to Sir George Bowes, one of the queen's staunchest supporters, indicate that the earlier date is correct.[49] In Stow's summaries, the rebels went to Durham on Monday 13 November; in the *Annales* it was 16 November. Two letters of Bowes giving the date as 14 November – which was Monday – would seem to deny each of Stow's efforts to date the event.[50] According to the summaries, the rebels proceeded to Darlington on 14 November; in the *Annales* it was 17 November. Again, the testimony of Bowes rejects both dates as he prefers 16 November.[51] According to the summaries, the siege of Barnard Castle, which was defended by Bowes, began on 23 November; in the *Annales* it began on 30 November. The two accounts agree that the siege lasted for eleven days before Bowes was forced to surrender, but his correspondence suggests that the siege began on the latter date.[52] Yet another discrepancy in dating concerns the departure of the queen's army from York. The summaries have 5 December, the *Annales* 11 December. The second date is confirmed by a letter from Sussex to Sir William Cecil on the 11th stating, 'This day the footmen be set forwards out of this city.'[53] Stow's chronology was obviously faulty, and the revised *Annales*, which appeared thirty-two years after his first effort, continued to include dates that are at variance with contemporary letters.

Since Stow not only enlarged and continued his chronicles but also revised his work, one finds different versions of the same event. In the summaries of 1573 and 1574, Stow gave the following account of events at Darlington: 'They went to Darlington and there had mass, which the earls and the rest heard with such devotion as they had.'[54] In the *Annales* of 1605 this awkwardly worded passage is replaced with a totally different account: 'The same night [16 November] they went again to Brancepath and on the morrow to Darlington where they had holy water but no mass for want of vestments.'[55] Sir George Bowes wrote to the Earl of Sussex on 17 November that mass was said at Darlington, but it is possible that he was misinformed and communicated a correct account of what happened to Stow at a later date.[56] These events at Darlington are of importance because, if no vestments were available, it must be concluded that the Elizabethan reformers had achieved a measure of success in a region that was strongly Roman Catholic.

Stow's narratives of the rebels' advance from Durham southward differ slightly from each other and to a greater degree disagree with the map of the Northern Rebellion included in Anthony Fletcher's *Tudor Rebellions*.[57] In the summaries as well as the *Annales*, Stow indicated that the earls of Northumberland and Westmorland parted and followed different routes after leaving Darlington. Northumberland went to Richmond and then on to Northallerton and Boroughbridge, while Westmorland travelled to Ripon. According to the summaries, the earls joined forces again at Boroughbridge, but the *Annales* reunites them at Ripon. Fletcher's map shows a single route to the south via Richmond and Boroughbridge and omits the earls' passage through Darlington, Northallerton, and Ripon. Variations may also be found in Stow's descriptions of what occurred at the end of the rebels' advance to the south. Each account takes the rebels as far south as Wetherby, but the *Annales* adds that 'some bands' entered 'Tadcaster and took 200 footmen, chasing their captains which were leading them towards York to the Earl of Sussex'.[58] In the *Chronicles* and *Annales* Stow revised downward the size of the rebel army; the summaries of 1573 and 1574 described a force of 2,000 horse and 5,000 foot, while by 1580 the numbers had shrunk to 1,600 and 4,000 respectively.[59] Stow never associated the Northern Rebellion with an effort to release Mary, Queen of Scots, and declare her heir to the throne, and he restricted the rebels' military objective to a march on York. In the earlier versions of the chronicles, he explained that they turned away from York because their minds 'suddenly altered', but in 1605 he wrote that they learned that Sir George Bowes had mustered 'great bands' in Durham and Richmondshire.[60]

An analysis of Stow's narratives of the rebellion of 1569 reveals chronological errors, irreconcilable differences in attempts to tell exactly what happened, and a failure to relate the rebellion to larger national political and religious issues. His chronicles would have been vastly improved if he had had access to the most important document for the study of the rebellion, the examination of the Earl of Northumberland, which is now contained among the State Papers Domestic at the Public Record Office.[61] Yet if Stow's history of the rebellion is compared with other Tudor chronicles, his work may be seen in a more favourable light. The second edition of Holinshed's chronicle offers a narrative very similar to Stow's *Summarie*, including the faulty chronology. In view of the great difference in size between the octavo *Summarie* and the Holinshed folio of 1,592 pages, the compilers of the latter clearly saw the rebellion as an event unworthy of a detailed narrative. Holinshed's one-page account of the Northern Rebellion stands in marked contrast with fifty-three pages on the rebellions of 1549 and twenty-four pages on Wyatt's Rebellion.[62] Stow's *Chronicles of England*, published in 1580, appeared early enough to have been consulted by the editors of Holinshed, but they preferred to follow the earlier summaries. Therefore, Holinshed's short, derivative treatment of the Northern Rebellion is scarcely an improvement on Stow.

William Camden's *The History of the Most Renowned and Victorious Princess Elizabeth*, first published in a Latin edition in 1615, gives an account of the Northern Rebellion that also suffers in comparison with Stow's *Annales*. Essentially a court historian, Camden was privileged to have access to the royal archives and the papers of Lord Burghley. He was educated at Oxford and held a comfortable sinecure as Clarenceux King of Arms at the College of Heralds, which freed him from the need to earn his living by writing history. Camden avoided Stow's chronological errors by giving no chronology at all. Neither did Camden trouble his readers with an itinerary of the rebel march southward. With the courtier's contempt for the common man, whom he called 'the silly multitude', combined with Elizabethan chauvinism, Camden wrote of 'Romish' intrigues and Spanish plots.[63] If the *Annales* offers an imperfect history of the rebellion, Stow attempted a detailed narrative, wrote with restraint, and used the language of his countrymen.

While there were rumours of conspiracies, ominous intrigues, and dark plots after 1569, no organized rebellion seriously threatened the country for the remainder of Elizabeth's reign. Stow took notice of a 'conspiracy in Norfolk' planned for Midsummer Day 1570 at Harleston fair where the rebels' 'devilish purpose under pretence against strangers and others' was to be proclaimed. What the modern historian Neville Williams called 'the fiasco of Harleston Fair' began on 16 May at Norwich with the battle cry, 'We will raise up the commons and levy a power and beat the strangers out of the city of Norwich.' Disaffected gentry, who supported the Duke of Norfolk and the Northern earls, wanted evil advisors removed from the queen's government and had plans to turn over the port of Yarmouth to the Spanish. When the leaders decided to appeal for popular support at Harleston fair on Midsummer Day, they found little support from people who might have been expected to favour the proposed expulsion of Huguenot weavers. According to Stow, news of the conspiracy was leaked by Thomas Kett, who was himself one of the conspirators. At an elaborate trial at Norwich conducted by Sir Robert Catlin, lord chief justice of the queen's bench, three leaders, John Throgmorton, Thomas Brooke, and George Redmen, were sentenced to be hanged, drawn, and quartered. While this incident coincided with issuance of a papal bull against Queen Elizabeth and the trial of the Duke of Norfolk, Stow failed to place it in a larger political context.[64]

The next year the Ridolfi plot, intended to depose Elizabeth and enthrone Mary Stuart, implicated the Duke of Norfolk. The plot itself was not mentioned in the *Chronicles* (1580), only the execution of Norfolk, but the *Annales* offers a short account of the trial and execution without any indication of its larger significance.[65] Although Stow's manuscript notes include fragments concerning the execution of Norfolk, there is no indication that he witnessed the event.[66]

During the 1580s Stow merely mentioned treasonous plots that had been foiled and referred readers to official accounts that were printed in the second edition of Holinshed. The Throckmorton plot of 1583 planned to free Mary Stuart and murder Queen Elizabeth. Francis Throckmorton, a Roman Catholic, conspired while living abroad, returned to England, and communicated with the Spanish ambassador, Mendoza.[67] Stow, declining to discuss the plot, directed his readers to the official version that was included in Holinshed:

> A discovery of whose [Throckmorton's] treasons practiced and attempted against the queen's majesty and the realm were in the month of June published and printed in a book entitled, A true and perfect declaration of the treasons practiced and attempted by Francis Throckmorton etc. And the same I have set down in the continuation of Reigne Wolfes chronicle.[68]

In March 1585 William Parry, MP, who schemed to assassinate the queen, was executed at Westminster. According to a modern authority, the plot provoked hysteria, but Stow offered merely five lines: ' "A true and plain declaration of the horrible treasons practised by W. Parry etc" I have set down the same book in the continuance of Reine Woolfes chronicle.'[69] The following year the Babington plot fatally implicated Mary Stuart, but Stow did not see it as such; instead he wrote that in July 1586 'diverse traitorous persons were apprehended' in a 'wicked and detestable' conspiracy against the queen that was intended to stir up a general rebellion. After the conspirators had been apprehended, joyful Londoners rang bells, lighted bonfires, and sang psalms. Stow in this instance provided readers of the *Annales* with the full text of a letter sent by the queen to the lord mayor expressing her pleasure with the city's loyalty and an effusive oration by James Dalton, a common councillor, praising the queen and denouncing the 'Romish' religion. After listing the fourteen men, including Anthony Babington, executed for complicity in the plot, Stow again referred his readers to the fuller account available in Holinshed's chronicle.[70]

The rising of the Earl of Essex in February 1601, perhaps the greatest non-event of the Tudor century, was also the last conspiracy of the Elizabethan era. Seen by historians as a court *putsch*, a mere riot, or a dazzling display of chivalry, it culminated in the execution of the queen's last favourite for treason.[71] Stow, who preferred the term 'rising', did not say whether he was actually an eyewitness to either the revolt or the trials that followed. His health may have forced him to observe events from a distance, yet he knew that Thomas Smith, sheriff of London, escaped from Essex through a back gate, and he was able to describe the 'gown of wrought velvet' and

Robert Devereux, Second Earl of Essex in a portrait painted by Marcus Gheeraerts the younger around 1597.

black satin suit that the earl wore at his execution inside the walls of the Tower of London.[72] Stow's accounts of the revolt in the *Summarie Abridged* (1604) and *Annales of England* (1605) were cautiously written and reflect the contemporary political sensitivity of the subject.

When Essex was called before the Privy Council in June of the previous year, Stow was characteristically vague and unhelpful, saying only that 'for matters laid to his charge he was suspended from use of divers offices'.[73] Stow, however, left no doubt that Essex and his small group of supporters conducted themselves in a 'warlike manner' and committed treason. Referring his readers to official accounts 'published by authority', Stow declined to discuss the trial of Essex but offered lengthy coverage of the execution including his confession and final prayer, eloquent words that broadcast his guilt throughout the land. Stow seemed to be defending the ineptitude of the executioner as he wrote that the head of Essex was 'severed from his body by the axe at three strokes, but the first deadly and absolutely depriving all sense and motion'. An unexpected surprise comes at the end of Stow's politically correct narrative when he

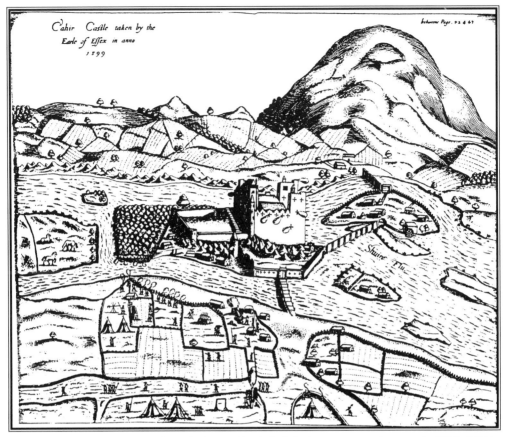

One of the few positive moments in the Earl of Essex's largely futile Irish campaign was the capture in 1599 of Cahir Castle, illustrated here in Stafford's Pacata Hibernia.

wrote that after the execution 'the hangman was beaten as he returned thence so that the sheriffs of London were called to assist and rescue him from such as would have murdered him'.[74]

Stow's account of the Essex revolt appears short and uninspired when compared with the work of William Camden. But Stow, unlike Camden, wrote for a large and potentially volatile audience that read only English. Camden's Latin account did not appear until 1627, over twenty years after Stow's last edition of the *Annales of England*.[75] Differences in social status between the two historians stand out, for while Stow wrote of the mob's attack on the executioner, Camden not only omitted this distasteful episode but stressed that no man of quality took up arms in support of Essex.[76] Although Camden had no more sympathy for the revolt than Stow, he praised the quality of the defeated earl, writing of his distinguished genealogy, his study at Cambridge University, and the Christian deportment expressed at his execution.[77] The

The execution of the Earl of Essex is illustrated here in the Shirburn Ballads, *one of the many popular ballads lamenting the death of this popular man.*

importance of upholding social hierarchy may also been seen in Camden's demeaning references to Henry Cuffe with whom he spoke before he too was executed. Secretary to Essex, the learned Cuffe, who has been portrayed as 'a sacrificial lamb offered up upon the altar of Tudor snobbery, social prejudice, and paranoia', probably gave Camden useful information about the Essex revolt, but the historian did not think that he was worthy enough to mention his first name. Stow, on the other hand, not only gave Cuffe's Christian name, but identified him as a gentleman.[78]

Although Stow never addressed the question of rebellion in theoretical terms, his manuscripts include a text of the polemical mid-Tudor ballad 'Vox Populi Vox Dei' that vigorously condemns the oppression of the poor commons by selfish landowners.[79] While the possession of a copied text does not prove that it reflects the owner's outlook, it is reasonable to argue that Stow agreed with the position of the anonymous author of 'An Apologie of the Cittie of London' that he included at the end of *A Survey of London*. The author, looking at rebellions from a moralistic perspective, asserted that two causes, ambition and covetousness, were of paramount importance. The first, ambition, 'reigneth in the minds of high and noble personages, or of such others, as seek to be gracious and popular, and have robbed the hearts of the multitude', but in London men shunned high office as well as popularity.

Covetousness, 'that other sire of rebellion possesseth the miserable and needy sort and such as be naughty packs [and] unthrifts'. In London, the author argued confidently, such persons did not hold sway because most people were of a 'competent wealth and earnestly bent to honest labour'. The author conceded that while London supported rebellions in the past, 'it resisted many and was never the author of any one'.[80] Here civic pride inspired the conclusion that London was distinguished for its integrity and orderly government, a view that Stow undoubtedly endorsed wholeheartedly.

When Stow himself wrote about Tudor rebellions, it was as a historian of contemporary events. His accounts of the Northern Rebellion and the rising of Essex were written in the immediate aftermath and undoubtedly recorded contemporary attitudes. The mid–Tudor rebellions, on the other hand, were viewed with the perspective and advantage of hindsight when Stow completed the 1605 edition of the *Annales of England*. While it is possible to identify many of the sources that he used, there is no way to determine what information he chose not to include in the chronicles, but the insertion of new material in later editions of the chronicles suggests that Stow had information that he initially declined to use. During each of the major rebellions, Stow had access to eyewitnesses and participants in events that are at best partially recorded in surviving records. The rebellions of 1549 were the only risings in which Stow found social and economic discontent. For him, enclosures were the primary cause, and the conflict was between the gentry and the commons. In later editions he added details of Robert Kett's wealth and thereby emphasized that the commons of Norfolk were led by a respectable man of property, not the rabble. Stow's criticism of the looting at Winchester Place during Wyatt's Rebellion suggests that while he sympathized with victims of oppression, he would tolerate neither wanton destruction nor mob violence.

Stow did not probe very deeply into the religious issues associated with the rebellions of 1549 but could not avoid the question in 1554. His approach to Wyatt's Rebellion could not have been more circumspect because, by following Thomas Cooper, he avoided the risk of saying anything new or potentially controversial. As Stow did not publish an account of that rebellion until 1565, he had no worries about Catholic censorship, but it is unlikely that the insecure Elizabethan government of the early years of the reign would have welcomed chronicle accounts showing a connection between Protestantism and rebellion. The late appearance of John Ponet, the rebel bishop, in Stow's work may therefore reflect self-restraint by the author. The religious issues of 1569 by contrast presented no ideological difficulties for Stow since contemporaries perceived the Northern Rebellion as a clear–cut conflict between the reformed religion and popish superstition.

The most sensitive topics addressed by Stow were political. On the issue of the legitimacy of rebellion, there was no scope whatsoever for questioning the Tudor doctrine that the subject must render complete obedience to the state. Secondary issues, however, posed serious problems for Stow. Without private wealth, he needed a patron, but the patronage of Robert Dudley, Earl of Leicester, may have affected his treatment of the Duke of Somerset in 1549 and Lady Jane, Leicester's sister-in-law, in 1554. Stow's silence regarding events in London in 1549 as well as in 1554 suggests not ignorance, but that he knew too much. Internal evidence indicates that whenever he touched on issues relating to the monarchy and royal succession he exercised the greatest restraint. Ambiguity and outright omission characterize Stow's treatment of the objectives of Wyatt, the role of Lady Jane and Princess Elizabeth in the rebellion, and the connection between the Northern rebels and Mary, Queen of Scots. His caution continued through the reign of Elizabeth as his chronicles escaped censorship by carefully avoiding insights damaging to the crown and government. An analysis of Stow's writing and rewriting of the history of the rebellions of his era supports the contention of Annabel Patterson that self-censorship and deliberate ambiguity were integral parts of communication during the early modern period.[81]

Modern historians have tended to regard Stow as a literary source rather than an eyewitness to contemporary events and have therefore neglected his chronicle accounts of rebellion. Because of space limitations, general accounts of Tudor rebellions by Penry Williams, Anthony Fletcher, and Perez Zagorin either relied on secondary accounts or preferred primary sources other than chronicles. One of these works, Fletcher's *Tudor Rebellions*, cites a number of chronicles, but not Stow. The two major books on Tudor historiography, F. Smith Fussner, *The Historical Revolution: Historical Writing and Thought, 1580–1640* and F.J. Levy, *Tudor Historical Thought*, give considerable attention to Stow but emphasize his treatment of ancient and medieval history.

The best example of the misuse of Stow by a historian of sixteenth-century rebellions may be found in Frances Rose-Troup, *The Western Rebellion of 1549*. In her effort to prove that the rebellion was caused exclusively by religious discontent, Rose-Troup examined an unusual assortment of twenty-two contemporary sources and concluded that only five failed to attribute the rising wholly to dissatisfaction with Protestant reforms. The five exceptions, however, included the major chroniclers of the period: Cooper, Grafton, Holinshed, Sleidan, and Stow.[82] Unfortunately, this crude and misleading effort at quantification was accepted by Tudor historians for over half a century. The leading authority on Wyatt's Rebellion, David M. Loades, consulted Stow's *Annales of England* but rejected his contention that the revolt was caused both by political and religious issues, while a critic of Loades, Peter Clark, used local archival sources to confirm Stow's view without actually citing his chronicles.[83] Modern historians of the rebellion of 1569, including R.R. Reid, Wallace B. MacCaffrey, and Mervyn James, practically ignored Stow and consequently avoided entanglement in his errors of chronology. However, Reid's conception of the rebellion as a 'popular movement' and James's argument that the Northern earls' authority and seigneurial administration were crumbling receive little support from Stow's writings.[84]

In the study of Tudor rebellions, Stow's chronicles have been under-utilized. Failing to recognize Stow as an authentic reporter of contemporary events, historians have given greater prominence to other sources, especially government records and letters of the aristocracy and gentry. These sources view rebellion from the perspective of the governing elite while Stow's writings reflect the outlook of ordinary men and women. C.L. Kingsford, editor of his *Survey of London*, exaggerated Stow's unfettered pursuit of the truth and his historical accuracy, but Kingsford's assessment of Stow's importance as a historical source needs to be vigorously reaffirmed for the study of Tudor rebellions.[85]

CHAPTER FOUR

A LAYMAN'S
REFORMATION

Stow was not only a chronicler of the Reformation era but also an eyewitness to the dramatic events that transformed England from a Catholic kingdom into the most influential Protestant state in Europe. Born about 1525, he was too young to recall Henry VIII's divorce of Queen Catherine, the fall of Cardinal Wolsey, and the break with Rome and, therefore, relied on Edward Hall's *Union of the Two Noble and Illustre Famelies of Lancaster and Yorke*, first published in 1548, and other chronicles.[1] For the period after the king's death in 1547, the situation was different. Stow was of course older, twenty-four, when the first *Book of Common Prayer* appeared in 1549; twenty-eight at the accession of Queen Mary; and thirty-four at the time of the Elizabethan settlement. Moreover, when he began to write, there was no published chronicle account comparable in stature to Hall that covered the reigns of Edward VI and Mary. For this period as well as the reign of Elizabeth, Stow was forced to rely on his own recollections and such contemporary documentation as he could acquire. As a zealous collector of manuscripts and a keen observer, ideally located in London, he was well qualified to write the history of an epoch of religious change.

The Reformation in England and elsewhere was largely 'the creation of the clergy', a privileged elite that experienced both gains and losses as a consequence of the religious upheaval,[2] and it was only natural that the clergy should have written the earliest accounts of the Reformation. From John Foxe to Gilbert Burnet, John Strype, and the Anglican apologists and controversialists of the nineteenth and twentieth centuries, clerical writers shaped the Protestant perception of the Reformation. Clerical influence also manifested itself in secular scholarship as witnessed by the work of William Camden, Thomas Cooper, Abraham Fleming, Richard Hakluyt, William Harrison, and Raphael Holinshed.[3] Clerics saw the Reformation as the great event of the sixteenth century because it freed England from the corruption and tyranny of Rome and established true religion. Their heroes were appropriately the bishops, preachers, scholars, and martyrs who created and guided the reformed Church. As the elect nation, the English had a solemn duty to protect and nurture the Church of Christ.[4]

Stow, however, stands outside the tradition of clerical historiography. He was not only a layman, but one who viewed the Reformation from the outside. Stow made no significant contributions to the success of the Reformation, and he neither gained nor lost status or wealth as a consequence of it. He did not join the great religious debates of his day and never wrote polemical works to praise or condemn government policy. Apparently satisfied with a life of historical scholarship, Stow did not seek to shape public opinion; neither did he aspire to a career of public service. Consequently, he survived the Protestant reforms of Edward VI, conformed to Roman Catholicism under Mary, and satisfied the government of Elizabeth that his personal beliefs and historical writings constituted no threat to the Church of England.[5]

Stow's interest in the Church derived from his love of antiquity. His manuscripts, chronicles, and *A Survey of London* document his interest in everything that was old. Churches interested Stow not as houses of worship or religious institutions but because they contained monuments of mayors and rich merchants. He collected data about foundations of churches and abbeys and compiled lists of the archbishops of Canterbury.[6] He rarely mentioned the religious work of bishops and parish clergy although *A Survey* dutifully recorded clergy buried at St Paul's.[7] Stow understood the Church as a historical institution that had existed for many years, and by the end of his long life, seems to have convinced himself that the Church could be at once historic and reformed.

Stow was one of a small group of lay chroniclers writing during the second half of the sixteenth century that included Henry Machyn, Charles Wriothesley, and Richard Grafton. Like Stow, these chroniclers did not write exclusively about religion. Indeed, their accounts raise questions as to whether they really comprehended the religious revolution that was unfolding before their eyes. An alternative conclusion, probably closer to the truth, is that Stow and his contemporaries spoke for the proverbial man in the street, who was less moved by the Reformation than either the Foxes, Latimers, and Gardiners or the modern historians of religion. In contrast to Stow, the writings of Machyn and Wriothesley remained in manuscript until the nineteenth century when they were printed by the Camden Society. While it is impossible to say why certain works were not published, it is unlikely that either Machyn or Wriothesley would have been very successful in the competitive market that Stow and Grafton entered. Machyn's diary – in reality more of a chronicle – would have required substantial editing to remove the tedious listing of burials, and his Catholic sympathies may have been too pronounced for the Elizabethan government.[8] Wriothesley, on the other hand, included more interesting materials in his chronicle than Machyn and remained within the fold of Protestant orthodoxy. The abrupt ending of Wriothesley's chronicle in September 1559 and his death in 1562 undoubtedly explain why it was unsuitable for publication.

The chronicles that were published during the sixteenth century, especially those that appeared in more than one edition, not only satisfied the government's requirements for religious and political orthodoxy but also appealed to the interests and needs of a growing reading public. This lay public had a voracious appetite for sermons and religious tracts, but its interest in secular works should not be underestimated. Chronicles responded to secular interests with accounts of the crown and court, military and naval campaigns, social conditions, and bizarre natural occurrences. At the same time chroniclers like Stow described the great religious changes of the Tudor century.

Following the death of Henry VIII in 1547, Stow witnessed the beginning of the Edwardian Reformation. In just over six years the English Church, despite vigorous opposition, moved far beyond the cautious reforms of the previous reign and took its place among the Protestant Churches of Europe. The short reign of Edward VI saw the most sweeping religious changes in English history as the Latin mass gave way to the English communion of the *Book of Common Prayer* and as a sacrificing, celibate priesthood gave way to legally married preachers and pastors.[9] The 1565 edition of the *Summarie of Englyshe Chronicles* notes only a few random examples of the externals of the religious revolution. Stow mentioned that processions were forbidden, that images were removed from churches, and that preachers attempted 'to persuade people from their beads and such like'. He took note of the dissolution of the chantries and saw the *Order of Communion*, the first liturgical innovation of the new reign, merely as an order 'for the use of the Lord's Supper that it should be in both kinds of bread and wine'.[10] The reader of the *Summarie* of 1565 learned nothing of the prayer books, nothing of the theological debates between the Catholic and Protestant clergy, and nothing of the parliamentary legislation permitting clerical marriage, except for a reference to the legitimacy of the children of priests.

Fifteen years later the greatly expanded *Chronicles of England* offered a more detailed portrait of the Edwardian Reformation, a portrait that was further enlarged in the *Annales of England* of 1605. Beginning on 11 April 1547, when compline was sung in English at the king's chapel, Stow recounted the changes in religious services. He may have been present at St Paul's early in September when he noted that the king's commissioners came to reform the 'ceremonies and superstition'.[11] It is not surprising that Stow, who was also a London topographer, carefully recorded the alteration and demolition of church buildings that changed the topography of the city. On 17 November 1547, workmen began to demolish the rood screen at St Paul's. By March of the following year Stow saw entire buildings pulled down. These included Barking Chapel near the Tower of London, the college church of St Martin's le Grand, and the parish church of St Ewine within Newgate. In April 1549,

> the cloister of Paul's church in London, called pardon churchyard, with the dance of death, commonly called the dance of Paul's about the same cloister costly and cunningly wrought, and the chapel in the midst of the same churchyard were all begun to be pulled down. Also the charnel-house of Paul's with the chapel there (after the tombs and other monuments of the dead were pulled down, and the dead men's bones buried in the fields) were converted into dwelling houses and shops.[12]

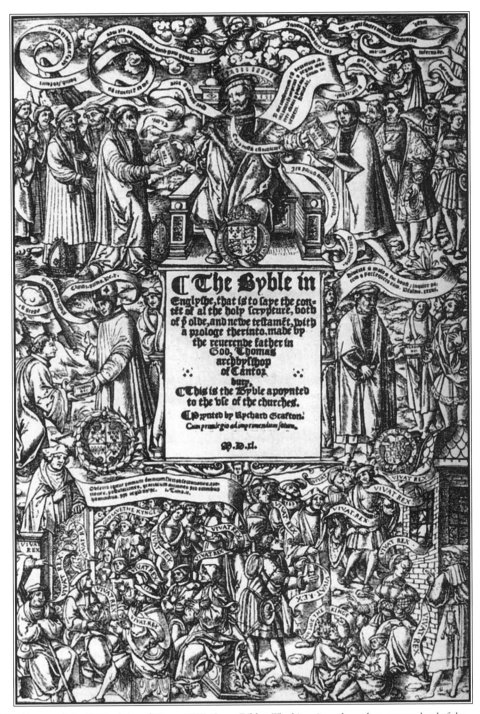

The title-page of the 1540 edition of Henry VIII's Great Bible. The king sits enthroned as supreme head of the Church, distributing copies of the Bible to Archbishop Cranmer and to Thomas Cromwell, who pass copies to the bishops and lords. The acclamation of the crowd needs no explanation.

A symbolic representation of the reign of Edward VI from the folio edition of Actes and Monuments *(1573). The engraving shows the pre-eminence of the Bible, the supreme importance of the sacraments of Baptism and Communion and the centrality of preaching to Protestant religion. In the background papists, purged from the English church, depart in 'the ship of the Romish Church'.*

Protestant iconoclasm, the needs of a growing urban population, and the residential building of the aristocracy, especially of Edward Seymour, Duke of Somerset and Lord Protector, all contributed to the destruction of London churches.[13]

Stow's account of the first phase of the Edwardian Reformation – 1547 to 1549 – failed to recognize Parliament's central role in the process of reform. He recorded that Parliament first met on 4 November 1547 and passed statutes dissolving the chantries, authorizing communion in both kinds, and repealing the Henrician act of six articles but did not include even brief summaries of these statutes. Neither the *Chronicles* nor the *Annales of England* mentions that the second and most important session of Edward's first Parliament began in November 1548. Stow noted the second session only in connection with the trial of the Protector's brother, Thomas, Lord Seymour of Sudeley.[14] The reader is not informed that two major statutes, an act of uniformity authorizing the first *Book of Common Prayer* and an act removing the penalties for clerical marriage, turned the Church of England in an entirely new Protestant direction. If Stow thought of Parliament as a major participant working in partnership with the crown and council in the process of religious reform, his chronicles fail to sustain that view of the Tudor constitution. Although Edward VI was only a child, Stow implied that religious policies emanated from the crown and that no significant differences distinguished proclamations based on royal prerogative from parliamentary statutes.[15]

Stow was unquestionably more impressed by the activities of London clergymen than by the work of Parliament, an attitude indicating that he spent the bulk of his time in the city rather than at Westminster. He noted the efforts of aspiring clergy to tune their doctrines to harmonize with government policy. In the spring of 1547 one cleric recanted his former teachings at Paul's Cross while another repudiated Catholic beliefs regarding images and the saints.[16] Although the government of Elizabeth investigated Stow for possible pro-Catholic sympathies, his brief account of the imprisonment of the two leading opposition bishops, Stephen Gardiner and Edmund Bonner, reveals no remorse for the demise of Henrician Catholicism.[17] In fact, Stow gave a fuller account of Hugh Latimer's sermon of 1 January 1548 when the Protestant reformer and future martyr preached for the first time in eight years.[18] Other Protestants whose sermons were noted by Stow during the first two years of the reign included Nicholas Ridley, Bishop of Rochester, and Miles Coverdale.[19] The chronicles, however, do not indicate that Stow was an enthusiastic churchgoer because he gives nothing like the complete listing of important sermons that can be compiled from other sources.[20] And only on rare occasions did he bother to give details about the contents of sermons that he heard.

Modern historians have often contrasted the moderation of the first phase of the Edwardian Reformation, the years 1547 to 1549, with the radicalism of 1550 to 1553. A.F. Pollard developed the distinction in

The title page of the first edition of Cranmer's Book of Common Prayer *(1549).*

England under Protector Somerset in an attempt to separate Somerset's protectorate from the government of John Dudley, Earl of Warwick and Duke of Northumberland. While Pollard was more interested in praising the virtues of Somerset than in analysing the development of religious policies, his division of the Edwardian Reformation into moderate and radical phases survived and received greater elaboration in other works, especially W.K. Jordan's history of the reign of Edward VI.[21]

As an eyewitness to the Edwardian Reformation, John Stow lends no support to the interpretation of Pollard and Jordan. In fact, Stow's *Annales of England* remind us that some contemporaries expected conservative – not radical – changes in religious policy.[22] The imprisoned Bishop of Winchester, Stephen Gardiner, for example, hoped the fall of Protector Somerset in 1549 would hasten his release. Stow printed a fragment of one letter and the complete text of another which Gardiner sent to the king's council. When the councillors received Gardiner's first letter from the Tower of London, they 'laughed very merrily thereat, saying "he had a pleasant head," for reward whereof they gave him leave to remain still in prison five or six weeks after'.[23] The case of Gardiner illustrates the essential continuity of religious policy during the reign of Edward VI. First imprisoned under Somerset, Gardiner remained in captivity until the accession of Mary. He was deprived of his bishopric in 1551 and replaced by John Ponet, a staunch Protestant who was sympathetic to the reform programme of Cranmer, Somerset, and Northumberland.

Stow's account of the second phase of the Edwardian Reformation recognized no change from moderation to radicalism and also indicated little interest in the theological and liturgical aspects of reform. The *Summarie* of 1565 remains thin on religious matters as before but includes a curious reference to parliamentary legislation (5 & 6 Edward VI c. 12) that made the children of priests legitimate, a point not made in later editions of the chronicles.[24] Perhaps by 1580 it was unacceptable to remind the clergy that their offspring had once been bastards under the law. Although Stow had noted the imprisonment of Stephen Gardiner, his actual deprivation from the see of Winchester rated a short account in the *Chronicles* and *Annales of England*.[25] Stow merely mentions the deprivation of George Day, Nicholas Heath, and Cuthbert Tunstall and deals perfunctorily with the fall of the bishop who should have been best known to him, Edmund Bonner, Bishop of London. If Stow's historical writing offers any insight into his own thinking, he must have felt little sympathy for the once-mighty prelates whose careers foundered under the Protestant regime.

Stow revealed the laity's interest in visible, external changes when he recorded the removal of the high altar at St Paul's on St Barnabas' Day, 11 June 1550. He noted that the saint's day was kept holy, but that at night, presumably after the last service, the altar was pulled down, and 'tables placed in their rooms'. Later, in early November 1552, he remarked that the upper choir at St Paul's 'where the high altar stood, was broken down and all the choir thereabout'. The new communion table was then set in 'the lower choir where priests sing'.[26]

Thomas Cranmer, Henry VIII's Archbishop of Canterbury, painted by Gerlach Flicke in 1546.

Similarly, Stow was less interested in the liturgical changes contained in the new *Book of Common Prayer*, introduced in 1552, than in ecclesiastical vestments. When the new prayer book was first used on 1 November, he saw that Bishop Ridley wore 'his rochet only, without cope or vestment'. The prayer book forbade the wearing of copes and communion vestments, and Stow also noted that the prebends of St Paul's left off their hoods and the bishops their crosses in accordance with the Act of Uniformity that enforced the provisions of the prayer book.[27] While theologians studied the significant changes embodied in the new communion service, Stow and many lay people were more impressed with alterations inside the churches and changes in the appearance of the clergy.[28]

Stow undoubtedly mourned the death of Edward VI in 1553, but he never shared the religious fervour of the Protestant preachers and writers who saw the reign of King Edward as a new dawn for the Church of Christ in England. He wrote sympathetically of the late king as 'a prince of such towardness in virtue, learning, and all godly gifts', but the words were not Stow's own. The same epitaph had appeared earlier in the chronicle of Thomas Cooper, a future Anglican bishop.[29]

Stow's description of the accession of Mary and the restoration of Roman Catholicism shows the extent to which he revised his chronicles and incorporated the work of other chroniclers into his own. In the *Summarie* of 1565 he wrote that 'all sorts of men almost did rejoice that the queen's majesty had recovered the crown'.[30] The use of the word *almost* is intriguing: the meaning, now archaic, is 'mostly all' or 'for the most part'. Stow therefore meant that most people rejoiced at Mary's triumph. The whole phrase, borrowed from Thomas Cooper, was deleted from the larger chronicle of 1580 in which Stow rewrote the introduction to the reign of Queen Mary. In 1553 everyone from Northumberland and the Protestant bishops to Stephen Gardiner understood that the accession of Mary endangered the Edwardian Church, but not everyone viewed the prospect of religious change in the same way. Stow recognized the different attitudes in 1565 as he completed his comments on rejoicing:

As all sorts of men almost did rejoice that the queen's majesty had recovered the crown; so many notwithstanding much feared alterations of religion by her.

Perhaps Stow expressed his own views when he added that 'people showed themselves so ready to receive their old religion that in many places' they restored altars and reverted to the mass and Latin services before Parliament repealed the Act of Uniformity of 1552, but his words were again those of Thomas Cooper.[31] If there was uncertainty about the permanent character of the Elizabethan Church and its attitude toward Catholic practices in 1565 when the *Summarie* first appeared, most of the doubts were gone in 1580 and entirely eliminated by 1605. In recognition of these changes, Stow's *Chronicles* (1580) and *Annales of England* (1605) omitted the references to popular support for the old religion.

A hint of Stow's sympathy for the traditionalism of the Henrician Church may be found in two entries in the *Summarie* of 1565. On 15 November 1553, he noted with apparent approval the restoration of anthem singing at St Paul's. The singing began after evensong in the choir when, Stow recalled, the cathedral was illuminated with cresset lights 'after the old custom'. Five days later he mentioned a procession in Latin at St Paul's in observance of St Andrew's Day, a service which was attended by the mayor and aldermen of London.[32] Although the *Annales of England* was a substantially longer and more detailed work, references to these two services were deleted.[33]

The Catholic Restoration, like the Edwardian Reformation, was legislated by Parliament in response to initiatives taken by the queen and council. The Catholic Restoration took place in two distinct stages. From the moment of Mary's victory over Northumberland it was assumed that Edwardian Protestantism was dead. As David M. Loades has said, 'The real issue was not the fate of Protestantism, but the extent of the reaction.'[34] The first step was quickly accomplished before the end of 1553 with the statute of repeal, which abrogated nine Edwardian statutes. To the queen's great dissatisfaction the royal supremacy remained in existence until January 1555 when the second and final step in the Catholic Restoration was taken. At that time Parliament, in return for a guarantee protecting purchasers of former monastic lands, repealed the remaining Henrician legislation and revived heresy statutes formerly used against the Lollards. The parliamentary legislation combined with the absolution pronounced by Reginald Pole, cardinal and papal legate, reunited the Church of England with the see of Rome.

The contribution of Parliament to the restoration of Roman Catholicism and the persecution of heretics was hardly a happy memory to Protestants of a later generation, who were taught that Parliament was the protector of the Protestant religion and the guardian of English liberties. While Sir Thomas Smith emphasized the supremacy of Parliament when he wrote that it was 'the most high and absolute power of the realm', his argument that 'the consent of Parliament is taken to be every man's consent' troubled Protestants who preferred to view the heresy statutes as instruments of either monarchical or papal tyranny.[35] Stow's references to the Marian parliaments in successive editions of his chronicles suggest that he was sensitive to Parliament's self-image and political posture.

The first act of repeal in 1553 received scant attention from Stow. In the *Summarie* of 1565, he categorized the statutes that were repealed and added that Parliament determined that religious services should be as in the last year of Henry VIII.[36] The *Annales of England* (1605) offers even less to the reader interested in the work of Parliament. Stow reported that Parliament was dissolved on 6 December and that on 21 December religious services were 'done in Latin as was enacted by the last parliament'. When reunion with Rome was accomplished the following year, Stow emphasized the contribution of Cardinal Pole and the queen, not Parliament.[37] The short *Summarie* in fact gives more information about Pole's work than the longer *Chronicles* and *Annales*.

The *Summarie* as well as the later versions state that Pole was 'restored to his old dignity that he was put from by King Henry'. The 'whole court of Parliament' then prepared a supplication repenting 'of that schism that they had lived in, and therefore desired the king, queen, and cardinal that by their means they might be restored to the bosom of the church and obedience of the see of Rome'.[38] Stow also summarized a sermon preached by Stephen Gardiner, the lord chancellor, at Paul's Cross on 2 December. In the *Summarie* he wrote that Gardiner declared that the realm was 'again restored and united unto the church of Rome'; in the *Annales* he stressed that the king and queen 'restored the Pope to his supremacy' while Parliament, 'representing the whole body of the realm, had submitted themselves to the same'.[39] As for the heresy statutes, the *Summarie* states that Parliament indeed passed the legislation, whereas the *Chronicles* and *Annales* make no reference to them. Nevertheless, Stow acknowledged the enforcement of the heresy statutes when he recorded the burning of John Rogers at Smithfield, London.[40]

Stow's history of the reign of Queen Mary is of interest not only because of the variations between the editions, but also because of the important topics that are completely omitted. Stow's lack of interest in the burnings is especially remarkable. He merely noted the burning of Latimer, Ridley, and Cranmer. There are no details of the charges against them, no reference to the heresy trials, and no details about their behaviour at the stake. Stow had a good opinion of John Bradford, 'a man of very sober and honest life' whom the bishops earnestly wished to 'recant and abjure his opinions', but did not explain how he knew Bradford was sober and honest or what opinions he was asked to recant.[41] Stow's neglect of Latimer, Ridley, and Cranmer in the chronicles might be explained by the fact that they were burned at Oxford, while Bradford died at Smithfield.

Stow's published works give no indication that he took a greater interest in the burning of London lay persons than in the burning of clergy. His earlier account of the two Edwardian martyrs shows no preference for religious radicals; he noted that Joan Bocher was burned for holding that 'Christ took no flesh of the virgin Mary' and dismissed George Van Paris as a Dutch Arian.[42] Stow's apparent indifference to the whole process of religious persecution is underscored by his terse entry for 27 June 1556: 'Thirteen persons being condemned for opinions concerning the sacrament were burnt at Stratford the Bow.'[43] Stow's unpublished manuscripts, however, reveal that he knew more about the burnings than he included in the chronicles. His notes record the charges against five men who were burned at Smithfield on 12 April 1557. One held 'that Christ was not yet come, another that he was not yet ascended, the third that he was not equal with the father in godhead'. Perhaps the most radical was a man who held that wives ought to be common to all men.[44] The manuscript notes also include an estimate of the number who died during the reign of Queen Mary:

> In the time of the reign of this queen there were burned and some also that died in prison for religion little under or over 2,000–2,040 men and women.[45]

The burning of bishops Latimer and Ridley at Oxford in October 1555, as engraved as an illustration for John Foxe's Actes and Monuments *(1563).*

Inevitably, Stow's inadequate treatment of the Marian burnings raises the question of what contact he had with John Foxe, the martyrologist, and the *Actes and Monuments*. C.L. Kingsford said that Stow 'seems to have been on good terms with Foxe', but fails to give an example of any connection, either personal or literary, between them.[46] Authorities on Foxe, whose career and writings have been studied extensively, also fail to mention any connections. On the other hand, Stow's associations with Matthew Parker, Archbishop of Canterbury, and the Earl of Leicester brought him close to those who were vigorous proponents of Protestantism.[47] As the first English edition of *Actes and Monuments* appeared in 1563, Stow had access to Foxe's work even if the two were not well acquainted.[48] Therefore, it would appear that Stow consciously chose to publish only the briefest account of the martyrs and to avoid a moral judgement on the Great Persecution.

Stow's chronicles have little to say about the activities of the Protestants who managed to avoid martyrdom. He was undoubtedly correct when he wrote that many people enthusiastically welcomed the restoration of the Latin services, but he cannot have been ignorant of those committed Protestants who gathered illegally for worship in London or fled abroad into exile.[49] The only Protestants mentioned by Stow during the reign of Queen Mary were either violent or mentally deranged. There was the violent mob that attacked a Catholic preacher at Paul's Cross in August 1553, the gunman who fired at another preacher in June 1554, and William Flower, who stabbed a priest with a wooden knife at St Margaret's, Westminster, at Easter 1555. Radical Protestants of the worst sort were almost certainly responsible for hanging a cat 'with her head shorn, and the likeness of a vestment cast over her, with her forefeet tied together and a round piece of paper like a singing cake betwixt them' in April 1554.[50] Stow also gave a detailed account of the unfortunate Elizabeth Croft, a 'wench' of about eighteen, who was used by Protestant troublemakers to make strange noises from inside a wall that were interpreted as supernatural voices condemning the mass, confessions, and other Catholic practices.[51] Stow acknowledged the Protestant exiles only after the accession of Elizabeth, when he noted that Richard Cox and several other clergy had recently returned 'from beyond the seas'.[52] Foxe was clearly better placed to write about the exiles, but Stow could easily have improved his chronicles by drawing from the *Actes and Monuments* or the *Brief Discourse of the Troubles Begun at Frankfurt*, first published in 1574 at Heidelberg.[53]

With the accession of Elizabeth in 1558, Stow moved from the recent past to his own times. For him the queen's reign was very much a living age, whereas the reigns of Edward VI and Mary could be viewed with a greater sense of detachment. Thus Stow wrote of Elizabeth, 'our most gracious sovereign lady', whose accession brought 'great comfort' to the people of England although he did not specify whether this meant religious comfort.[54] Although he continued to be a dispassionate chronicler of events past, he associated the accession of Elizabeth with religious change. In the first paragraph of the *Chronicles* and the *Annales of England* he mentioned the royal proclamation that forbade preaching and alteration of religious ceremonies, except in the queen's chapel. The *Summarie* of 1565 – but not later versions – interjects that the accession was joyful to those who had fled to Germany 'for religion's sake'.[55]

Stow proceeded to trace the well-known events that culminated in the Elizabethan religious settlement. His account of the work of Parliament remains as inadequate as for the previous reigns. The *Summarie* mentions only the restoration of the royal supremacy, while the *Chronicles* and the *Annales* offer little more:

> In this parliament the first fruits and tenths were granted to the crown and also the supreme government over the state ecclesiastical. Likewise, the *Book of Common Prayer* and the administration of the sacraments in our vulgar tongue was restored to be done as in the time of King Edward the Sixth.

The *Annales* is also marred by careless chronology where the account given above is followed by a lengthy section on the Westminster disputation which actually took place before Parliament completed its religious legislation.[56]

Unlike Sir John Neale, Stow found neither romance nor major legislative achievements in the first Parliament of Elizabeth I. If the legislature held a 'dramatic secret' that explained the mystery of the religious settlement, he did not attempt to discover it. Neither did Stow anticipate Neale's conclusion that the queen sustained a defeat at the hands of Parliament.[57] His attitude toward the religious settlement, so far as it is revealed in the chronicles, is closer to the revisionism of Winthrop S. Hudson in that both see the settlement as an anticipated series of events favoured and supported by Elizabeth and her closest advisors. Far from being bold or innovative, it was merely the restoration of the Church of Edward VI.[58] If Stow failed to sense the parliamentary drama, he also failed to perceive the theological issues involved in the preparation of the Elizabethan prayer book. Both Neale and Hudson as well as William P. Haugaard and other scholars examined the important Eucharistic controversy that arose in the preparation of an acceptable liturgy.[59] Stow, on the other hand, was content to write that on 'the 8th of May being Whitsunday the service in churches began according to the *Book of Common Prayer* set forth and established by this last parliament correspondent to that of King Edward's time'.[60]

It would be erroneous to suggest that Stow analysed the Elizabethan religious settlement with the same intensity and thoroughness as modern scholars. His chronicles, however, do contain the authentic voice of a contemporary lay witness whose response to the Elizabethan settlement needs to be heard along with modern parliamentary and church historians. To Stow the work of Parliament was not very important, the policy to alter religion was that of the queen, and the programme of religious reform was merely a revival of what had begun during the reign of Edward VI. The Eucharistic debate was important to theologians and clergy, but not to most of the laity. What mattered to Stow was that Latin services gave way to the vernacular. Like Hudson, he was interested in the new preachers appearing in London pulpits and the Catholic bishops committed to the Tower of London.[61]

As during the religious changes of the reigns of Edward VI and Mary, Stow took particular note of the external and visual aspects of the Elizabethan settlement. On 9 January, he saw the broken image of St Thomas Becket at the mercer's chapel. Later, on St Bartholomew's Eve (23 August), he saw the burning of roods and images in St Paul's churchyard and noted that elsewhere in the city copes, vestments, altar cloths, books, banners, and sepulchres were burned. By September, when an obsequy for the deceased King Henry II of France was held at St Paul's, the new religious order was established. Three new bishops, Matthew Parker of Canterbury, William Barlow of Chichester, and John Scory of Hereford, were seated in the Bishop of London's seat in the upper choir wearing only surplices with doctor's hoods about their shoulders. And the service was 'the dirge of the evening song in English' conducted according to the *Book of Common Prayer*.[62]

The east end of Winchester Cathedral after the Reformation. In the foreground is the medieval tomb of William Rufus, but in the background all is new: the simple communion table and the ten commandments affixed to the reredos behind.

After the Elizabethan settlement was completed, Stow's interest shifted to its enforcement, and in so doing he compiled extensive information about persons who were dissatisfied with the state Church. Under English statutory law these men and women were criminals who received appropriate punishment for their offences, but from their own perspective they suffered persecution for their commitment to Roman Catholicism or radical Protestantism. Stow seems to have become more sensitive to religious persecution in England as he grew older, because his chronicles recount the fate of Roman Catholics and Protestant non-conformists more carefully during the reign of Elizabeth than during the reign of Mary. Modern terms such as Puritan, Separatist, and recusant were not part of Stow's historical vocabulary, and he preferred to deal with people as individuals or as members of small groups, although 'Anabaptist' was a word that he used.

In a carefully balanced narrative, Stow noted that twenty-seven members of a Dutch Anabaptist congregation were arrested and imprisoned on Easter Sunday 1575. Four bore faggots and recanted at Paul's Cross where they repudiated the following heretical positions:

That Christ took not [sic] flesh of the substance of the blessed virgin Mary.

That infants of the faithful ought not to be baptized.

That a Christian man may not be a magistrate or bear the sword or office of authority.

That it is not lawful for a Christian to take an oath.

After renouncing these beliefs, the Dutch Anabaptists further confessed that the whole doctrine and religion established in England was received and preached in the Dutch Church and that these teachings were in conformity with 'the word of God'. They agreed to submit themselves to the discipline of the Dutch Church and abandoning all Anabaptist errors affirmed that they would 'most gladly be a member of the said Dutch church from henceforth'.

Later, on 21 May, Stow wrote that eleven Dutch Anabaptists – ten women and one man – were condemned to be hanged by the consistory of St Paul's. He did not indicate whether these persons were from the same congregation as those previously apprehended. 'But after great pains taken with them,' he added, 'only one woman was converted, the other were banished the land.' Holinshed's chronicle adds that the nine women were led away by sheriff's officers, while the man was tied to a cart and whipped. All were taken from Newgate to the 'water's side' where they were shipped away never to return. Two Dutch Anabaptist males were burned to death the following July at Smithfield, and Stow's comment that they 'died in great horror with roaring and crying' suggests that he may have been an eyewitness to the executions.[63]

Stow's approach to the Anabaptist persecution was that of a detached reporter. It has been argued that the two burnings were the first executions for heresy since the death of Queen Mary, but Stow characteristically failed to put his account into historical context. There is also the possibility that opposition to the Dutch Anabaptists was caused as much by the fact that they were foreigners as by their religious beliefs. Foreign churches in London had to defend themselves from English prejudices against their poorer members who were believed to pose an economic threat, but Stow's description is free from any stain of chauvinism.[64]

Readers of the *Annales of England* might well have concluded that Stow had little knowledge of another group of radicals, the Family of Love, because of perfunctory references to a group of five who repudiated the teachings of Hendrik Niclas at Paul's Cross in 1575 and a brief reference to a royal proclamation in October 1580 against the sect.[65] His manuscript notes show that he had more information about the Familists than he selected for inclusion in published chronicles. Harleian MS 247 at the British Library includes extensive uncatalogued notes on the royal proclamation,[66] while other manuscripts indicate that Stow was familiar with the beliefs of the sect and a few of its members. The notes relate to the confession of an apprentice glover, Leonard Romsye, formerly a member of a congregation at Wisbech, Cambridgeshire. Although the confession was allegedly voluntary, it has been argued that Romsye wished to damage his employer, John Bourne.[67]

Stow was sufficiently interested in the Family of Love to copy seventeen articles in which Romsye revealed his understanding of Familist teaching[68] as well as a second document, 'Rumsays Articles against the Preachers'. In the latter document an informant said that Romsye told him that many people at Bury St Edmunds held the opinions of a radical preacher, Matthew Hamon, but added, 'I did not credit him in all his speeches.' It was also alleged that Hamon's followers had influence with the justices of the peace.[69] In May 1579 Matthew Hamon, a ploughwright of Hethersett, Norfolk, was convicted for denying that 'Christ be our saviour' and burned at the stake. Stow did not say that Hamon was a Familist, and indeed the teachings ascribed to him included the extreme positions that the New Testament was a mere fable and that Christ was an abominable idol.[70] Since neither manuscript relating to the activities of Leonard Romsye was incorporated into the *Annales of England*, it might be asked whether Stow himself had a personal interest in the teachings of the mysterious Family of Love or whether he merely wished to avoid heaping abuse on a small persecuted sect of religious radicals that he pitied rather than admired.[71]

In 1583 Stow alerted his readers to the influence of Separatism (although he did not use the word) in East Anglia when he noted that Elias Thacker and John Coping were hanged in Suffolk for 'spreading certain books seditiously penned by one Robert Browne against the Book of Common Prayer . . . , their books so many as could be found were burnt before them'.[72] Diarmaid MacCullogh argued that the Separatists were an embarrassment to Puritan leaders at Bury St Edmunds while W.K. Jordan contended that the Separatists were 'technically convicted of treason for having assailed the royal supremacy, but their heretical beliefs cannot be disentangled from their civil offence'. John Coping or Coppin was a layman of Bury St Edmunds who refused to permit his newly born child to be baptized by an unpreaching minister in 1578. Both he and Elias Thacker were imprisoned for unorthodox words and behaviour. They were subsequently charged with heresy and dispersing books of Browne and Robert Harrison and hanged at Bury. Stow may have learned of this incident through the book trade because Thacker and Coppin were associated with a third man, Thomas Gibson, a local bookbinder, who was released after demonstrating that he fully accepted the royal supremacy.[73]

A manuscript narrative of the trial and execution of the London Separatist leaders, Henry Barrow and John Greenwood, in 1592 provides details not found in the

Annales of England and suggests that Stow may have been an eyewitness to the executions.[74] The first part of the narrative, which is not in Stow's hand, states the Barrow and Greenwood were indicted and found guilty of a felony but does not examine the legal issues involved. The second and third sections are in Stow's hand and describe the executions. Here we learn that Barrow and Greenwood were originally to be executed on 31 March 1593. They were brought to Tyburn, 'the halters put about their necks and fastened to the gallows' where they stood for more than half an hour. Each had offered his last prayers when a stay of execution was delivered. The execution was rescheduled for the following Friday, 6 April, at which time Stow summarized their last words and noted that they refused to say the Lord's Prayer, protesting that they preferred a prayer that was inspired by 'the spirit of God'. He added, 'The same day (as I remember) a Welshman, [John] Penry, publisher of books entitled Martin Marprelate, was apprehended', but other sources suggest that Penry was arrested earlier.[75]

The first part of the manuscript describing the trial of Barrow and Greenwood, is very similar to the account published in the *Annales*,[76] but the second part includes the last words of the condemned men that were not printed. The third part of the manuscript is especially interesting because it may be the only account of Barrow and Greenwood's appearance at Tyburn on 31 March, stating that they were fastened to the gallows for more than thirty minutes before they were granted a stay of execution.[77] It was obviously dangerous for Stow to write anything that might encourage sympathy for Separatists, and this may explain why the lengthy ordeal at the gallows was omitted. Stow was neither a Separatist nor a Separatist sympathizer, but his non-judgemental manuscript narrative reflects a sense of compassion for suffering people that runs through most of his historical writing with the notable exception of the Irish.

When Matthew Hamon, the ploughwright of Hethersett, Norfolk, was burned at Norwich in 1579,[78] Stow meticulously listed the heresies that he had published:

The New Testament and Gospel of Christ are but mere foolishness, a story of men, or rather a mere fable.

That man is restored to grace by the mere mercy of God, without the mean of Christ's blood, death, and passion.

That Christ is not God, nor the Saviour of the world, but a mere man, a sinful man and an abominable idol.

That all they that worship him are abominable idolaters;

And that Christ did not rise again from death to life by the power of his Godhead, neither that he did ascend into heaven.

That the holy ghost is not God, neither that there is any such holy ghost.

That baptism is not necessary in the Church of God, neither the use of the Sacrament of the body and blood of Christ.

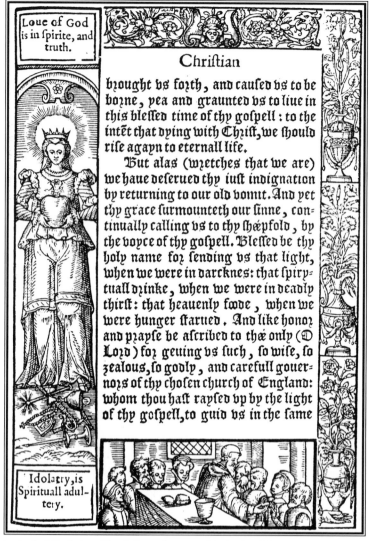

Holy Communion in the Elizabethan Church depicted in part of the border of the 1578 edition of John Daye's Booke of Christian Prayers. *The large communion cup and the loaf of bread contrast with the Catholic chalice and wafer shown among the pile of idolatrous relics of popery on the left.*

The positions attributed to Hamon suggest that he was an Arian, but he also spoke blasphemously of Queen Elizabeth and her privy councillors. After both of his ears were cut off, he was burned in the castle ditch at Norwich.[79] Stow's account of the execution of Hamon appears in the *Chronicles of England*, published in 1580, and was later included in the second edition of Holinshed, where it was mistakenly attributed to Abraham Fleming by Annabel Patterson.[80]

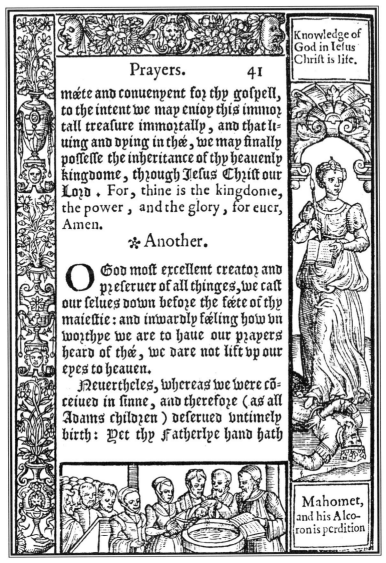

Baptism in the Elizabethan Church, from Daye's Booke of Christian Prayers.

Matthew Hamon was not an isolated figure in rural Norfolk because in 1583 another Arian, John Lewes, 'an obstinate heretic, denying the Godhead of Christ, and holding diverse other detestable heresies, (much like to his predecessor, Matthew Hamon)', was burned at Norwich.[81] Six years later Francis Kett, a physician of Wymondham, appeared before Edmund Scambler, Bishop of Norwich, for holding 'divers detestable opinions against our Saviour' before being burned near Norwich.[82]

The grandson of Robert Kett, the tanner and leader of the Norfolk Rebellion of 1549, Francis Kett was educated at Cambridge where he received a BA, MA, and MD (1581).[83] Although Kett has been accused of atheism, the charges against him clearly indicate that he had adopted Arian views.[84]

In April 1561 Stow recorded the punishment of two London radicals, William Geffrey and John Moore. Geffrey was whipped from the Marshalsea in Southwark to Bedlam without Bishopsgate for proclaiming that Moore was 'Christ our Saviour'. After long imprisonment at Bedlam, Geffrey, in the presence of Moore, was whipped again until he confessed that Christ was in heaven. Subsequently Moore was whipped until he made a similar confession, and then both were returned to prison where they had been confined for the previous eighteen months.[85] Stow offered no comments on the punishment of the false messiah and his disciple, but his inclusion of the incident without comment opens the door to speculation about his own interest.[86]

Perhaps the most extraordinary radicals whose careers were chronicled were two London gentlemen, Edmund Coppinger and Henry Arthington, and William Hacket of Oundle, Northamptonshire, a yeoman. As Coppinger and Arthington walked through the streets of London in 1591, they proclaimed that 'Christ was come'. Standing in an empty cart near the Cross in Cheap where large crowds had gathered, they said that William Hacket represented Christ 'by partaking a part of his glorified body by his principal spirit and by the office of severing the good from the bad with his fan in his hand'. Stow chose to 'overpass' their words against the queen and the council, but added, 'This strange accident being quickly blown through the city, all was in a buzz, and a kind of astonishment what to think of the matter.'[87] Two of the queen's council were dispatched to London where they arrested the culprits, whose examinations Stow also omitted from his chronicle.

William Hacket was tried for treason because he spoke traitorous words, 'razed and defaced her majesty's arms, as [sic] also a certain picture of the queen's majesty and did maliciously and traitorously thrust an iron instrument into that part of the said picture that did represent the breast and heart of the queen's majesty . . . '. Stow may have been among the 'incredible multitude' present in the streets as Hacket was led off to execution. *En route* to Cheap he cried out 'jehouah, messias, jehouah, messias'. Refusing to ask the queen's forgiveness, he 'fell to railing and cursing of the queen's majesty most villainously and then began a most blasphemous and execrable prayer against the divine majesty God'. Stow went on to explain that 'they had much ado to get him up the ladder where he was hanged and after boweled and quartered'.[88]

Edmund Coppinger died in Bridewell on 29 July after refusing food, while Henry Arthington was held 'long after' at Wood Street in hope of 'perfect repentance'. Stow advised readers of the *Annales of England* that more might be found in Richard Cosin, *Conspiracie for Pretended Reformation* (1592) and took his own advice since his account draws heavily from this polemical book. Stow's use of Cosin, however, was selective as he omitted his denunciation of Hacket as 'an unlettered maltster'.[89] Modern historians generally accept contemporary assessments of this bizarre episode and suggest that Hacket may have been a psychopath, but W.J. Sheils connected him with Separatists and Extremists at Oundle. 'Whether the conspiracy was an aberration is questionable,' he argued, 'for it had roots firmly in local puritan developments.' Hacket had been imprisoned previously in Northampton jail after claiming to have assumed the spirit of John the Baptist. When he arrived in London he fell in with two other zealots, Coppinger and Arthington, and tried to assist imprisoned classis leaders.[90]

Stow's references to the persecution of Roman Catholics during the reign of Elizabeth reflected the official policy of the queen's government and the Church of England. He boasted of his loyalty by reminding readers that he had included books defending the use of torture and condemning the Throckmorton Plot (1584) in the second edition of Holinshed's chronicle.[91] Stow's references to individual victims were short, but the sheer number of entries listing executed priests could not fail to impress his readers with the simple truth that large numbers of Roman Catholic clergy were prepared to die for their religious principles. Stow's brevity is especially apparent in his accounts of the executions of two of the most prominent Jesuits, Edmund Campion

The persecution of English Catholics under the Elizabethan regime depicted in a French book of 1592. The subject matter was deemed so inflammatory that the English ambassador ordered its suppression.

and Robert Southwell. In the case of Campion, who was executed in 1581, Stow referred his readers to the second edition of Holinshed, 'Look more in my continuation of Reine Woolfes chronicle'. This was a work that had been previously castrated because of its tactless account of Campion's execution. The death of Southwell in 1594 received even less attention and was merely the execution of 'a Jesuit that long time had lain prisoner in the Tower of London'.[92]

Stow sometimes withheld information that was available to him. His manuscripts include the following details about the death and burial of Edmund Bonner, the former Bishop of London, in September 1569:

> . . . deceased Edmund Bonner, doctor of civil law, bishop of London, in the prison of the Marshalsea who was privily buried about midnight next following being Tuesday at might in St George's church among two thieves who died in prison. . . .

While Bonner was hated by Elizabethan reformers for his role in the Marian persecution, it is difficult to understand why news of his death needed to be suppressed, especially at the beginning of the seventeenth century when he had been dead for nearly forty years. Nevertheless, Stow's chronicles as well as both editions of Holinshed's chronicle failed to include a notice of Bonner's death. *A Survey of London*, on the other hand, lists Bonner among the spiritual governors of the city and gives the place and date of his death.[93]

Catholic victims of the Elizabethan persecution included a Lincolnshire priest, Thomas Woodhouse, who was executed for treason in 1573 after long imprisonment at the Fleet.[94] On Palm Sunday the same year several priests were arrested for celebrating mass in private chapels in London. In addition to the illegal services, a search of chapels revealed various books in Latin, beads, and palms.[95] John Slade, a schoolmaster, and John Bodie, MA, were condemned of high treason and hanged for maintaining Roman authority at Winchester and Andover, respectively, in 1583. Stow probably knew a London printer, William Carter, who was hanged in 1584 for printing a seditious book, *A Treatise of Schisme*.[96] Stow listed the execution of many Jesuits and seminary priests but only two women, both of whom were described as 'gentlewomen'. Margaret Warde died because she had 'conveyed a cord to a priest in Bridewell, whereby he let himself down and escaped', while Ann Line was hanged for 'relieving a priest' contrary to the law.[97]

In dealing with Catholics Stow offered a series of politically correct anecdotes that viewed their offences as violations of parliamentary statutes. Nevertheless, his accounts of barbaric executions as well as references to Holinshed's chronicle would have been of assistance to anyone who wanted to attack the Elizabethan persecution of Catholic priests and laypeople. Like Holinshed's chronicle, the *Annales of England* was a compendium of historical data readily available for reinterpretation. But Stow also included substantial information in the shorter chronicles for the benefit of a larger reading public that could not afford the price of a quarto volume.

While it is very clear that Stow's perception of the English Reformation differs substantially from both contemporary and modern writers, it is arguable that he should not be viewed as a historian of the Reformation at all but merely as a citizen who chronicled day-to-day affairs without really understanding the significance of the religious revolution through which he lived.[98] Such an argument would appropriately emphasize his apparent lack of interest in important aspects of the Reformation, his indifference to major theological and liturgical issues, and his neglect of the

John Whitgift, Archbishop of Canterbury 1583–1604. Stow was a great admirer of Elizabeth's third archbishop and the Annales of England *was dedicated to him.*

role of the Reformation in foreign policy and national security. On the other hand, the Reformation is too important to English society to be left exclusively to learned clerics and religious authorities.

Like most lay people of his era, Stow was never fully engulfed by the Reformation. The investigation of his alleged Catholic sympathies, for example, led to no charges and appears to have had no effect on his work as a historian. Nevertheless, the changing religious climate influenced Stow's personal life and writing. In the chronicles and *A Survey of London*, he showed little more than nostalgia for the pre-Reformation Church. While he admired monasteries and other old religious buildings and criticized their desecration, he did not lament the demise of traditional religious practices or condemn the disappearance of old bones 'hanged up for show' in a London parish church.[99] His published works were scarcely the best contemporary examples of anticlerical propaganda, but they expressed attitudes characteristic of that genre. Stow's personal religion included elements of applied Christianity with an emphasis on charitable works and compassion for the suffering.[100] His family life, especially during the controversy with his brother, reveals the strong influence of the reformed Church. He knew the English Bible and referred to it in his writings.[101] A moralistic, sober, and righteous man, Stow displayed a remarkably tolerant attitude toward radical Christians and Arians; and his non-judgemental account of the notorious stews of Southwark would hardly have won the approval of Puritan clergy.[102] Stow's major contribution to an understanding of the Reformation is that he offers the perspective of a literate lay person outside the governing elite to a subject that has been seen traditionally from different vantage points. His interests, priorities, and emphases differed from those of the major Protestant and Catholic writers, but they must be considered seriously in any complete history of the Reformation in England.

CHAPTER FIVE

ENGLISH POLITICS AND BRITAIN

Although John Stow lived outside the governing elite and never travelled outside England, he had a keen interest in English politics and the British Isles. Stow wrote about the Tudor monarchs and followed the work of politicians but as a citizen historian did so from a distance. His political interests were surprisingly unconventional as they differ from traditional thinking about the institutional basis of government, especially Parliament. Throughout his long life, Stow dutifully collected narratives of medieval Wales and Ireland and was also a careful observer of contemporary diplomatic and military affairs. Stow understood that the British Isles were peopled by Scots, Irish, Welsh and Cornish, as well as the English, but he revealed a deep-seated patriotism with approving and uncritical accounts of English military operations in Scotland and Ireland.

1. MONARCHS AND MINISTERS

Monarchs and their ministers lay at the very heart of early modern English political life. They dominated society and shaped foreign and domestic policies. Modern historians, including the much maligned Whigs as well as revisionists and Tories, assign great importance to individual kings and queens and the great and not so great men called to give counsel. Living in a society where freedom of expression was unlawful, Stow was unable to write as he wished about monarchs and the governing elite, yet his restraint in lavishing uncritical praise on the great and powerful exceeded that of many of his contemporaries. The chronicler Edward Hall was certain that the deceased Henry VII would 'sit on the right hand of our saviour' and wrote eloquently of the death of his son, Henry VIII:

> Now approached to this noble king, that which is by God decreed, and appointed to all men, for at this season in the month of January, he yielded his spirit to almighty God and departed this world.

Stow declined to speculate on the final destiny of the first Tudor king and was content to record that Henry VIII died at Westminster on Friday 28 January 1547, 'beginning the year at Christmas' after reigning thirty-seven years, nine months, and 'odd days'.[1]

Edward VI as Prince of Wales, c. 1542, after Hans Holbein.

Edward VI, who succeeded his father when he was only nine years old, was the first king whose reign Stow experienced in its entirety. In his account of the reign he did not have access to the principal source for the reign which is the manuscript chronicle or journal written in the young king's own hand. Stow's earliest chronicle, the *Summarie* of 1565, devotes fourteen folios to the reign and owes a good deal to the earlier efforts of Thomas Cooper and Richard Grafton.[2] In his own work, Stow did not attempt to demonstrate that the young king possessed precocious genius that allowed him to govern the country. Neither did he argue that the king was merely a puppet manipulated by those closest to the throne. In Stow's narrative, government was conducted in the name of the king, but there was no effort to present him as a mature political leader. Stow did not anticipate the modern debate on the 'real' Edward although he provided historical data upon which these arguments could be based. In the last edition of the *Summarie Abridged* (1604), he offered a short, matter-of-fact account of the reign of only eighteen pages in which he noted the young king's untimely death without sentimentality and offered no eulogy.[3] The *Annales of England*, on the other hand, contains a fuller narrative as well as important documents and letters, including one in which Protector Somerset told John Dudley, Earl of Warwick, during the political crisis of 1549 that there had been 'so great a friendship and amity betwixt us, as never for my part to no man was greater'.[4]

Stow, who was old enough to be a credible eyewitness to the events of Edward's reign, never suggested that the king was sickly or suffered from ill health before January 1553. In fact, he noted that the king was conducting business at Whitehall as late as April 1552.[5] In the *Annales*, Stow remembered Edward chiefly because of his charity to Bridewell and St Thomas's Hospital in Southwark.[6] At the end of the reign, when Dudley, now Duke of Northumberland, was allegedly manipulating the dying king to transfer the crown to Lady Jane Grey, Stow simply avoided the controversial question of the succession by stating that Edward provided for the succession by issuing letters patent granting the throne to Jane. Stow lamented that Edward died 'in this his youth a prince of such towardness in virtue, learning, and all godly gifts, as seldom hath been seen the like' but did not spell out exactly what his godly gifts actually were.[7]

The influence of Stow's patron, Robert Dudley, Earl of Leicester, may explain why the *Annales of England* offers the most sympathetic interpretation of Northumberland's political career to be found in any sixteenth-century chronicle. Over the centuries opponents of Northumberland's son, the Earl of Leicester, supported by historians such as William Camden and Sir John Hayward, helped create and sustain the durable legend of the wicked duke, but Stow cannot be counted as one of the myth makers.[8]

Whereas Hayward detested both Protector Somerset and Northumberland, Stow's sympathy for Northumberland did not require him to blacken the reputation of the lord protector. Lacking close contacts at court, Stow was convinced that Somerset was 'elected' protector in 1547.[9] The *Annales* implies that the protector's younger brother, Thomas, Lord Seymour, was guilty of the charges brought against him since he 'wrote a letter unto the Lady Mary and Lady Elizabeth, the king's sisters, that they should make some stir against the lord protector and revenge his death'.[10] The *Summarie Abridged* (1604) carried only a short account of the overthrow of Protector Somerset in 1549 in which there is no indication of a coup or a conspiracy organized by Dudley, but the *Annales* suggests that the king's council opposed Somerset because of his misgovernment. It prints an important letter from Somerset to Dudley, lists the charges against Somerset, and includes his submission.

Robert Dudley, Earl of Leicester, in a miniature by Nicholas Hilliard dated 1576.

Somerset was released following a short period of imprisonment and restored to the king's council in 1550, but he never recovered his dominant position as lord protector. Although he seemed willing at first to accept a position of diminished authority, Somerset attempted to reassert himself. Political rivalries reappeared leading to his trial and execution in 1552. In an account not dissimilar to that found in the king's journal, the *Summarie Abridged* repeats what must have been the official version of the trial, namely that Somerset was 'arraigned at Westminster and condemned of felony'. The *Annales*, however, includes a full account of the trial as well as a fascinating description of the execution on Tower Hill that Stow himself attended.[11] In an unpublished manuscript, Stow noted that Somerset was executed to the 'great discontent of the Protestants', but this observation is not found in the *Annales*.[12]

After the king died of tuberculosis in 1553, the *Annales of England* cast Northumberland in a more heroic role than Queen Jane. According to Stow, her father, the Duke of Suffolk, initially was to lead the expedition against Mary, but Jane – 'with weeping tears' – insisted that he remain at her side in London.[13] The council, praising Northumberland's wisdom and knowledge effusively, persuaded him to take command. Before leaving Northumberland spoke movingly to the assembled councillors:

> My lords, I and these other noble personages with the whole army that now go forth as well for the behalf of you and yours as for the establishing of the Queen's highness shall not only adventure our bodies and lives amongst the bloody strokes and cruel assaults of our adversaries in the open fields, but also we do leave the conservation of ourselves, children, and families at home here with you, as altogether committed to your truth and fidelities.[14]

Stow reproduced this speech from an original manuscript, Harleian MS 194, that came into his possession and was very likely preserved for posterity by his efforts.[15] Northumberland's prophetic comment that no one said God speed us as his army rode out of London to apprehend Mary was also incorporated into the *Annales of England* from the same manuscript. In Stow's account the deceased king's councillors not only failed to send military assistance to Northumberland, but also changed their minds about the succession and gave their support to Princess Mary.[16] While Stow did not offer an apology for Northumberland, he included documents and details that make the duke's actions more understandable.

Unlike other popular writers of the period, Stow did not contribute to the romanticization of Lady Jane as a role model for Protestant women.[17] Stow's Lady Jane was much like the historical Jane, a devout, intelligent, and well-meaning young woman, whose father thrust her into a major political crisis that she did not understand. Essentially a pawn in the hands of the politicians, she survived the abortive attempt to make her queen in 1553 only to be drawn into Wyatt's Rebellion the following year. Stow reported Jane's courage with compassion as she viewed the decapitated corpse of her husband, Lord Guildford Dudley, before dying herself but carefully avoided exaggerating her historical role. Since a sixteenth-century historian could not rehabilitate a loser, Stow, accepting the ultimate success of Queen Mary against both Northumberland and Wyatt, expressed relief that Jane's short reign ended 'without bloodshed as many feared'.[18]

If Stow's King Edward wore none of the interpretive costume designed by later historians, his Queen Mary (1553–8) also failed the reader looking for early evidence of the myth of Bloody Mary.[19] Nowhere is his determination to avoid religious controversy more visible than in his account of the restoration of Roman Catholicism under Mary. Although his manuscripts leave no doubts that Stow knew about the burnings, the published chronicles do not offer the slightest hint that Stow lived through the greatest religious persecution in English history.[20] His impartial account not only skirts religious issues but also contains little, if any, bias against England's first female sovereign. A bare hint of criticism against Philip occurs in Stow's announcement of the queen's death on 17 November 1558:

> King Philip being absent out of the realm and Queen Mary being dangerously sick ended her life at the manor of St. James by Charing Cross. . . .[21]

The second edition of Holinshed's chronicle to which Stow was a major contributor boldly emphasized the bloodshed and tyranny of Mary's reign while Edmund Howes inserted the following critical comments on her religious policy in his continuation of the *Annales of England*: 'The news of Queen Mary's death was deadly unto all abbots, priors, and prioresses, etc who saw their sudden desolation before their face. . . .'[22]

Stow seems to have had little interest in the personal lives of either Edward or Mary, and he did not traffic in court gossip. The queen's marriage to King Philip rated only a paragraph in the *Annales*, but Stow understood that the Spanish marriage was 'grievously taken

Mary Tudor, painted by Antonio Mor, 1519–75.

of divers men' and that it and opposition to the re-establishment of Roman Catholicism led to Wyatt's Rebellion early in 1554.[23] Stow was probably in the congregation at St Paul's on 28 November 1554 when a letter was read from the council 'the tenor whereof was that the Bishop of London should cause Te Deum to be sung in all the churches of his diocese with continual prayers for the Queen's majesty which was conceived and quick with child'.[24] We know that no child was born because the queen was not pregnant, but Stow was content to drop the issue and not engage in any guesswork or speculation. Since Stow always found space in his chronicles for subjects that interested him, his avoidance of sensitive questions may be attributed to a Tudor commitment to national unity or perhaps a determination to write what would later be called politically correct history. As Stow's last edition of the *Annales of England* was published at the beginning of the seventeenth century, it is difficult to believe that the government of that day would have objected to a mildly critical account of Mary's religious policies or simple recognition of her childlessness.

Stow noted that Queen Mary reigned 'five years, four months, and odd days' and that Cardinal Pole, Archbishop of Canterbury, died the same day in 1558, but omitted a eulogy or an assessment of her reign. He devoted nearly forty pages of the *Annales* to the reign, slightly more than given over to Edward VI. Mary's half-sister and successor, Elizabeth, understandably received greater attention from Stow, over 350 pages in the last edition of 1605. As Stow compiled his account of Elizabethan England, the most contemporary part of his history, he gave about equal coverage to the first and last decades of the reign; the 1570s received the shortest account, while greatest attention went to the decade of the 1580s when England sent an army into the Netherlands and defended itself against the Spanish Armada.

Although Stow was in no way a critic of Queen Elizabeth, his enthusiasm for Gloriana was surprisingly restrained in an age given to passionate devotion to the monarch.[25] He not only knew little of the queen's personal life but seemingly failed to understand that the Duke of Anjou came to England seeking her hand in marriage. In 1579 Stow praised the queen's 'noble courage' as she comforted a bleeding waterman shot accidentally through both arms as he rowed the royal barge on the Thames. 'She bade him be of good cheer', he wrote, 'and said he should want nothing that might be for his ease.' Stow noted, however, that the reckless gunman, Thomas Appletree, who was sentenced to death, received the queen's pardon as the hangman was placing the rope about his neck. Appletree may have deserved pardon, but he was a man of some standing as he was a servant to Henry Carey, Lord Hunsdon, cousin to the queen. The shooting victim whom Elizabeth comforted so courageously remained nameless, and Stow did not say whether his wounds proved fatal.[26]

Throughout the chronicles Stow made favourable references to Elizabeth's presence at national celebrations and spectacles. She attended a service of thanksgiving at St Paul's in 1588 after the defeat of the Spanish Armada. In 1596 Stow noted the celebration of her accession on 17 November to which he referred as a 'day of great triumph for the long, prosperous and triumphant reign' of the queen but did not say whether he was in attendance. Three years later, on 13 November, the mayor, aldermen, sheriffs, and commons of London, 'all well mounted on horseback, as of late times had been used, for honour of the queen, by commandment, received her at Westminster by torch light'. Stow's insertion of the words 'by command-ment' does more than hint that the reception was government inspired while his account of the forty-first anniversary of Elizabeth's accession the same year spoke of 'great jousts and triumphs' that lasted several days.[27]

Elizabeth I in a full-size portrait of about 1575, attributed to the great miniaturist Nicholas Hilliard.

Stow's response to the queen's death is the strongest indication of either his lack of devotion to her or a sense of disillusion with the last years of the reign. The dead Gloriana rated only short entries in the *Summarie Abridged* (1604) and *Annales of England* (1605), the last two historical works that he published. He probably watched the funeral procession as it passed from Whitehall to Westminster Abbey, and he estimated that 1,600 mourners dressed in black attended her funeral where the sermon was preached by the deceased queen's almoner, Anthony Watson, Bishop of Chichester.[28] There is no indication that Stow was one of the mourners in the abbey or that he grieved or was in any way affected by the queen's death.

It is far from clear how many contemporary readers would have agreed with Stow that the date of the queen's death on Thursday, 24 March 1603, the eve of the Annunciation of the Virgin Mary, was memorable because

Thursday hath been a fatal day to King Henry VIII and all his posterity, for himself died on Thursday the twenty-eighth of January, King Edward on Thursday the sixth of July, [and] Mary on Thursday the seventeenth of November.[29]

Inclusion of such trivia may be taken as further evidence that the end of the age of Elizabeth was not in Stow's estimation an earth-shattering event. When Edmund Howes revised and enlarged the *Annales of England*, he altered Stow's curious account and added an effusive, three-page commemoration of the queen. 'Her subjects' love daily increased upon her without ceasing or intermission, during all her whole reign,' he wrote, 'and so continued during her life and after.'[30] It was Howes, not Stow, who helped create the myth that romanticized Elizabeth and her reign, and when a modern biographer, Paul Johnson, invoked the name of Stow as one who praised the deceased queen, he was really quoting Edmund Howes.[31]

Despite his advanced age and traditional mentality, Stow looked forward enthusiastically to the new era of the Stuarts. James I was proclaimed 'to the comfort of the whole realm', and to Stow the prospect of a male sovereign was especially enticing:

> This change was very plausible, or well pleasing to the nobility and gentry, and generally to all the commons of this realm among whom the name of a king was then so strange as few could remember. . . .[32]

The old man seems to have celebrated the accession of James I from a distance because his comments on the coronation, which took place on St James' Day, 25 July, are very

A king and one of his subjects, from the Roxburghe Ballads.

brief. He probably watched the mayor and aldermen dressed in resplendent gowns depart by barge from the Three Cranes stairs, but he did not see Archbishop Whitgift crown the new king at Westminster Abbey.[33] As John Stow ended his long life in 1605, it is not possible to know whether his enthusiasm for the Stuarts would have survived or whether he would have joined Howes and others who longed for 'good Queen Bess'.[34]

In contrast to historical writing where great men, especially political leaders, parliamentarians, and diplomats, stand at the centre of the historical stage, Stow's chronicles assign the now famous workhorses of Elizabethan government, figures such as William and Robert Cecil, Francis Walsingham, and Nicholas Bacon, supporting historical roles. A sixteenth-century reader of Stow's chronicles, unlike the reader of modern texts, would not have learned how William Cecil, Lord Burghley,

William Cecil, 1st Baron Burghley, painted by an unknown artist in 1580.

weathering countless crises, shaped government policy from the accession of the queen until his death in 1598. Stow did not recognize that Burghley's 'capacity for work, his care for detail, his grasp of difficulties amounted to genius'.[35] Neither did he follow Burghley's long career, and his death was briefly recorded in the last edition of the *Summarie Abridged* while the *Annales* more generously characterized him as a famous councillor renowned for his wisdom throughout Europe.[36] Military commanders campaigning in the Netherlands or fighting on the high seas impressed Stow more than clever politicians aspiring to become statesmen. As he had no appetite for power politics, factionalism, and intrigue, he had little in common with politique historians such as Sir John Hayward. Twentieth-century academic historians gradually abandoned the view that a few great men shaped history in favour of an appreciation of hard-working experts, who managed an emerging bureaucracy, but Stow had little interest in the technical aspects of statecraft.

2. GOVERNMENT

While Stow recognized the symbolic and political role of Tudor monarchs and gave their ministers the social prominence they deserved, his interest in the government was limited. His writings show no great interest in the major institutions of central government including the privy council, Parliament, courts of justice, or the exchequer. Policy-making, legislation, royal administration, and court politics were unquestionably of little importance to him. If the sixteenth century witnessed the growth of a modern bureaucracy and the emergence of a better governed state, these achievements have impressed twentieth-century historians more than John Stow.

To Stow the English Parliament was neither a major event nor an institution of great importance. He had no interest in decisions to summon Parliament or in elections to the House of Commons. Sir Thomas Smith was correct when he wrote that the consent of Parliament was taken to be the consent of everyone, but Stow saw it as remote and separate from persons like himself.[37] The mechanics of Parliament, including relations between the Lords and Commons, did not concern him. In 1554 Stow noted that 'the whole court of Parliament' desired King Philip and Queen Mary to be restored to the obedience of the see of Rome, a request that later parliamentary historians were anxious to overlook.[38]

The Parliament of 1571 rated only a few lines in the *Annales of England*:

> The second of April at Parliament began at Westminster, wherein was granted to the queen's majesty (toward her great charges in repressing the late rebellion in the North and pursuing the said rebels and their fautors which were fled into Scotland) by the clergy a subsidy of 6s. in the pound and by the temporalty two fifteenths with a subsidy of 2s. 8d. in the pound.

Stow's account of the Parliament filled only five lines and was followed by a notice of similar length describing jousting in which the Earl of Oxford won the 'chief honour'. During the same year a bizarre tale of armed combat over disputed lands filled several quarto pages.[39] He carefully noted that a number of Parliaments, including those of 1571, 1585, and 1593, levied taxes but never argued that the taxes were unnecessary or unjust. In the Parliaments of 1585 and 1593 he gave particular prominence to the queen's speech, and in 1598 he noted that people were killed trying to see the queen; but the parliamentarians themselves weren't important enough to mention.

Such a reading of English constitutional history flies in the face of the great weight assigned to the subject by historians as diverse in outlook as A.F. Pollard, J.E. Neale, and G.R. Elton. It is easy enough to conclude that Stow was a mere tailor with no understanding of the constitution, but a more significant question is the extent to which his views represented the outlook of inarticulate common people, who have been largely ignored by constitutional historians. Stow, like the ordinary man, entertained no parliamentary ambitions. Without legal training, he had little appreciation of the finer points of the legislative process. Nor was he important enough in the affairs of London to influence the agenda of the city's representatives in the House of Commons. Since the great majority of English people were in the same position as Stow, it is not unreasonable to argue that he represented their thinking more accurately than the parliamentarians whose special pleading often represented the self-interest of the governing elite as much as the people of England as a whole.

Stow's *Survey of London* offers invaluable information about the government of the capital, but local government elsewhere interested him very little. As a Londoner who seems to have travelled around the country very little, he had a poor understanding of county politics and the operation of local government. He compiled a fascinating narrative about the terrible murder of Thomas Arden, but anyone interested in the quarter sessions at Faversham or law enforcement in Kent would have to look elsewhere.[40] While the chronicles include anecdotes on subjects such as conspiracies and riots from many English counties, their political focus is on central government, military affairs, and foreign policy. The reader of Stow's chronicles quickly discovered that local politics and society were topics reserved for writers such as William Lambarde and John Hooker and that Stow never troubled himself with the administrative or legal aspects of government at any level.

3. BRITAIN AND BRITISH POLICY

Although Stow was English and wrote for an English public, he was aware of a larger British environment that included Wales, Scotland, and Ireland. In both the *Chronicles of England* and the *Annales of England* Stow offered descriptions of Scotland, Wales, and Cornwall. Britain, he began, 'which by two names is called England and Scotland is an island in the ocean sea situate right over against France'. He continued, 'One part . . . the Englishmen do inhabit, another part the Scots, the third part Welshmen, and the fourth part the Cornishmen; all they either in language, conditions, or laws do differ among themselves.'[41] Sixteenth-century readers interested in their own times who looked beyond Stow's introduction found that he gave more attention to Ireland than to either Wales or Cornwall, although his manuscript collection included accounts of medieval Wales as well as Ireland.

Stow understood and never questioned the extension of English rule over Cornwall and Wales. While he offered a geographical description of Cornwall and made a few brief comments about its economy, he was most attracted to its language, which in his view was 'far dissonant from English', but very much like Welsh. Tudor Cornwall had no political existence because the Normans had reckoned it to be 'one of the counties or shires of the country'. Stow had more sympathy for the Welsh as a conquered people probably because of his familiarity with the writings of the medieval scholar

Gerald of Wales. He thought the Welsh language had Trojan and Greek roots and criticized its pronunciation:

> The Welshmen do not pronounce their speech so pleasantly and gently as the Englishmen do, because they speak more in the throat and contrariwise, the Englishmen rightly following the Latins do express their voice somewhat within the lips which to the hearers seemeth pleasant and sweet.[42]

By incorporating Wales into England, the Tudors deprived it of its national identity and began a programme of modernization under English auspices. The goal of English policy was the creation of an English empire in the British Isles, but only Wales suffered military conquest during the middle ages. Of the British nations, Wales, after Cornwall, was the weakest and posed the least threat to English domination. During the second half of the sixteenth century the Tudor monarchs took little interest in the region and left the governance to gentry who in return for loyalty to the crown were left largely to their own devices.[43] As a backward but peaceful country without a government, Elizabethan Wales failed to attract Stow's attention, and his attitude mirrored the thinking of most of his English contemporaries.

In the introduction to the *Annales* Stow left little doubt of the subordinate place assigned to Scotland:

> Scotland another part of Britain (whereof in this place I have thought good to treat at large that no further mention of the situation thereof might be made hereafter) began sometime at the hill called Grampius. . . .

His four-page account emphasized topography, but the people were not ignored. Stow conceded that Scots were 'hard to be vanquished at any time by reason the woods and marshes be at hand for refuge and hunger eased with venison and fish'. Acknowledging differences between the northern and southern parts of the country, he observed that Scots in the south were 'well nurtured, and live in good civility and the most civil use the English speech', but in the north lived 'a very rude and homely kind' of people called the 'redshanks or wild Scots'. Stow conceded that Scots were 'very wise as their learning declareth, for to whatsoever art they do apply themselves, they easily profit in the same'; and he concluded approvingly that they 'generally be observers of Religion'.[44]

While the Scotland of Stow's day was of greater importance to England than Wales, he showed little interest in the invasion and occupation of Scotland by the Duke of Somerset in 1547. After England won a great victory in the field and killed as many as 14,000 of the enemy, Stow was content to refer the interested reader to 'Master Patten his booke extant entituled, The Expedition into Scotland'. Stow not only declined to incorporate any of the vivid details from William Patten's eyewitness account in the *Annales of England*, but he also did not use a two-folio narrative included in his own manuscripts.[45] The Elizabethan attack on Scotland in 1560 was altogether different, because Stow offered a narrative of no fewer than ten pages in the *Annales*. Here he considered the controversy between England and France, listed the 'lords of Scotland that made suit for aid against the Frenchmen', meticulously followed military operations, and enumerated thirteen articles of the treaty of Edinburgh. Although Stow showed no great animosity toward the Scots, he revealed none of the pro-Scottish enthusiasm that colours the writing of the Jacobean historian Sir John Hayward. To Stow the Scots were victims of French aggression, and it was the latter power that really mattered because they threatened an invasion of England. Unlike modern historians, Stow saw only the 'malicious purpose' of the queen's adversaries;[46] he was not interested in the formulation of Scottish policy and knew nothing of divisions within the English privy council.[47]

Although Stow saw little significance in Mary, Queen of Scots' escape to England in 1568,[48] he was drawn to the punitive raids of the Earl of Sussex and Lord Hunsdon into Scotland in 1570 after the Northern Rebellion ended. He gave the reader no rationale for the attack beyond the fact that the Scots had 'received our English rebels' but described in depressing detail how the English 'burned, overthrew, razed, and spoiled' Scottish castles and towns.[49] As warfare of this type had been going on for decades, Stow saw the conflict as part of the normal relationship between the two countries and omitted from his narrative any consideration of the cost in property damage and human lives. Three years later Stow responded to the siege of Edinburgh Castle in a similar vein. Taking advantage of French weakness, England destroyed the remnants of Mary Stuart's cause in Scotland.[50] In a matter-of-fact account, Stow related the surrender of the castle and enumerated the reasons for its delivery to the English. His narratives of military operations in Scotland consistently emphasize the deeds of great men, peers and gentry drawn from the governing elite, and remind us that in these matters the citizen historian, deferring to his social betters, offered no independent perspective.[51]

The murder of Lord Darnley and the execution of Mary, Queen of Scots are major historical events that underscore Stow's deferential mentality and his extreme caution when writing about the monarchy. He sought refuge in brevity when he wrote of the death of Darnley, 'before named king of Scots, by Scots', who was 'shamefully murdered, the revenge whereof remaineth in the mighty hands of God' (but no more!)[52] The execution of Mary Stuart in 1587 was handled in the same way. Stow gave the time, date, and place of execution in one short paragraph, adding that the execution itself was witnessed by 300 gentlemen 'of the country near adjoining'. He explained that Mary died 'according to sentence lately given by the nobility' and that she was given a royal burial at Peterborough. Stow assumed that the reader knew why she was executed and offered no help to anyone interested in the legal aspects of the case. By arguing that Mary had been sentenced to death by the nobility, Stow conveniently absolved Queen Elizabeth of all responsibility.[53]

After the execution of Mary Stuart, Stow's interest in Scotland diminished, and he gave greater attention to English relations with Ireland. Despite his interest in the Irish writings of Gerald of Wales (Giraldus Cambrensis), his approach to sixteenth-century Ireland was episodic and anecdotal. To Stow, Ireland was little more than an unruly dependent kingdom requiring military force to maintain the queen's legitimate authority,[54] and he accepted without question the legitimacy of Elizabethan policy in Ireland. The brutal murder in 1567 of Shane O'Neill, who had 'most traitorously rebelled against the queen', was treated as a colourful anecdote by Stow and inserted in the *Annales of England* between accounts of a fire in Suffolk and the creation of a peer at Westminster. After suffering defeats at the hands of an army commanded by the 'valiant' Sir Henry Sidney, lord deputy of Ireland, O'Neill tried to cultivate the friendship of a band of 'wild Scots'. Unfortunately, O'Neill had previously killed the father and uncle of one of the Scottish leaders. According to Stow, O'Neill received entertainment at the Scots' camp and enjoyed the 'quaffing of wine', but later the son of the man who had been killed, 'burning with desire of revenge', provoked a brawl and 'hewed in pieces' O'Neill and most of his followers.[55]

In 1572 Thomas Smith, younger son of the privy councillor and scholar of the same name, attempted to establish 'a colony of Englishmen to inhabit the Ardes [Ards] in Ulster'.[56] Stow observed that the elder Smith was 'carefully tending the reformation of Ireland', but the self-educated citizen historian probably did not appreciate that his study of Caesar and Cicero according to the highest standards of Renaissance humanism inspired him to create a Roman-style colony in Ireland that could be governed by his son. Stow, the chronicler, also overlooked a colourful anecdote when he failed to note that the younger Smith's project ended abruptly when he was attacked and killed by disaffected Irish who boiled up his body and fed it to their dogs.[57]

Stow stressed the influence of the Pope on 'certain companies of Italians and Spaniards' – actually only about sixty men – who fortified themselves near Smerwick in 1579. But he hastened to add that the Pope's banner did not survive as English forces attacked. All the Irish men and women, Stow reported triumphantly, were hanged, while the foreign soldiers were put to the sword.[58] When the Earl of Desmond, the Irish rebel who had previously joined the foreign invaders, was killed a few years later Stow gave the notice of his death slightly less space than a preceding entry that reported the hanging of a London horse thief.[59]

A good example of Stow's approach to Anglo-Irish relations appears in his long narrative of the campaigns of Sir Richard Bingham (1528–99), a career soldier who was determined to make the Irish conform to English practices and customs.[60] It is far from clear why Stow took an interest in Bingham, who feuded continuously with other officials while serving as president of Connaught, but he wrote in the *Annales* that because of the 'great troubles' in Ireland, he undertook to 'set down the causes and foundations thereof with all the particular services and successes, as I have received them, confirmed under the hands and testimonies of diverse captains and gentlemen employed in the said service'.[61] Since Stow never travelled to Ireland, he relied on others to supply him with information about the Irish wars. His published account is based on a manuscript that he said was abridged 'out of a larger treatise which I received at the hands of one who was present'. Although the manuscript upon which Stow based

Sir Richard Bingham in 1564, by an unknown artist.

his text has not been located, it was published in 1849 as *Docwra's Relation of Service Done in Ireland*. The author, Sir Henry Docwra (1560?–1631), served in Ireland under Bingham and later fought in Spain and the Netherlands with Essex.[62] In Stow's notes Bingham assumed heroic proportions as one of the major figures in the English civilizing mission in Ireland.

A vivid picture of English policy in Ireland emerges as Sir Richard Bingham's men marched through Connaught in 1585–6. We learn that his principal objective was to 'strengthen the government and weaken the Irishry'. To achieve this goal Bingham worked to 'take away the greatness' of Irish lords and increase the queen's revenue. It was quickly discovered that because the Irish were 'wiser than we take them to be', they fell into rebellion when discontented and misgoverned.[63] Bingham's approach was simply to use military force when the Irish resisted and not worry about the number of casualties. Therefore through his 'wonderful care and industry' the rebels were defeated, their leaders hanged, and peace restored.[64] Bingham's greatest triumph was the slaughter of the Scottish allies of the Irish in September 1586:

The number of fighting men slain and drowned, as hath been well known and tried out, were fourteen or fifteen hundred, beside horse and foot boys, women, churls, and children were as many more, so as in the whole there died of them that day and the day after in their flying homewards, three thousand persons, and of the English companies were not slain past two persons. . . .[65]

Stow's historical methodology was as straight forward as Bingham's military strategy because he merely reproduced Docwra's firsthand report and accepted its conclusions unequivocally.

While Stow was unquestionably ignorant of a country that he had never visited, his uncritical acceptance of information supplied by Docwra not only reflects English chauvinism but also illustrates one of the worst examples of his historical scholarship. In dealing with other subjects where he had firsthand knowledge, he wrote with compassion and understanding for suffering people although he never questioned the legitimacy of Tudor policy or the need for law and order.[66] Stow's account of Sir Richard Bingham's campaign reveals dramatically the prejudice and ethnocentricity that constitute the darker side of Elizabethan England.

Stow's interest in Brian O'Rourke, who rebelled against English land seizures in 1589, was limited to his trial in London two years later. He quoted extensively from the indictment against O'Rourke without saying how he obtained the information. The charges stated that the Irish rebel tried to deprive the queen of her 'regal seat', sought destruction of her royal person, and raised forces against her. After the defeat of the Armada, he had assisted the Spanish fleet in Ireland. O'Rourke received a letter of congratulation for his services to Spain from Philip II and later 'procured and caused' Thady O'Hart and others to enter into rebellion against the queen. The list of offences included burning, killing, stirring rebellion in Scotland, and offering to bring Ireland under the subjection of the king of Scotland. Stow must have been present when Brian O'Rourke was executed because he described graphically how the traitor was hanged until he was half dead, then cut down, and 'his members and bowels' taken out and burned. He revealed a remarkable degree of boldness as he quoted O'Rourke's last words in which he denounced James VI of Scotland and defiantly refused to ask the queen's forgiveness.[67]

In 1599, when the Earl of Essex led an army of 16,000 men, the largest force ever sent to Ireland, against the Earl of Tyrone, Stow said very little about what actually happened there. As Essex, lieutenant and lord high marshal, left in March, Stow wrote that he rode through London accompanied by a great train of nobles and gentlemen *en route* to Ireland. When he suddenly returned to London on Michaelmas Eve, 28 September, Stow remarked cautiously that he was 'of late greatly feared to have entered England by force of arms'. After an acrimonious interview with the queen at Nonesuch Palace and a meeting with the privy council, Essex was committed to house arrest at the residence of the Lord Keeper, Sir Thomas Egerton. Stow treated the Irish campaign of Essex in two short, unconnected paragraphs that tell nothing about the events that led to his disastrous revolt a few months later.[68]

At the end of his history of the reign of Elizabeth, Stow inserted a nine-page letter from Ireland describing the victory over the Spanish at Kinsale in Munster. To meet the most formidable challenge to English authority in Ireland that had yet occurred, the government dispatched 20,000 men.[69] Stow explained that because he had received 'small intelligence worth the noting' from Ireland during the wars of Essex and Mountjoy, he decided to 'set down the copy of a letter from a soldier of good place in Ireland to his friend in London' celebrating the great victory over the Irish rebels and their Spanish allies in 1602. The undated letter was dedicated to 'Sir W.D. Knight', but the author, an actual participant in the battle, cannot be identified.[70] It begins with a reference to an earlier letter of 19 December 1601 and reports the landing of a 'new supply' of 2,000 Spanish soldiers with more to come. Although the English army was weary as a result of a long winter's siege, the enemy was engaged and defeated. Twelve hundred Irish rebels died after having been abandoned by their own leaders. In addition to the men killed in battle, the writer noted that the Irish prisoners were hanged. The Spanish, finding their Irish allies 'not only weak and barbarous, but perfidious friends', offered to negotiate terms of surrender to the English. Unlike the Irish, the Spanish were treated honourably and permitted to return to Spanish ports with all their arms and equipment.[71] The letter ends with an eloquent paragraph rejoicing at the deliverance of the English from 'this troubled cloud of most likely perilous danger'. It went on to pay tribute to the queen's 'magnanimity and princely resolution' and to the great honour of the English generals and men. Perhaps feeling that he could add little to this triumphant conclusion, Stow was content to mention only the great celebration in London complete with bonfires that took place on 18 January 1602. The *Annales of England* gives no indication that the aged historian participated in the festivities.[72]

Stow regarded Ireland not as a colony, but as an extension of England, a region governed by the same laws that applied in England. Therefore Irish rebels, like their English counterparts, Robert Kett and Sir Thomas Wyatt, were rebels against the crown and entitled to no mercy. Stow relied heavily on information supplied to him and showed little ability to evaluate it critically and formulate his own conclusions. His episodic accounts, though rich in details, convey no idea of English objectives or policy in Ireland. Stow was, of course, writing of the exploits of Essex and Mountjoy at the end of his life when he was well past his prime as a historian. It must be remembered that these accounts are among the most contemporary that have survived since he died in 1605, only three years after the Spanish surrender at Kinsale, and consequently they exhibit all of the shortcomings of contemporary history. Stow was also writing about the most emotional and controversial subject in English history, and if his scholarship falls short of expectations, many other English writers fared little better when addressing the Irish question.

As Stow wrote about English politics and the challenge of maintaining influence throughout the British Isles, he was a traditional English patriot, who loyally supported his sovereign, government, and military forces. With limited understanding of the Welsh, Scots, and Irish, he expressed the conventional prejudices of his day that these peoples should acknowledge the superior position of England and defer to English rule. He was not much interested in national politics, court intrigue, or the danger of militarization during the last decade of Elizabeth's reign,[73] and it is likely that he had a superficial and unsophisticated understanding of the institutional foundation of national government. Stow was far more interested in people and events than institutions of either central or local government. Although a fervent supporter of law and order, he was a stranger to the complexities of English law, the formulation of national policy, and the emergence of a modern nation.

CHAPTER SIX

LONDON SURVEYED

While Stow's chronicles have been neglected in favour of Holinshed, *A Survey of London* (1598, 1603) stands as Stow's most influential work and is the basis of his scholarly reputation.[1] To Charles L. Kingsford it was 'the book of a life; on it the author's peculiar title to fame now rests'.[2] A.L. Rowse said *A Survey* was a classic, 'one of those rare books the author was born to write', and Steve Rappaport wrote that 'only the writings of John Stow are extensive enough to provide a sense of what life in London was like in the sixteenth century'.[3] Ian Archer praised the book as a 'celebration of the city's traditions' but has also contributed to a critical reassessment. He challenged Stow's views about declining charitable giving and noted that he failed to analyse the ills of society, while M.J. Power showed that Stow's descriptions of London neighbourhoods were impressionistic as well as erratic.[4] Stow might well have challenged modern critics as vigorously as he engaged his contemporary rival, Richard Grafton, but he would also be pleased that his work continues to attract attention after four centuries.

It was the author's modesty and personal self-effacement that were most striking to the reader of *A Survey* who began with Stow's dedication to Robert Lee, lord mayor of London. Not claiming any originality for his enterprise, Stow began by saying that he was inspired by William Lambarde's *Perambulation of Kent*, first published in 1576. He saw *A Survey* as a topographical work rather than a history and hoped that it might give courage to his friend, William Camden, 'to increase and beautify his singular work of the whole [*Britannia*] to the view of the learned that be abroad'. Stow would have preferred another person, 'some excellent artisan', to have written about London. His reluctance is understandable because no significant description of London had been written since the twelfth century when William Fitzstephen produced his classic account. As a better qualified scholar was not available for the task, the citizen historian offered his own qualifications. During his lifetime, Stow had seen many of the antiquities of London with his own eyes and spent long years searching historical records. 'Divers written helps are come to my hands', he added, 'which few others have fortuned to meet withal.' With these assets he chose to pursue the work after 'my plain manner' rather than leave it undone.

Stow correctly categorized his book as chorography or topography, a type of antiquarian scholarship dating from the fifteenth century and advanced by John Leland, who scoured the country seeking manuscripts for the *Collectanea* and *Itinerary*, neither of which was published in the author's lifetime. William Lambarde and William

A
SVRVAY OF
LONDON.

Conteyning the Originall, Antiquity,
Increafe, Moderne eftate, and defcription of that
City, written in the yeare 1598. by Iohn Stow
Citizen of London.

Since by the fame Author increafed,
with diuers rare notes of Antiquity, and
publifhed in the yeare,
1603.

Alfo an Apologie (or defence) againft the
opinion of fome men, concerning that Citie,
the greatneffe thereof.

VVith an Appendix, contayning in Latine
Libellum de fitu & nobilitate Londini: Written by
William Fitzftephen, in the raigne of
Henry the fecond.

Imprinted by Iohn Windet, Printer to the hono-
rable Citie of London.
1603.

The title page from the 1603 edition of John Stow's A Survey of London.

Camden followed in this tradition thereby establishing the precedents fully recognized by Stow and followed by seventeenth-century writers who produced topographical histories of most English counties.[5] F.J. Levy found a relationship between *A Survey of London* and Camden's *Britannia* (1586) despite the differences in purpose and contents:

> Camden, at least in the beginning, was most interested in restoring the past, Stow in showing the historical antecedents of the present. None the less, the structure of the *Survey* was based on that of *Britannia*. Both books opened with general sections, in the one case of history, in the other of description mixed with history. Then they settled down to their proper business, the detailed examination of the ground. With that, it must be admitted, the similarity became less obvious. Stow knew his London better than Camden knew England, and he made much greater use of records.[6]

Stow recognized a sense of patriotic duty to what he called 'my native mother and country'. While the learned Camden could instruct educated people on the continent as well as in England with *Britannia*, written in Latin, Stow's duty was to his fellow citizens at home, whose language was English. Lacking a classical education and associations with Italian humanists, Stow could make no contribution to civic humanism, but no Renaissance scholar was more devoted to an urban culture than he.[7] In *A Survey* he attempted the discovery of his London, but as he wrote of London, he also wrote for England.[8]

1. STRUCTURE

As neither edition of *A Survey of London* offered a formal introduction or maps to assist the stranger who was unacquainted with the city, Stow thought exclusively of an English or possibly a London readership. The book began with an account of London's antiquity that boldly compared it to ancient Rome.[9] Almost as an afterthought Stow inserted an apology for the city at the very end. Not written by Stow himself, the apology was a bold discourse with distinct commonwealth overtones written twenty years earlier. The learned, but unidentified author who gave it to Stow was a student at Oxford during the reign of Queen Mary.[10] Stow's organizational approach stands in marked contrast to a lengthy introductory chapter on the significance of London included in a modern collection of essays analysing the growth of the metropolis. Although Stow's thoughts are unknown, he may have felt unqualified to write a learned defence of the city, or perhaps he – unlike modern authors – thought the significance of London was self-evident.[11]

Stow began writing *A Survey of London* in 1590 when he was about sixty years of age. After eight years of work, he published the first edition in 1598, followed by an expanded second edition five years later. Kingsford noted that 'the main framework of

A Survey was based on a perambulation of the several wards of the City, which Stow accomplished with scrupulous care and verified from his ample collections'. Stow visited churches, examined city records, and attempted to consult records of the city companies.[12]

Studying the manuscript of *A Survey of London*, British Library, Harleian MS 538, Kingsford commented

> From the state of the original manuscript we may conjecture that Stow first set out in a fair hand the result of his perambulation. This he then proceeded to complete with additions and interpolations drawn from his own large storehouse, and written on the margins, or between the lines, or on slips pasted in, at such length as often to double the original contents of the page. The draft thus prepared differs a good deal from the printed work as well in matter as in the arrangement which was finally altered for the better.[13]

This manuscript is an incomplete draft that may be supplemented by an account of the borough of Southwark in Harleian MS 544.[14] It is likely that the two texts are part of the same draft. In any case, Stow made numerous changes in his work before it was printed in 1598; for example, the first two folios of the introduction were corrected and rewritten while the position of the histories of Southwark and Westminster was reversed.[15]

On the title page of the enlarged, second edition of 1603 Stow drew the attention of his readers to new material referred to as 'divers rare notes of antiquity' but did not say that the new edition contained over ninety more pages than its predecessor (the first edition runs to 484 pages of text; the second edition is 580 pages long). The additions included a section called 'Of Charitable Alms in Old Times Given', a curious note on the Devil's appearance ('an ugly shapen sight') at St Michael Cornhill,[16] and an account of city government, a subject not included in the first edition because Stow hoped another writer would do this.[17]

As Stow enlarged *A Survey*, he also carefully revised the entire text. For example, he reorganized his account of the medieval Jewish community giving the topic considerably greater coherence and prominence.[18] Stow also responded to criticism of the 1598 edition by eliminating disparaging references to the vintners as a company that hindered his research and to other critics as 'unthankful men'. Kingsford concluded that while Stow improved his book in the second edition, 'both the original draft and the first edition contain peculiar matter which we should have been sorry to lose'.[19]

A Survey of London, like the chronicles, demonstrates the author's critical use of sources. Stow, for example, questioned the old notion that Julius Caesar founded the Tower of London because he 'remained not here so long, nor had he in his head any

Norden's map of London, dated 1593, with the arms of the City livery companies on the left and right.

such matter but only to dispatch a conquest of this barbarous country'.[20] He drew on the humanistic scholarship of Sir Thomas More by citing his history of Richard III and included references to his own chronicles as well as Holinshed.[21] The book also demonstrates Stow's lifelong interest in manuscripts because it included the first printed text of William Fitzstephen, *Descriptio Nobilissimae Ciuitatis Londoniae* (*A Description of London*), a topographical history of London written in the twelfth century. Working with his own Latin manuscript – thought by him to be the only surviving copy – Stow made only 'a few alterations of his own, but these are of very minor importance'. The text printed by Kingsford is not that of Stow, and according to Sir Frank Stenton, 'It is uncritical and his notes as to readings are not always accurate.'[22]

2. SOCIAL CRITICISM

It was perhaps inevitable that an old man should reveal nostalgia as he reflected on the London of his youth. His memory reached back over a half century to the era of Thomas Cromwell and included a recollection of the cleaning of the city ditch in

1540.[23] Stow recalled that a farm where he 'fetched many a halfpenny worth' of milk as a youth was rented first for grazing horses and later for garden plots and that the farmer's son was living like a gentleman from the income.[24] The rural environment of the city is also apparent in an amusing story about the pigs of St Anthony's hospital. 'Amongst other things observed in my youth,' he wrote, 'I remember that the officers charged with oversight of the markets in this city did divers times take from the market people pigs starved or otherwise unwholesome for man's sustenance.' One of the proctors of St Anthony would tie a bell about the pig's neck and let it feed on the dunghills. If anyone gave the pigs bread or other food, 'such would they know, watch for, and daily follow, whining till they had somewhat given them'. The practice gave rise to a proverb, 'such a one will follow such a one, and whine as it were an Anthony pig'. Stow added that if a pig grew fat, 'as oft time they did', the proctors would use it to feed the inmates of the hospital.[25] Pessimism resulting from the economic tension of the 1590s may have coloured his thinking when he observed that the quaffing of beer and wine had declined among the poorer sort because of high prices and that 'the frequenting of schools and exercises of scholars in the city, as had been accustomed, hath much decreased' since the time of Fitzstephen because of the growth of universities.[26] Stow did not welcome many of the changes that had transformed London during his long life, and Kingsford's somewhat romanticized account of his memory of the good old days may not be far wide of the mark.[27]

Stow was not merely a romantic antiquarian opposed to change because *A Survey of London* includes numerous examples of social criticism. He absolutely detested the construction of high towers on private residences because they allowed the privileged occupant to overlook his neighbours and invade their privacy. The first of these that he 'ever heard of in any private man's house' was a brick tower built by a mayor of London, Sir John Champneis, but Stow noted that 'this delight of the eye was punished with blindness some years before his death'.[28] Subsequently, Richard Wethell, a merchant tailor, also built a high tower; his punishment, Stow assured his readers, was gout in both his hands and legs. In fact, Wethell became so badly crippled that 'he could neither feed himself nor go further than he was led, much less was he able to climb and take the pleasure of the height of his tower'.[29] As Stow walked through the streets of the city, he also saw many examples of wanton destruction and vandalism that he condemned. At St Bride's church a partition built with materials originally intended for the Duke of Somerset's house in the Strand was erected between the old and new parts of the building in 1557. Many years later, in 1596, 'one willful body began to spoil and break the same' but was forced by the high commissioners to make repairs.[30] Individual monuments built inside parish churches seemed to be completely unprotected from vandals, and Stow vigorously denounced their destruction. Monuments had been removed and defaced at St Michael Cornhill, the church where

Stow's father and grandfather were buried, and at another church the builder of a large chapel had constructed his own image 'fair graven in stone' over the porch, but Stow found it 'defaced and beaten down'.[31]

Stow's keen eye and intimate knowledge of London enabled him to identify and criticize the destruction of historical sites as well as the urban blight that was a consequence of rapid growth. But Stow was not a problem-solver who offered practicable solutions that would have been helpful to the mayor and aldermen. He combined the understandable anger of an older citizen watching his own environment being transformed with large doses of moralizing that reeked of self-righteousness. While moralizing may be a legitimate aspect of social criticism, Stow often projects a sanctimonious image that, while always placing him on the high ground, was hardly one of the more attractive features of his character.

Stow declined to offer solutions to the urban problems of Elizabethan England, but he was unequivocal about the kind of people and behaviour that had made London a great city. In a chapter entitled 'Honour of Citizens and Worthiness of Men in the Same', he quoted approvingly Fitzstephen's reference to three 'famous kings', persons who in reality never occupied the throne of England: Maude, the 'empress' (i.e. Matilda, daughter of Henry I), 'King Henry', son of Henry II, and Thomas Becket, Archbishop of Canterbury.[32] Although obviously not a monarch, St Thomas of Canterbury was a distinguished Londoner even if not the best choice for enthusiastic praise after Henry VIII's repudiation of papal authority. Stow then gave the names of sixty-seven men and five women who exemplified the honour and worthiness of the city. It was not surprising to find chroniclers and scholars such as Robert Fabyan, Edward Hall, and John Colet remembered, but the latter was cited for founding St Paul's school for 153 poor men's children, not for his scholarship. While William Walworth, mayor in 1381, distinguished himself by arresting Wat Tyler, 'a presumptuous rebel', most of the men and women mentioned in *A Survey* practised the kind of good lordship that Stow praised in his chronicles. These honoured citizens and their wives founded schools, relieved the sick and poor, and performed other acts of charity. Stow truly believed that the greatness of London derived from virtuous citizens who invested their wealth for social betterment, not the warrior kings and nobles whose deeds came to be celebrated in traditional historical works.

3. THE JEWISH COMMUNITY

A Survey of London included an intriguing and unexpected account of the Jewish community. The official exclusion of Jews from England in 1290 meant that this subject ought to have been of little interest to a sixteenth-century writer, but as Cecil Roth observed, 'The exclusion of the Jews from any land, however rigidly it may be prescribed by law, is unlikely to be absolute.'[33] Elizabethan London had a community

A traveller at the city gates, seeking access to London, from the Roxburghe Ballads.

of eighty to ninety Portuguese 'New Christians', some of whom maintained close relations with their co-religionists on the continent. Diplomatic privilege permitted Jewish worship in 1592, and there is contemporary evidence that the Passover was celebrated in London homes. In *A Survey* Stow admitted no knowledge of Elizabethan Jewry, but the trial and execution of Dr Roderigo Lopez, 'a Portingale (as it was said)', in 1594 for conspiring to poison the queen, recorded in the *Annales of England*, leaves little doubt that Stow was aware of the Jewish presence.[34] David S. Katz, however, has argued that it was not Lopez's Jewish origins that lay at the heart of the prosecution but his secret contacts with Spain.[35] Stow's familiarity with Jewish traditions led him to the vigorous medieval community that had been expelled over 200 years before his birth. His own curiosity about the Jews resulted in different versions of their history in the two editions of *A Survey*.

London Jews appear early in Stow's work because in the chapter on the London wall he noted that barons revolting against King John entered London, 'first took assurance of the citizens, then brake into the Jews' houses, searched their coffers to fill their own purses, and after with great diligence repaired the walls and gates of the city with stones taken from the Jews' broken houses'. This episode must have had a powerful impact on Stow since he refers to it no fewer than three different times in *A Survey*. He went on to explain that the stones were used either to build or to repair Ludgate. In 1586, when the gates were taken down, there was found couched within the wall a stone taken from one of the Jews' houses on which was graven in Hebrew characters the following inscription: 'this is the station or ward of Rabbi Moyses, the son of the honourable Rabbi Isaac'. It had been fixed on the front of one of the houses as a note or sign that such a person lived there. Stow had undoubtedly seen the inscription and included the text in both Hebrew and Latin.[36]

His survey of the Jews in England concluded with an account of their former quarters, the Old Jewry in Coleman Street Ward.[37] According to Stow, William, Duke of Normandy, first brought them from Rouen, and his son and successor, William II, 'favoured them so far that he swore by Luke's face his common oath, if they could overcome the Christians, he would be one of their sect'. Readers of *A Survey* learned that subsequent monarchs were uniformly hostile. Henry II 'grievously punished' the Jews for corrupting the coin, while Richard I forbade them as well as women from attending his coronation for fear of 'enchantments'. When Jews broke the king's commandment to avoid the coronation,

> many Jews were slain, who being assembled to present the king with some gift, one of them was stricken by a Christian, which some unruly people perceiving, fell upon them, beat them to their houses, and burned them therein or slew them at their coming out.[38]

Persecution continued through the reigns of John, Henry III, and Edward I when, according to Stow, 15,060 Jews were expelled.

Stow not only revealed the official anti-Semitism of English kings, but he also drew attention to similar acts committed by the nobility and citizenry. In addition to the outrages of the rebel barons during the reign of John, Stow described the destruction of the synagogue by London citizens in 1262:

> On the south side of this street [Lothbury] . . . be some fair houses and large for merchants, one that of old time was the Jew's synagogue, which was defaced by the citizens of London after that they had slain 700 Jews and spoiled the residue of their goods.[39]

Ranging far beyond London, he noted that Jews were robbed and spoiled at Norwich, Bury St Edmunds, Lincoln, Stamford, and King's Lynn. The notorious massacre at York in 1190, in which men, women, and children died, was described but not dated.[40] Henry III founded a house for converted Jews in Chancery Lane, 'where it came to pass that in short time there were gathered a great number of converts', but after the expulsion of 1290 'the number of converts in this place was decayed'. In 1377 the house came into the possession of the master of the rolls. Despite the closing of the house for converts, Stow found record of one convert, William Piers, who was baptized in 1381 (5 Richard II) and received two pence a day for life from the king.[41]

Interwoven with the story of Jewish persecution were numerous anecdotes drawn from medieval anti-Semitic folklore. In an account of Newgate prison, Stow included the hanging of an unidentified number of Norwich Jews in 1241 for circumcising a Christian boy. As further punishment, their house, called the Thor, was demolished, and London Jews were forced to pay 20,000 marks at two terms in the year or else be kept in prison.[42] Later 202 Jews were brought from Lincoln to Westminster for crucifying a child named Hugh, and eighteen were hanged.[43] There was also the bizarre story of a Jew who fell into a privy at Tewkesbury on Saturday and would not be taken out because of the Sabbath (43 Henry III). According to Stow's tale, Richard Clare, Earl of Gloucester, kept him in the privy until the following Monday, by which time he had died.[44] During the reign of Edward I, Stow recorded that a child was crucified at Northampton 'for the which fact many Jews at London were drawn at horse tails and hanged'.[45]

Stow wittingly or unwittingly brought sixteenth-century English readers face to face with the horrors of medieval anti-Semitism. The revised second edition gave greater emphasis to the plight of the Jews and included incidents far beyond the confines of London. Medieval chronicles provided Stow with information about the distant past, but for Jewish survivals of his own times Stow relied on his own knowledge of the city. In addition to the Hebrew inscription mentioned above, he noted that the corner house at the end of Bassinghall Street, 'an old piece of work builded of stone', formerly belonged to a Jew named Mansere.[46] Stow not only knew the location of the 'Old Jewry' but also confidently traced the occupancy of the former synagogue by friars, a nobleman, and a fifteenth-century mayor, concluding that 'it is now a tavern and hath to sign a windmill'.[47] Although Stow presumably had never seen a functioning synagogue, he rejected the notion that another building called Bakewell Hall had once been a synagogue. 'But that this house hath been a temple or Jewish synagogue (as some have fantasied) I allow not,' said Stow, 'seeing that it had no such form of roundness or other likeness, neither had it the form of a Church for the assembly of Christians which are builded East and West. . . .'[48] Despite his extensive acquaintance with Jewish traditions and artefacts, Stow failed to mention any living member of the Elizabethan community. Perhaps to have done so would have jeopardized people who had placed their trust in him.

4. CULTURAL LIFE

Stow recognized London as a cultural centre, but his unfamiliarity with the continent precluded comparisons with Paris, Florence, Venice, or other European cities. His perception of cultural life emerges from individual observations scattered through *A Survey of London*. As a mere citizen, he did not participate in the high culture of Elizabethan London, and his associations with the cultural elite were limited primarily to persons engaged in historical studies. Stow knew little first-hand of university life, yet he confidently boasted that law students in London actually constituted a third university:

> There is in and about this city a whole university, as it were, of students, practisers or pleaders and judges of the laws of this realm not living of common stipends as in other universities it is for the most part done, but of their own private maintenance, as being altogether fed either by their places or practice, or otherwise by their proper revenue, or exhibition of parents or friends: for that the younger sort are either gentlemen, or the sons of gentlemen, or of other most wealthy persons.[49]

He went on to list the fourteen houses or inns of court that were in existence at the end of the sixteenth century. Stow's definition of a university is inadequate and his understanding of legal education leaves much to be desired, but a reader of *A Survey* came away with the clear impression that the lawyers and legal students enhanced London's reputation as a centre of learning.

In other areas of cultural life, Stow thought London's lamp had burned brighter in the past. The grammar schools, for example, had suffered because of the growth of the universities although the city had benefited from public lectures in surgery, mathematics, music, divinity, and astronomy endowed by wealthy Elizabethans.[50] The most notable patron, Sir Thomas Gresham, gave the Royal Exchange and other property to endow seven lectures to be presented daily in term time at his house in Bishopsgate Street. The lectures were to be delivered in Latin in the morning and repeated in English in the afternoon. The destruction of libraries was a cultural loss that troubled Stow deeply. He noted that the great library of the former Grey Friars, founded by Richard Whittington in 1429, measured 31 by 129 feet and that the books of the library at St Paul's had largely disappeared.[51] Many of the confiscated volumes ended up in the hands of private collectors such as Protector Somerset, who took the books from the chapel adjoining Guildhall.[52] To Stow the essence of London's culture lay in its schools, libraries, and old buildings, but the world of Renaissance art, music, and literature was beyond his realm of appreciation.

St Paul's Cathedral as engraved by Visscher as part of his famous 1616 panorama of London. The building is still in substantially its medieval form and as it appeared to Stow, before the 'classical' modifications by Inigo Jones.

Stow considered popular culture and recreation under the heading of 'sports and pastimes' and began his account with an approving quotation from William Fitzstephen, who wrote

> Let us now come to the sports and pastimes, seeing it is fit that a city should not only be commodious and serious but also merry and sportful.[53]

In this category Stow included cock-fighting, bear-baiting, ball games, dancing, wrestling, and marching, as well as stage plays. He emphasized the relationship between sports and social class when he wrote, 'The ball is used by noblemen and gentlemen in tennis courts, and by people of meaner sort in the open fields and streets.'[54] Gender was also important since Stow thought that sports were particularly the realm of young males. Sliding on the ice was suitable only for children, but in hawking and hunting 'many grave citizens at this present have great delight and do rather want leisure than goodwill to follow it'.[55] He approved of manly recreations such as marching, wrestling, and shooting that contributed to national defence and lamented that the enclosure of common lands had encouraged archers to 'creep into bowling alleys and ordinary dicing houses' nearer home.[56] When Stow was young, maidens played on a timbrel and danced for garlands outdoors in the sight of their masters and dames. These activities had been suppressed, but he suspected that 'worse practices within doors are to be feared'.[57] Although prostitution was very much part of London popular culture, Stow understandably did not regard it as a legitimate pastime. His approach to the subject was legalistic and rather detached, but he avoided a strong moral condemnation. There was also a trace of English chauvinism as he noted in the margin that 'English people disdained to be bawds. Froes [frau/frow] of Flanders were women for that purpose.'[58]

Stow regarded recreation as secondary to work and not an end in itself. Religious holidays were an appropriate occasion for sport but only after evening prayer. Every nobleman of 'honour or good worship' was expected to celebrate the feast of Christmas with enthusiasm and generosity. In preparation for the festivities, citizens

London entertainers: in this case the illustration in Kempes nine daies wonder *(1600) shows William Kemp the Morris man, who famously danced from London to Norwich.*

decked their houses and parish churches with 'holm, ivy, bays, and whatsoever the season of the year afforded to be green'.[59] May Day had formerly been another day of fun for all, but Stow noted that since the insurrection of youths against aliens – Evil May Day – in 1517, the government had curtailed merry-making in the interest of law and order.[60] Stow does not seem to have participated in recreational activities himself and was less approving of organized fun – especially for adults who had a job to do – than his medieval predecessor, William Fitzstephen.

5. CONCERN FOR THE ENVIRONMENT

As a sober, practical man, Stow had a higher regard for the environment than for pleasure and amusement. He understood the importance of fresh clean water for the well-being of London and dealt with the subject at length.[61] Originally supplies came from wells and the river while small ponds provided water for horses. By the end of the thirteenth century, growth of the city was beginning to cause concern about the quality of the water supply. Lead conduits operated by gravity were constructed to convey water from distant wells. The earliest of these was an underground conduit built about 1285 that brought 'sweet water' from Paddington to a cistern in West Cheap.[62] From that date until Stow's own time, new conduits were built including that of William Lambe in 1577. A gentleman of the chapel of Henry VIII as well as a citizen and cloth worker of London, Lambe spent £1,500 of his own money to rebuild a conduit of 2,000 yards in length that supplied water to Holborn Cross. Before his death in 1580, Lambe received further praise from Stow for bequeathing to his company former monastic property worth £50 a year. The bequest was 'to the intent they shall hire a minister to say divine service there', but Stow also noted that the property included its own well.[63]

New German technology improved the city's water supply in 1581 when Peter Morice, founder of the London Bridge Waterworks, built a pump operated by a water-wheel in one of the arches of London Bridge. According to Stow, Morice's pump conveyed Thames water in lead pipes over the steeple of St Magnus church at the north end of London Bridge into houses in Thames Street, New Fish Street, and Grass Street. The river water also cleaned the channels of nearby streets, but Stow lamented in *A Survey* that in recent years the practice had been discontinued 'through whose default I know not'.[64] While Morice's company may not have lived up to all of Stow's expectations, it operated for many years and proved to be highly profitable for the owner's family. Several years later in 1594, Bevis Bulmer, an English gentleman, built the first mechanical pump driven by horses that supplied a 120-foot tower with water from the river. Stow referred to the tower as a 'large house of great height, called an engine for the conveying and forcing of Thames water to serve in the middle and west parts of the city'.[65] Stow is a good example of a scholar and historian whose interest in the water supply did not extend to curiosity about how the new technology actually

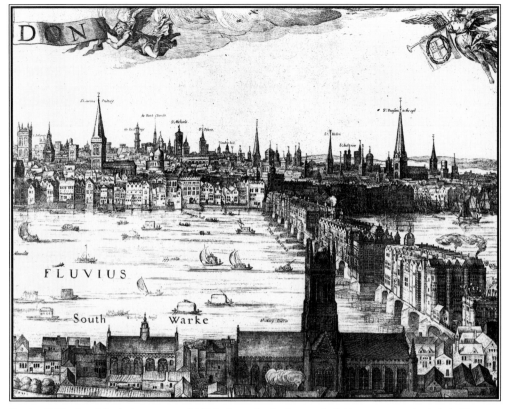

London Bridge from Visscher's panorama of 1616. As can be clearly seen, the bridge was very extensively built-up, with structures up to four and five storeys in height. At the entrance to the bridge on the south side of the river, the gatehouse is topped with the heads of traitors.

worked. His descriptions of the pumps built by Morice and Bulmer are brief and unhelpful to anyone seeking to understand their operation.[66]

Stow's interest in London's water supply was his major environmental concern, but *A Survey of London* offers other examples of his sensitivity to what is often thought to be an innovation of the twentieth century. While modern writers speak of pollution and create scientific euphemisms, Stow preferred simple, honest English and wrote of 'filth'. It was the filth of the tanners that caused the course of the river of the Wells in the western part of the city to be 'sore decayed'.[67] The town ditch, originally 200 feet wide and intended for the defence of the city, was in Stow's day badly neglected and 'forced either to a very narrow and the same a filthy channel or altogether stopped up for gardens planted and houses builded thereon . . . to what danger to the city I leave to wiser consideration and can wish that reformation might be had'.[68] Stow remembered that the ditch was cleaned in 1540, 1549, and 1569 and once contained a 'great store of very good fish of diverse sorts as many men yet living who have taken and tasted them can well witness'. Since 1569 economic interests had prevailed with the result that the cost of cleaning was thought to be too burdensome while handsome profits were made 'by letting out the banks with the spoil of the whole ditch'.[69]

8. CRITIQUE

While Stow's knowledge of London appears to be encyclopaedic, glaring omissions may be found. Charles L. Kingsford noted that these topics included William Shakespeare as well as other Elizabethan dramatists and writers, the theatre, and Sir Francis Drake.[70] For Stow the theatre ranked along with cock-fighting, and while he had some interest in medieval drama, he wrote dismissively of his own times: 'Of late time in place of those stage plays, hath been used comedies, tragedies, interludes, and histories, both true and feigned: For the acting whereof certain public places have been erected.'[71] The very idea of London as a theatrical city would have repelled him as he declined to mention the opening of the Globe and other Elizabethan theatres.[72] For details of the marriage of Henry VIII and Catherine of Aragon, which was of such importance to the Reformation, Stow merely referred his readers to Edward Hall's chronicle.[73] He never really assessed the impact of the Reformation on London, and religious controversy plays a role no larger than that of the theatre in his vision of the city.

Unfortunately, Stow was no more skilled as a historian of London architecture than he was as a chronicler of an urban reformation. One learned that the spire of St Paul's Cathedral was 260 feet high but nothing that evoked the magnificence of the great gothic structure. Westminster Abbey was similarly ill-served. While Stow certainly appreciated that the abbey was famous for the coronation and burial of English kings, he gave no indication of its size and seemed to be more interested in the cost of construction than aesthetic appreciation of its beauty. More impressive to Stow, the citizen historian, were ten dwelling houses and fourteen shops in Goldsmith's Row that he regarded as the most beautiful in England.[74]

One of the most disappointing sections of *A Survey* is that dealing with London politics and political leaders. Stow's chapter in the first edition, 'The Temporall Gouernment of this City, Somewhat in Briefe Manner', begins with the Britons, Romans, and Saxons, includes an inaccurate listing of mayors and other officers, and ends with a statement that another work is in preparation

> Thus much for the chief and principal governors of this famous city, of whose politike government, with the assistance of inferior officers, their charges for keeping of the peace, service of the Prince, and honour of this city, much might have been said, and I had thought to have touched; but being informed that a learned Gentleman, a Citizen born, minded such a labour and promised to perform it, I have forborne, and left the same to his good leisure.[75]

By 1603 the 'learned gentleman', James Dalton, had died. Stow chided the unfortunate man who, by promising more than he could perform, forced Stow to address the subject himself. Unfortunately, he was no longer equal to the task because age had begun to take its toll of his once sturdy constitution. Stow explained that he had been visited with sickness so severe that his feet, 'which have borne me many a mile have of late years, refused once in four or five months to convey me from my bed to my study'. The best he could do was use old notes that he had previously collected to be 'chaptered'. Recognizing that his work was 'unperfected', he asked readers 'to pardon me that want not will to pleasure them'.[76]

Forced to rely on old notes, Stow produced a short, disjointed descriptive account of the aldermen, city officials, and livery companies. The reader seeking a systematic analysis of London politics, the city's relations with central government, or the role of the companies would be required to look elsewhere.[77] Illness and old age were not the only handicaps that impaired Stow's ability to handle the subject. As a citizen historian whose world was well removed from the mayors and aldermen who governed the city, he lived outside the governing elite. Rather than feeling a sense of alienation, Stow seems to have been content with a simpler existence as a historian and antiquarian. He summed up his own way of life when he alerted readers to the deficiencies of his compilation of the precedence of livery companies. 'The 23rd of Henry VIII, these companies had place at the Mayor's feast in the Guild hall in order as followeth, I speak by precedent,' Stow wrote, 'for I was never [a] feast follower.'[78]

Although Stow recognized London as 'the most noble of all other cities of this land and the prince's seat', *A Survey of London* did not communicate effectively to the outsider either its significance as the national capital or its role in international trade.[79] His description of the city of Westminster, covering only twenty-seven pages in the 1603 edition, greatly underestimates its importance as the centre of national government. Since no introduction was offered, the author must have assumed that readers knew the queen's court and government were situated there. Stow, like most Londoners, knew the royal court at Whitehall Palace only from the outside. He wrote that Henry VIII had built a sumptuous gallery and a beautiful gate-house there but was himself a stranger to the corridors of power. To him the gallery was important because 'the princes with their nobility used to stand or sit and at windows to behold all triumphant joustings and other military exercises'.[80] Unlike a contemporary such as Sir William Paget, who was privileged to have direct access to Henry VIII and Edward VI, Stow did not understand the court as the centre of decision-making and political power.[81]

While the court was at Whitehall, royal government was located at the palace of Westminster. This in Stow's judgement was the queen's 'principal palace'. He had unquestionably ventured inside as he knew that it was the 'usual place of pleadings and ministration of justice' and that 'many parliaments have been kept there'.[82] In a detached and non-judgemental way, he observed that the Star Chamber received its distinctive name because 'the roof thereof is decked with the likeness of stars gilt' and that it was a court where

> Pliants heard of riots, routs, and other misdemeanours, which if they be found by the king's council, the party offender shall be censured by these persons which speak one after another, and he shall be both fined and commanded to prison.[83]

Stow wrote about the national capital more as a historian focussed on past centuries than as a contemporary reporter because his narrative said nothing about any aspect of royal government during the reign of Elizabeth.

In recent years modern historians of London and urban culture have begun a critical reassessment of *A Survey of London*. Perhaps the most severe critic, M.J. Power, observed that the work has rarely been subjected to 'systematic scrutiny' and is biased in favour of the city in that less attention is given to newer suburbs. He found that London seems to have possessed a wealthy centre and western suburb and uniformly poor eastern and southern suburbs and went on to argue that Stow's description of houses was erratic because he 'gives us an impression of the obvious concentrations of traders, craftsmen, and food and drink purveyors, not a thorough survey'. Power criticized Stow's handling of the monastic dissolution because he recounted 'unemotionally' the fortunes of each site 'unless the new development was of a kind he disapproved'. By the end of the sixteenth century the social elite were beginning to abandon city residences to merchants or more humble tenants, but, according to Power, Stow 'gives very little hint of such strain or the fear accompanying it'. 'We can only conclude,' he argued, 'that Stow, despite his age and occasional doubts, must have seen his city through rose-tinted spectacles.'[84] Power's latter statement cannot stand unchallenged because Stow saw social problems very clearly and showed great compassion for the sick and poor not only in *A Survey*, but also in his chronicles.

A Survey of London portrays a city blessed with social stability. The Elizabethan reader interested in social unrest in the capital would have learned more from Stow's *Annales of England* than from *A Survey*. Modern scholarship has confirmed his perception of law and order because Ian Archer and Steve Rappaport, using a wide range of archival sources, arrived at conclusions very similar to those of Stow. Stow dismissed the Evil May Day riots of 1517 as nothing more than an insurrection of youths, a judgement accepted by Rappaport, who commented that the disturbance lasted only four hours and claimed not a single life.[85] *A Survey* passed over in silence tensions arising from the rebellions of 1549 as well as the economic problems of the 1590s. Rappaport similarly minimized the disturbances of the 1590s, arguing that while unrest existed among the young, 'boys will be boys'.[86] Although Archer criticized Stow's failure to provide a detailed analysis of London's social ills and rejected aspects of Rappaport's arguments, he concluded that stability was accomplished through the solidarity of the ruling

A London watchman illustrated in the Roxburghe Ballads. *He is carrying a lantern in his left hand and a bell in his right. Like many, or all, of the illustrations in the* Roxburghe Ballads, *this illustration is copied from another contemporary book – in this case* The Belman of London, *1608.*

elite.[87] Stow's judgements, however, have not stood unchallenged, for several modern historians have identified a European crisis of the 1590s that reached far beyond the confines of London.[88] Roger Manning not only emphasized significant social instability in the capital but characterized the London riots and rebellions of 1595 as 'the most dangerous and prolonged urban uprising in England between the accession of the Tudor dynasty and the beginning of the Long Parliament'.[89]

Modern historians' continuing use of *A Survey* as an authority underscores its enduring importance and regrettably has also resulted in its misinterpretation. Like later editions of the *Annales of England* that included additions by Edmund Howes, *A Survey* also contained the work of other authors. Steve Rappaport, attempting to support his views about social stability, wrote

Indeed there is little evidence in general that London was a city only of extremes, of a few rich and many poor, of a privileged elite and unprivileged masses. That extremes existed we can be sure, but between them lay the majority of the men and women who lived, worked, and raised families during the twelve decades when the Tudor kings and queens ruled in England, the 'middling sort' of people who in Stow's words, 'do far exceed the rest'.

A London comedian from the Roxburghe Ballads.

Whether this happy state of affairs actually existed is a subject for further study, but the authority cited was not John Stow but the anonymous author of the commonwealth discourse included at the end of the book.[90] Roger Manning was also drawn to the discourse and employed it to show that Stow believed that a large urban population need not lead to unrest as long as a city was well governed.[91]

A Survey of London contributes to a broad and inclusive concept of nationhood and patriotism. Richard Helgerson, whose interests in *Forms of Nationhood: The Elizabethan Writing of England* are confined to the intellectual elite, neglected Stow, who nevertheless contributed significantly to Spencer's 'kingdom of our own language' by writing a history of London in English. Although *A Survey* was not published until 1598, Stow was at work decades before Helgerson's 'culturally uprooted young men who began writing England in the last decades of the sixteenth century . . .'.[92] The author of *A Survey*, a citizen historian, was neither privileged, young, nor culturally uprooted. By writing exclusively in English, Stow made a greater contribution to establishing a true English cultural identity than Renaissance humanists who believed in the superiority of classical Latin. His identification with London and England was one and inseparable. As he wrote in the introduction to his book, 'I have attempted the discovery of London, my native soil and country.'[93]

Although Stow's *Survey* is of limited scope compared with the large topographical works of William Camden, John Speed, and Michael Drayton, his contribution to an Elizabethan national culture was substantial. Camden's *Britannia*, first published in Latin in 1586 and not translated into English until 1610, stands as eloquent testimony to the vitality of Latin scholarship among the educated elite of the sixteenth century. Its English translation in 1610 made the work accessible to a larger reading public only after James I had claimed the throne of Tudor England for the Stuarts. Speed's *Theatre of the Empire of Great Britain*, first published in English in 1611 and curiously translated into Latin five years later, contributes to Jacobean but not Elizabethan literature, while Michael Drayton's *Poly-Olbion*, published in 1612 and dedicated to Henry, Prince of Wales, similarly belongs to the age of the Stuarts. Stow's Elizabethan credentials are unimpeachable, and his love of country was second to no one. His writing of England in its native language owed nothing to courtly patronage and laid claim to the capital city and nation for the ordinary citizen.[94]

CHAPTER SEVEN

EUROPE AND A
WIDER WORLD

Stow's chronicles and historical writings offer substantial accounts of English relations with Europe and the wider world. Of the European states, France, Spain, and the Netherlands obviously loom the largest, although he also dealt with Germany, Denmark, Sweden, Russia, and Poland. The Italian states are virtually ignored, but Stow included a few references to the Muslim world. Using an approach that is descriptive rather than analytical, he failed to consider specific English interests abroad or the structure and operation of the European state system. Nevertheless, the reader of the latest edition of his chronicle – whether a London investor or a country gentleman living in a remote part of rural England – received an abundance of current information about European affairs as well as English adventures in the New World.

When Henry VIII died in 1547, England's principal ally was the powerful Habsburg ruler Charles V, whose authority extended from Germany to the Netherlands and Spain and beyond the Atlantic to Mexico and South America. The Reformation under Henry VIII and Edward VI damaged the Habsburg alliance, but the marriage of Queen Mary to Charles V's son and heir, Philip, in 1554 brought England and Spain into a more intimate relationship than had previously existed. Stow observed cautiously that the queen's marriage was 'grievously taken of divers men' but declined to denounce Spain even in the last revision of the *Annales of England*.[1] In a similar manner he indicated that Sir Thomas Wyatt and his collaborators in rebellion opposed the Spanish marriage and spoke against the 'miserable tyranny of strangers' without offering any significant anti-Spanish rhetoric of his own.[2] When the Spanish alliance led to war with France in 1557, Stow offered no explanation of the causes of the conflict and merely reported that a town was taken, listed distinguished French prisoners and, perhaps most interestingly, noted that Lord Henry Dudley, son of the recently executed Duke of Northumberland, was slain.[3]

The loss of Calais, England's last fortress on the continent, to France in January 1558 made a greater impression on Stow. He meticulously recounted military operations leading to the surrender of Calais and concluded

The loss of this town seemed strange to many men of great experience, the same town being so many years so strongly fortified with all munitions that could be devised should now in so short space be taken of our enemies without fight or slaughter. . . .[4]

A detail from an engraving by Moulet showing the fall of Calais in 1558.

Stow as well as Queen Mary and her government expected Philip to use Spanish arms to assist in the recovery of Calais, but peace was concluded in 1559 with France in possession of the town.

During the 1570s the Netherlands was the major source of contention between England and Spain. R.B. Wernham argued that the Queen Elizabeth's policy during these years was 'primarily directed at getting Spain to agree to an early withdrawal of its military forces and a return to the largely home-ruling Netherlands of Charles V's time'. To this end she dispatched Thomas Wilkes to Spain in 1577 to alert Philip to the danger of French intervention if he failed to reach a reasonable settlement. Without placing this embassy in a historical context, Stow included

> a declaration sent by the queen's majesty of England unto the King of Spain containing a justification of her proceedings with the states of the Low Countries.

Diplomatic instructions running to nearly five pages in the quarto *Annales of England* followed and provided far more undigested details than any general reader could possibly have wanted, but Stow failed to mention that the Wilkes mission achieved absolutely nothing.[5]

The war between England and Spain, unlike the complexities and uncertainties of diplomacy, was a subject better suited to a citizen historian and chronicler.[6] Stow produced the last edition of the octavo *The Summarie of the Chronicles of England* in 1590, only two years after the battle of the Armada.[7] His was the first English chronicle to appear after the great victory at sea, and with Richard Grafton dead there was no active competitor for the chronicle market. The second edition of Holinshed's chronicle offered no competition since it ended in 1587 and was never extended. Stow began his account of the Armada with a description of English preparations by land and sea. The camp at Tilbury included 200 light horse from Suffolk, 5,000 footmen from Kent, as well as men from numerous other counties. London provided 16 ships and 4 pinnaces to the fleet while Bristol, Plymouth and towns like Barnstable supplied smaller numbers. The narrative moved on to Plymouth where, on 23 May 1588, Charles Howard, the Lord Admiral, assembled 'a most royal fleet of about one hundred sail'. As he described the fighting along the south coast, he gave special attention to Sir Francis Drake's capture of a galleon of 1,150 tons, a prize that included a Spanish general, 304 soldiers, 118 mariners, and 46 pieces of brass ordnance. Stow's source was a book in Spanish belonging to Anthony Radcliffe, a London alderman. Of the later stages of the battle he said less and completely overlooked the storms that destroyed the remnants of the defeated Armada. However, Stow never doubted the magnitude of the English triumph as he wrote that God had given 'a wonderful victory, yea such as (by the report of some) of that great fleet (the like whereof was never seen in Europe) there returned home not forty ships and caravels, and the men that came home in them, died immediately at their landing'.[8]

After victory had been achieved, the queen travelled to the great camp at Tilbury where 'she passed through every rank . . . to their great comfort and rejoicing'. Stow did not say whether Elizabeth actually spoke to her men, although she spent two nights there as the guest of Edward Rich, a justice of the peace.[9] In London there were three services of thanksgiving. On 28 August, Dr Alexander Nowell, preaching at Paul's Cross before the lord mayor, aldermen, and the companies apparelled in their best liveries, exhorted those assembled to give laud and praise to God for the victory given to 'our English nation'. At a subsequent service on 8 September, eleven ensigns taken from Spanish ships were displayed first on the lower battlements of St Paul's Cathedral and later on London Bridge. During the service a man raised a streamer with an image of the Virgin Mary holding her son in her arms over the pulpit. The queen, accompanied by the privy council and nobility, made a triumphal procession to St Paul's Cathedral on Sunday 24 November for a service that ended official celebrations in London.[10]

When the first edition of the *Annales of England* appeared in 1592, Stow offered an enlarged and significantly revised account of the battle of the Spanish Armada. His zeal for improving his work is fully demonstrated here as he introduced a major new authority, Petruccio Ubaldini (?1524–1600?). A Florentine Protestant living in England, Ubaldini had a strong animosity toward Spain. He interviewed Sir Francis Drake and Lord Howard and produced two Italian texts that survive in the Royal Manuscripts at the British Library. As there is no evidence that Stow read Italian or knew Ubaldini, he probably used the English translation of the second text by Robert Adams that appeared as *A Discourse Concerninge the Spanishe Fleete Inuading England 1588* . . . in 1590.[11] In the expanded narrative Stow gave greater attention to Spanish preparations. Sensing the strategic importance of the Armada, he wrote that the queen knew of the great fleet supported by the Duke of Parma's army in the Low Countries that intended to conquer England. 'It was never known in the memory of man', he wrote, 'that so great preparation was ever heretofore at one time made out' either by Philip or Charles V.[12] He went on to describe in far more detail the battles at sea that forced the Spanish to return home over a route around Ireland, a disastrous journey as violent storms destroyed many Spanish ships. Still Stow knew that even these sources were incomplete; and when the sources failed, he honestly admitted it, saying, 'I know not and therefore leave any further to write of that matter.'[13]

While the defeat of the Armada was a great victory for England, it marked the beginning, not the end of a long and costly conflict with Spain. To present the English position on the war as effectively as possible the queen published *A Declaration of the Causes Moving the Quenes Maiestie . . . to Send a Navy to the Seas* . . . in 1596. Stow printed the text in the *Annales*, explaining that it declared the need to prepare the navy for further conflict against Spain 'to the intent that it shall appear to the world' that England was acting defensively. The declaration, issued by the Earl of Essex and Lord Howard, referred to the Spanish attack in 1588 but said nothing about the intentions of the English.[14]

The queen's declaration set the stage for an attack on the Spanish port of Cadiz, but before describing this, Stow leapt forward to a 'great triumph' made at London in August 1596 to celebrate 'the winning, sacking, and burning' of Cadiz. Then back-tracking, he inserted an eleven-page narrative written by an unidentified 'gentleman who was in the voyage'.[15] The narrative named the leaders of the expedition, Lord Howard and the Earl of Essex and other commanders whose numbers included Sir Walter Raleigh, described the organization of the fleet, and traced its successful journey from Plymouth. After an attack on Spanish shipping, the English sacked and occupied the city but subsequently abandoned their prize because of a shortage of food and water and returned home. The account ended by concluding that God had blessed the queen and her ministers in 'all her designs and enterprises' and made her 'the mirror of all princely felicity in this world'. Stow added nothing of his own about the significance of the expedition for Essex and the war against Spain. He concluded abruptly saying, 'thus far of the expedition to Cadiz'.[16]

The Spanish Armada and the English fleet off Calais on 6 August 1588, shown in Pine's engraving from the House of Lords' tapestries.

Stow continued his coverage of the Spanish war with the attempt to occupy and garrison the Azores in 1597. Six thousand men were recruited, including 500 knights and gentlemen to serve under the Earl of Essex. Other notables in the expedition were Lord Thomas Howard, Lord Mountjoy, and Sir Walter Raleigh. A large fleet sailed from Plymouth but was forced to turn back after 'a fierce and tempestuous storm'. Extensive damage delayed the expedition for six weeks. After burning the town on Fayal Island, the English attacked Spanish ships returning from Havana. A force of 2,000 was landed at Villa Franca, but the army 'feasted themselves and seized wheat, woad, and other merchandise' that was loaded into 'private men's ships that followed for that purpose'. The fleet, according to Stow, 'looked out for the coming of our land army but all in vain, for they neither came nor sent and thus was a great piece of service very unfortunately neglected and lost'. A command was given 'that all sorts should with speed repair aboard their ship', and thus, owing to the weather and season, the fleet returned to England.

Stow, declining to probe more deeply into what modern historians have regarded as a fiasco, recommended to his readers Sir Arthur Gorges' eyewitness account of the Azores expedition; he had, said Stow, 'largely written and learnedly discoursed' in his book, *A Plaine and True Relation of the Voyage Made unto the Isles of the Azore*.[17] Stow's comment is of interest because, according to Samuel Purchas, who published a text of Gorges in *Purchas His Pilgrimes* (1625), it was written in 1607 and dedicated to Prince Henry.[18] It appears that the book referred to by Stow has not survived. On a lighter note, Stow added – perhaps sarcastically – in the *Summarie Abridged* of 1604 that 'many left their feathers' in the Azores and returned without much 'jollity'.[19]

Stow gave his readers full accounts of English military encounters with Spain, but he did not altogether neglect the tortuous process to make peace with his country's adversary. Two years after the peace of Verain between Spain and France in 1598, the French invited England to negotiate with Spain. English ambassadors including Sir Henry Neville and Robert Beale were sent to Boulogne. Stow noted that Elizabeth made claims dating back before the time of Charles V based upon the learned authority of 'Volanteran' or Raphael Maffeius.[20] A quarrel ensued over the question of precedence with the English citing the position of the Pope during the reign of Henry VII, but Spain would not concede precedence or even equality to Elizabeth. The conference settled nothing, and the ambassadors returned to England.[21] Peace with Spain was delayed until the next reign when, on 19 August 1604, a proclamation read at the cross in West Cheap by William Segar, garter king at arms, announced a 'joyful peace' between the two countries. Stow printed the proclamation and noted that the articles of peace had been printed by Robert Barker, printer to the king. It must be assumed that Stow along with other Londoners rejoiced to hear the proclamation announcing the end of the long conflict with Spain.[22]

While relations with England's major ally, Spain, deteriorated and culminated in open war in the 1580s, the reign of Elizabeth saw gradual improvement in relations with the country's traditional enemy, France. But Elizabeth's reign began with a legacy of hostility toward the French, and Stow echoed conventional thinking when he denounced 'malicious and devilish' enterprises of the French king that included support for the 'treason' of Northumberland, Wyatt's rebellion, and the conspiracy of Sir Henry Dudley against Queen Mary.[23] The loss of Calais at the end of her reign was a painful reminder of England's weakness with respect to France and her dependence on the Spanish alliance.

In 1562 England intervened in the first French War of Religion and began what Wallace MacCaffrey called the 'Newhaven Adventure'.[24] Stow followed these events with extraordinary interest and inserted in the *Annales* a long text or 'book' explaining why Elizabeth was obliged to arm 'certain of her subjects for defence both of her own estate and of the most Christian King Charles IX, her good brother, and his subjects'.[25] Following this document Stow offered a still longer narrative of military operations that followed the English occupation of Newhaven, or Le Havre as it was known outside England.

Considering that the government's bold plan to intervene in French affairs by assisting the Huguenots proved to be a dismal failure, it may be asked why Stow chose to devote over fifteen pages of the *Annales* to it. The answer would seem to lie not in the abortive Newhaven Adventure itself but in its political and military proponents, the Dudleys, with whom Stow had close ties. This episode allowed Lord Robert Dudley, son of the late Duke of Northumberland, to make his political debut while the military operations in France served to showcase his brother, Ambrose, Earl of Warwick.[26] According to Stow's glowing account, Ambrose Dudley landed in Newhaven 'where he was most joyfully received with a great peal of artillery'.[27] The narrative that followed is replete with incidents of English bravery, but it provides a wholly inadequate picture of the overall military operation. Stow dutifully noted that Warwick's men captured 300 sheep, successfully intercepted shipments of wine, and skirmished with the French forces; he also found space to record that Ambrose Dudley was created a Knight of the Garter on 1 May 1563. Under attack by superior French forces and dying from the plague, the English at Le Havre capitulated. 'Glad was he', wrote Stow, 'that could get soonest out of the unwholesome air; many sick persons yet were left behind, impotent, and not able to help themselves a ship board.'[28]

Stow's account of the Newhaven Adventure ends with the proclamation of 'an honourable and joyful peace' with France in 1564. The reader learns that peace was proclaimed to the sound of a trumpet at Windsor Castle, but nothing was revealed regarding the terms of the treaty itself. Although the Treaty of Troyes may have been joyful in that it ended the fighting, its provisions offered little else to the English. The French reoccupied Le Havre, the alliance with the Huguenots disintegrated, and Calais still remained in French hands. Modern historians interpret the Newhaven Adventure as a tactical political triumph for the Dudleys. Stow, however, did not mention the name of his deceased patron, Robert Dudley, in the long and curious version of these events that appeared in the 1605 edition of the *Annales of England*, and while Ambrose Dudley was cast in a favourable light, it would be a rare critical reader who could find anything heroic about his performance at Le Havre. Stow's earlier work, the *Chronicles of England* (1580), dedicated to Leicester, who was then alive and flourishing, surprisingly carried only a short, disjointed account of the Newhaven Adventure.[29]

Stow revealed the breadth of his reading as well as the ability to utilize non-English sources for relations with France when he quoted Peter Ramus' (1515–72) 'commentaries on wars of France'. The work to which he referred was probably Jean de Serres, *The Fyrst Parte of Commentaries, concerning the State of Religion and the Common Wealthe of France* (1573), a work that was once attributed to Ramus.[30] Stow criticized what he thought was Ramus' interpretation of the attempt of the Huguenot refugee, the Count of Montgomery, to relieve Rochelle. He failed to achieve his objective but took Belle Isle. The queen subsequently denied French accusations of English involvement.[31]

Stow's interest in Anglo-French relations included great emphasis on ceremony and pageantry. His preoccupation with the external aspects of foreign policy rather than the substance is apparent as he described the embassy of the Earl of Lincoln to Paris in 1572. Of feasting and sumptuous entertainments he tells much, but provisions of the Treaty of Blois relating to a defensive league against Spain are omitted.[32] When French commissioners arrived at Dover in April 1581, Stow dutifully listed members of the embassy and later noted that their English hosts prepared 'a triumph in most sumptuous order' but added, 'more at large I have set down in the continuance of Reine Woolfes Chronicle', which was his shorthand for the second edition of Holinshed's chronicle.[33] The visit of the French nobles was but a prelude to the main act, the arrival of the queen's suitor, the Duke of Anjou, younger brother of the French king.

Anjou arrived in London at the beginning of November 1581 and pursued – unsuccessfully – his courtship until February of the next year. For reasons that are not readily apparent, Stow never actually acknowledged that Anjou had come to England seeking marriage. Perhaps a man with few contacts at court didn't know what was happening or possibly he thought it dangerous to speculate on such a sensitive subject. What interested Stow most about Anjou's visit was the procession of the queen and her court from Westminster to Canterbury where she 'feasted all the French nobility'. After Elizabeth left, Anjou went on to Sandwich where he embarked accompanied by Robert Dudley, Earl of Leicester, and an entourage that sailed to Flushing in no fewer than fifteen ships.[34]

Robert Glover, Somerset herald and a friend of Stow, may have provided him with a long account of the embassy of Henry, Earl of Derby, to France in 1585 to bestow the order of the garter on Henry III. Each stage of the embassy's progress from London to Dover, Calais, and Clermont to French court was fully described. Derby eventually saw the king at the Louvre where the embassy was received 'with great courtesy and as amiable countenance as could be'. The king accepted the garter at the Augustine friars church. The embassy then returned home over the same route. Much of the ceremony was repeated eleven years later in 1596 when William Segar, Somerset herald, gave Stow a nine-page report of the embassy that presented the garter to Henry IV and sought his confirmation of a league of amity against Spain. Led by the Earl of Shrewsbury, the embassy made its way from Dover to Dieppe and on to Rouen where the English ambassadors met the king. Stow, hoping to delight readers hungry for Renaissance pageantry, gave careful attention to the procession of Norman clergy and nobility, the presentation ceremony, and the exchange of gifts.[35]

As he recorded the latter years of Elizabeth's reign, Stow continued to find military aspects of the French alliance less interesting than the pageantry. The city of London recruited 1,000 men in September 1589 to assist Henry of Navarre, who was 'then challenging the crown of France as the rightful inheritor by lawful succession', but

Stow offered only a few lines to describe a complex diplomatic question that has been called 'a novel experience' for the government. The dispatch of 3,000 footmen under Sir John Norris to Brittany in April 1591 similarly rated only a short notice while a modest paragraph informed readers that a larger force of footmen, horsemen, and pioneers accompanied the Earl of Essex, 'a young nobleman of great valour and expectation', to France in July of the same year. Stow's account ended on a sombre note as he recorded the death of the earl's brother, Walter Devereux, who was slain 'with a small shot before Roane [Rouen] in Normandy'.[36]

The Netherlands was the third major area in Europe that attracted extended interest from Stow. In this strategically located and economically advanced region vital interests of England, Spain, and France intersected. The Netherlands had been an important market for English wool and cloth for centuries while the dukes of Burgundy were a major ally against France. The last duke died in 1477, and Flanders and Brabant became part of the Habsburg empire. When the nobility of the Low Countries began to resist Spanish policies, the growing conflict offered opportunities as well as dangers to both England and France.[37]

As a Londoner Stow could claim special interest in policies that affected trade in woollen cloth. His chronicle account of Philip's proclamation forbidding the importation of English cloth into the Netherlands in 1563 can be traced to a longer narrative in the manuscript. Although it is not known how information in the manuscript came to Stow, he used it as a source for the *Annales*. He rejected the Spanish argument that the embargo was caused by the plague in London and noted with approval that the English cloth fleet went to Emden rather than Antwerp the following year.[38] Stow made a rather matter-of-fact reference to the arrest of all Spanish subjects in England – including the ambassador – early in 1569 as a reprisal for alleged Spanish mistreatment of English merchants in the Netherlands, but he did not place the episode in historical context, an omission suggesting that he gave little thought to larger English interests in the Netherlands.[39]

England's initial response to the revolt in the Netherlands was to join with France in order to force Spain to accept a negotiated settlement. Therefore, the queen supported her suitor, the Duke of Anjou, as governor of the Low Countries and leader of the rebels against Spain. Although many questioned his ability, Stow was enthusiastic about his prospects and convinced that after arriving in Dunkirk he had 'gotten the hearts of the people'.[40] Stow dutifully reminded readers of the *Annales* that a fuller account of Anjou's successes might be found in Reine Woolfes' chronicle. Lost in the myriad of details offered by Stow and completely obscured by his optimism was the simple fact that Anjou's best efforts achieved nothing. Before Anjou's death in July 1584, the Duke of Parma captured Ghent, Bruges, and Brussels and isolated Antwerp.[41]

The fall of Antwerp to the Spanish and death of William the Silent forced Queen Elizabeth to intervene. In June 1585 deputies from the estates of the Low Countries

The sack of Antwerp by Spanish troops in 1576 in a contemporary engraving.

arrived in London where they received accommodation at the queen's expense. They presented 'the sovereignty of those countries' to the queen in a French oration that Stow 'set down in Reine Woolfe,' but readers of the *Annales* had to make do with an English version denouncing the 'execrable assault committed upon the person of the late prince of Orange'. Arguing that the people were reduced to 'perpetual servitude worse than that of the Indians under the importable yoke of the detestable inquisition of Spain', the deputies begged the queen to accept them as her subjects and to defend

156

The assassination of William, Prince of Orange (the Silent) by the French fanatic Balthasar Gerard in July 1584. In the following year Antwerp fell to the Duke of Parma.

the reformed religion. Elizabeth agreed to 'incline her heart to the ease and relief of the said oppressed people' and authorized the publication of a book explaining her reasons that was printed in Latin, Italian, and English. Stow did not include the queen's response in the *Annales* but reminded readers that he had 'set down the same in Reine Woolfe's chronicle'.[42]

Stow's account of English military operations began with a matter-of-fact entry in the *Annales* that 'certain soldiers' were pressed in July 1585 for service in Holland and Zealand. More fanfare was attached to the departure of Leicester who had been appointed as the queen's lieutenant general:

> On the sixth of December the right honourable Robert Dudley, Earl of Leicester, lord lieutenant general (after he had taken his leave of her majesty and the court) with his train (which was great) entered the town of Colchester in Essex, where the bailiffs and brethren in scarlet gowns and multitudes of people met him and so with great solemnity entered the town where he lodged that night.[43]

Robert Dudley, Earl of Leicester, depicted in a Dutch engraving of c. *1585–7 as governor of the Netherlands.*

Leicester made his way to Harwich where he sailed with a large and distinguished entourage to Flushing. Using information provided by Henry Archer, his friend and kinsman, and William Segar, Stow followed Leicester from one triumph to another, emphasizing feasting and celebration at Christmas but culminating in the occupation of the 'strong fort' of Nijmegen with the loss of forty men.[44]

After inserting twenty pages devoted to English and Irish affairs, Stow returned to the Low Countries where information provided by Henry Archer highlighted the deeds of Leicester and Sir Philip Sidney. Archer followed Leicester from town to town as he made his progress through the Netherlands, but the focus shifted to the noble Sidney, who in a moving oration exalted the English and denounced 'men of false religion, enemies to God and his church'. Included within a nationalistic narrative are a few critical comments aimed primarily at soldiers of the lower classes. Readers learned that the town of Neuce was lost on 16 July after a long assault by the enemy, but was 'forthwith burned down to the ground by lackeys and boys belonging to our soldiers; there remained whole but eight houses'. The campaign also included the abuse of women as Dowsborough fell to the English: 'The women that passed with the soldiers, it was a grievous thing to see, how they were ransacked till the earl of Essex and diverse other gentlemen came.'[45]

The account of the campaign in the Netherlands reached its climax with the death of Sidney. Fighting with a host of brave men including Lord Willoughby, the Earl of Essex, and Sir William Russell, Sidney

> so behaved himself that it was wonder to see, for he charged the enemy thrice in one skirmish, and in the last charge he was wounded with a musket shot through the thigh to the great grief of his excellency and of the whole camp, who being brought to my lord lieutenant, his excellency said, 'O, Philip, I am sorry for thy hurt,' and Philip answered, 'O, my lord, this I have done to do your honour and her majesty service.'

Sidney was taken to Arnhem where he died but not before demonstrating godliness and valiant courage that astonished the preachers and surgeons alike.[46]

Leicester remained in the Netherlands until November 1586 but returned the following June. For Stow, Leicester's second tour of duty was anticlimactic. He reported that Leicester 'took shipping at Margate in Kent towards the Low Countries where he remained not long but returned' and then immediately moved on in the narrative to mention nothing more momentous than a late spring and cold summer.[47] Stow not only declined to note Leicester's failure to relieve the siege of Sluys and his inability to assert his authority over the States-General, but he also avoided any reference to the results of Leicester's efforts to implement English policy in the Netherlands. Whereas modern historians have roundly condemned Leicester and everything he stood for, Stow could hardly have turned upon his patron and the favourite of the queen. The abrupt and unsatisfying end of his long account of Leicester's campaign may have been Stow's way of anticipating the judgement of later historians, but it is also arguable that he felt sympathy for a patron who had failed to achieve military and political objectives in the Netherlands that were unattainable given the resources and priorities of Elizabethan England.[48]

In his chronicles Stow rated relations with Germany as of about the same importance as those with Poland, Russia, and Denmark. Although these countries remained at peace with England throughout the second half of the sixteenth century, the war with Spain strained relations with Poland and Denmark. Distance limited contact with these countries largely to trade and ceremonial expressions of goodwill, but England took initiatives to strengthen economic ties with Russia.

Stow's interest in Germany is suggested by an entry of only one sentence in the *Annales*, mentioning a memorial or 'solemn obsequy' at St Paul's on 2 October 1564 for the deceased emperor, Ferdinand I. What is intriguing is that Stow minimized the story by not using all of the information available to him. A manuscript volume of historical memoranda that almost certainly belonged to Stow tells more about the emperor's memorial service. According to Stow's memoranda, the lord high treasurer, William Paulet, Marquis of Winchester, was chief mourner at a 'certain kind of evening prayer'. A communion service with a sermon by the Bishop of London followed the next day. The fact that the queen was absent on both occasions suggests that Stow may not have been alone in his attitude toward the Habsburg monarchy.[49] Decades later, Henry IV, who came to the French throne in 1589, wanted military assistance from German Protestant princes against the Catholic (Holy) League. Elizabeth was prepared to offer up to £15,000 but really preferred to make a smaller contribution. In 1590 the queen dispatched Sir Horatio Palavicino, who travelled to Torgau with a commission to negotiate with the German princes. Stow thought the mission achieved 'good success' because an army of 'Almaine' horsemen was levied and sent into France to assist Henry IV. Stow was probably unaware that squabbling over the amount of the English subsidy damaged Palavicino's reputation with the queen and did nothing to increase her popularity with the German Protestants.[50]

The distant kingdom of Poland interested Stow only when the war with Spain disrupted normal trade relations. In 1583 he mentioned the goodwill visit of the Baron of Lasco, who stayed at Winchester House in Southwark while in London. The baron, according to Stow, 'well viewed the order of our English court and nobility', visited Oxford, and then returned home.[51] Relations between the two countries had deteriorated by 1597 when Paul Dzialynski, an ambassador from Sigismund III, made an oration to the queen in Latin complaining that Poles were forbidden to trade with Spain but added diplomatically that the king would not take reprisals against England for losses sustained, because he was a man of patience and restraint. Nevertheless, the ambassador wanted the English to make reparations for losses suffered by Polish merchants. It was the ambassador's opinion that the queen's war with Spain should not disrupt Polish trade with that country.

The queen replied angrily in Latin saying that she was greatly offended and could not believe the king really favoured the extreme argument put forward in the ambassador's oration. She noted that the Polish king was young 'and not by blood but by election, and newly elected'. The queen argued that it was unlawful to trade with Spain during time of war. Some issues she agreed to assign to the privy council. 'In the meantime,' Elizabeth said abruptly, 'farewell and be quiet.' Here the queen treated the representative of a weak and distant country with consummate contempt. He was later called before the privy council where he met with Lord Burghley, the lord treasurer, and his son, Sir Robert Cecil, the principal secretary. After the ambassador protested that he had been properly commissioned in Poland, he received what Stow called 'a large answer in the name of her majesty' that defined the English position fully as set down in 'a book entitled *A Treatise of Commerce*'.[52]

The arms of the Muscovy company in an engraving from the 1633 edition of John Stow's A Survey of London.

Unlike France or Spain, Russia posed no military threat to sixteenth-century England. Merchants looked to Russia as they sought new markets for woollen cloth. As a Londoner, Stow was understandably attracted to this vast and exotic empire to the east. In 1553 he mentioned the early trading venture to Muscovy that Sebastian Cabot organized. Individual merchants investing £25 each sent three great ships 'for the adventure of the unknown voyage to Muscovy'; this mission led to the creation of the Muscovy company two years later.[53]

Stow's fascination with Russia undoubtedly encouraged him to include an elaborate description of the wreck of an English ship carrying a Russian ambassador to London:

The Edward Bonaventure traversing the seas four months, finally the tenth of November the said year 1557 arrived within the Scottish coasts where by extreme storms, the said ship being beaten from her ground, tackles, was driven upon the rocks on shore, where she brake and split in pieces. . . .

Although the 'rude people of the country' rifled and carried away the ship's cargo, the Russian ambassador miraculously survived. As soon as the merchant adventurers for Russia learned of the disaster, they sent two men with sufficient money to escort the ambassador to England. Once safe in London, he was lavishly entertained by Queen Mary and King Philip, and Stow carefully itemized the luxurious gifts that were exchanged.[54]

Manuscript notes giving eyewitness accounts of the burning of Moscow by the Tartars in 1571 provide further evidence of Stow's interest in Russia, but information about a major disaster that claimed twenty-five English lives was entirely omitted from the *Annales of England* as well as the two editions of Holinshed's chronicle.[55] Written in Stow's hand, the notes were published by the Hakluyt Society in *Early Voyages and Travels to Russia and Persia*. They consist of two short narratives, the first of which the editors identified as a letter to Lord Burghley from Thomas Glover, an agent of the Muscovy Company who managed to escape from the cellar of the English House.[56] The editors cited the calendared version of a letter in the State Papers Domestic but must not have examined the manuscript at the Public Record Office because Stow's version differs significantly from it.[57] Stow would have had no access to the correspondence of Burghley, although it is more likely that he saw another letter written to the Muscovy Company. According to the Hakluyt Society editors, Thomas Glover also sent information about what had happened in Russia to Sir William Garrard, a former lord mayor and governor of the company. If Garrard received the letter, he may have passed information about the fire directly to Stow. The second part of Stow's narrative – according to the editors – reached London by means of Nicholas Proctor, later chief agent of the company at Moscow, who fled the city eight hours before the gates were closed. The most puzzling aspect of the Hakluyt Society text is that the editors failed to indicate that Stow's narrative could be found in Harleian MS 247 at the British Library.[58]

Stow's description of the arrival of ambassadors from the new Russian emperor, Boris Godunov, for a visit that lasted from September 1600 until February the following year was factual, but lacking in any pro-Russian sentiment. Arriving at Tower Wharf, they were received by aldermen, Muscovy merchants, and about 200 men from the principal London companies. It was nearly a month later when they had an audience with the queen. The Russian ambassadors were still in London on 17 November when the queen celebrated her 'holyday', the forty-second anniversary of her accession to the throne, with jousting at Whitehall. Stow noted that the celebration attracted 'so great an assembly of people as the like hath not been seen in that place before', and he breathed a sigh of relief when:

There was no harm that happened (thank be God) considering the multitude, but that one arm or branch of a great elm broke which stood in the park by being overladen with people and from whence there fell three men that were sore bruised and dangerously hurt.[59]

When Edmund Howes enlarged the *Annales* after Stow's death, he made major changes to Stow's text. Howes' account began exuberantly saying that the new emperor, Lord Boris Pheodorowich, had 'won the people's hearts'. He noted that the ambassadors brought a message of goodwill to the queen confirming the charter of English privileges and asked her to send to the emperor 'some men of quality, as doctors of physicke, learned men, and skilful artificers'. But Howes' sympathy for Russia was short-lived because his narrative ended with a dramatic reassessment of the emperor: 'Concerning the rest of this smooth-face usurping tyrant, look in the 3. year of King James' where his ambassadors were entertained at the expense of the merchant adventurers.[60] The ruler who had won the hearts of the people had become a tyrant.

While no crisis affected English relations with Denmark, Stow followed relations between the two countries closely although he showed little interest in the complex issues that lay behind the pageantry of diplomacy.[61] At the beginning of Elizabeth's reign Danish objections to English trade with Russia via the North Cape strained diplomatic relations between the two countries while England attempted to draw Denmark into a Protestant alliance. In 1582 Stow noted that English ambassadors went to Denmark to present the Order of the Garter to King Frederick II but advised his readers that he had written 'more at large' in the 'continuation of Maister Reine Woolfes chronicle'.[62]

Stow returned to Danish affairs only after the Armada when Arnold Whitfield (Witfeldt), the Danish 'chancellor of the realm', came to England as ambassador.[63] Whitfield arrived in 1597, and although he received better treatment than his Polish counterpart when the issue of trade with Spain was discussed, the queen showed him little respect. The new Danish king, Christian IV (1588–1648), offered to negotiate peace with Spain, but the aging Elizabeth argued that he was too young to understand the conflict. Moreover, she insisted that England did not crave peace, for, as she exclaimed, she had 'never endured one hour of fear'. The ambassador wanted 'open traffic' with Spain because Danish goods had been seized in the narrow seas. The queen protested that she knew of no losses but promised redress and satisfaction. The ambassador had an audience on the queen's birthday and used the occasion to praise her lavishly as a 'gracious creature' with whom God had glorified the world.[64] While Stow quoted the words spoken, he did not give the source of his information. Lord Zouche headed a delegation to Denmark the next year. The queen sent congratulations to Christian IV, who had recently married the daughter of the Marquis of Brandenburg, but the major issue affecting relations with Denmark was a complaint of English merchants 'touching a late arrest and detention of their goods in the sound' to the value of 100,000 tallers (thaler). After the English made allegations of fraud against Danish customs, the king offered restitution of only 30,000 tallers. The English rejected the offer, but the ambassadors were sent back to Denmark the next month. When the king increased his offer by 10,000 tallers, it was accepted, and payment was made to the merchants concerned.[65]

Elizabeth was dead and James VI of Scotland had succeeded to her throne when William Segar (d. 1633), now garter king at arms, gave Stow an eyewitness account of the Earl of Rutland's embassy to Denmark to attend the christening of Queen Anne's nephew, the son of Christian IV, and to present the garter to the king. Sailing from Gravesend at the end of June 1603, Segar wrote that they anchored safely in the Sound of Denmark after seven days at sea, 'the winds and weather being favourable'. The ambassadors landed at Elsinore a few days later and then went to Copenhagen where they had an audience with the king. Segar was present at the audience and offered many details as well as his own personal observations. In his judgement Danish women were 'both for habit and behaviour . . . the most modest women in the world'. He gave an unusually meticulous account of the christening where prayers were said in Latin and Danish, and water was put on the child's head with the sign of the cross. Afterwards Segar complained that he was offended by the Danes' raucous celebration: 'It were superfluous to tell you of all superfluities that were used,' he said, 'and it would make a man sick to hear of the drunken healths: use hath brought it into fashion, a fashion made it a habit, which ill beseems our nation to imitate.'[66] While in Denmark the English saw the ships and munitions of the king, examined fortifications at Elsinore castle, and enjoyed stag hunting, and Segar presented the Order of the Garter to the king. The embassy returned to England landing at Scarborough, Yorkshire, on 30 July after fourteen days at sea.[67]

William Segar's narrative of the embassy to Denmark in 1603 became available to Stow only after the 1605 edition of *Annales* had 'passed the press', and four pages of new material were inserted out of chronological order at the end. Stow's determination to include the most recent events and incorporate new material in chronicles suggests that to the very end of his life he was actively collecting historical records so that his chronicles might be as up to date and complete as possible. While a modern historian can only applaud Stow's determination to update his work, it might be argued that in view of the relative importance of Danish affairs at this time, Segar's account would have benefited from critical editing. Stow's interest in Sweden was slight compared with Denmark, but one entry in the *Annales* affords an interesting glimpse of Stow's use of historical sources. There he wrote that John, Duke of Finland, second son of the King of Sweden, came to London in 1559 hoping to negotiate the marriage of his brother to the queen and cited an important Latin work, 'Johannes Lewencii comment, de bellis Moscorum', as his authority.[68]

Stow's vision of international relations was largely restricted to Western Christendom, but he noted rejoicing with 'banqueting and bonfires' at the defeat of the Ottoman Turks in 1571 by 'the Christian army by sea', although he neglected to mention that the victorious Christian army was Spanish.[69] Many years later an embassy from the King of Barbary attracted his attention. In August 1600 Mully Hamer Xarise, ambassador from Abdola Wayhet Anowne, King of Barbary (sent from the 'King of

Maroco in Barbaria'), accompanied by two merchants and thirteen other persons arrived in London. They were conveyed in four coaches to the Royal Exchange and lodged in the house of Anthony Radclife, a merchant taylor and alderman. The ambassadors were entertained by the court at Nonesuch, and the queen received them at Oatlands. Stow's short account was greatly enlarged by Edmund Howes, who not only added details but also revealed a distinct dislike for the Muslim visitors. Notwithstanding many kindnesses and 'all other provision for six months space at the queen's charge', Howes wrote, 'such was their inveterate hated unto our Christian religion and estate as they could not endure to give any manner of alms, charity, or relief' to the poor. He went on to reveal that the Barbary ambassadors sold their 'fragments' to those who could pay the most. When killing their own meat, whether sheep, lamb, or poultry, they faced southward. Without giving a source, Howes said, 'They use beads and pray to saints.' As the ambassadors finally left the country, they took 'all sorts of English weights, measures, and samples of commodities'. Howes believed that they poisoned their interpreter, who was born in Granada, because he commended the estate and bounty of England. Although their chief 'pretence' was to require continuation of queen's favour to their king, the diplomatic mission also involved espionage. Howes was convinced that they were more like spies than legitimate ambassadors because they omitted nothing that might 'damnify the English merchants'.[70]

Stow recognized a world beyond Europe by writing about overseas exploration and trading ventures. He was a London chronicler, but his world reached westward to the Indies, North America, and the Pacific Ocean. Although his large circle of acquaintances does not seem to have included the writers who promoted English overseas expansion, it appears that he assisted Richard Hakluyt by letting him use his copy of Fabyan's chronicle to obtain information about the early voyage of Sebastian Cabot.[71]

After explorers of the Muscovy Company failed to find a north-east passage to China, efforts shifted toward the discovery of a north-west passage to the same destination. In 1576 Martin Frobisher (1535?–94),[72] supported by the queen, the Earl of Warwick, and several London merchants, including Michael Lok (who later ended up in debtor's prison), sailed for North America hoping to discover a passage to 'Cataya' or China. Sailing to the north-west, Frobisher explored along the Labrador coast, crossed Hudson Strait, coasted along Baffin Island, and entered an inlet now called Frobisher's Bay. According to Stow, Frobisher found the land inhabited by 'savage people', one of whom was caught and brought back to England. But Stow was more interested in reports that Frobisher's men found 'a piece of black stone, much like sea-cole in colour' (black pyrites). When this was 'brought to certain goldfiners in London to make assay', an Italian goldsmith and alchemist optimistically thought it contained gold, 'but other said the contrary and so it proved'.[73]

Encouraged by an outbreak of gold fever in London, Frobisher undertook a second voyage in 1577 and sailed from Harwich towards Cataya, following the same route as the previous voyage. He failed to find a north-west passage but returned to Milford Haven in Wales, bringing what he thought to be gold as well as a man, woman, and child, none of whom survived in captivity. His ore, in Stow's words, was not gold but 'dross'.[74] The next year Frobisher made a third voyage to Cataya with 'fifteen sail of good ships'. In the *Chronicles of England* of 1580, Stow wrote that Frobisher and his men 'fraught their ships with gold ore out of the mines', but later, amending his assessment in the *Annales*, he concluded that the gold ore 'proved worse than good stone whereby many men were deceived to their utter undoings'. The latter account suggests that Stow eventually lost faith in Frobisher and hopes of finding gold along a north-western route leading to Asia. George Best, who accompanied Frobisher and whose narrative was incorporated in the second edition of Hakluyt's *Principall Navigations*, however, conveyed a great deal of optimism and showed substantial support for the third voyage, but Stow used virtually nothing of Best's work in his account of the voyage.[75]

Stow offered readers of *Annales of England* a useful, if uninspired, summary account of Sir Francis Drake's famous voyage around the world in 1577–80. His manuscripts contain a shorter description of the voyage; both accounts are based on Hakluyt's *Principall Navigations* and include an assessment of Drake's achievement from William Borough's *Evaluation of the Variation of the Compass* . . . (1581):

> Our countryman, Sir Francis Drake, for valorous attempt, prudent proceeding and fortunate performing his voyage about the world, is not only become equal to any of them that live, but in fame far surpassing.

By relying on the evaluation of Borough, Stow avoided giving his own opinion of Drake and the significance of his circumnavigation of the world.[76]

Stow presented Drake's voyage to the West Indies in 1585 with about as much enthusiasm as the voyage of circumnavigation. He wrote that Drake, accompanied by 2,300 men and 25 ships and pinnaces, attacked Cartagena and Santo Domingo before burning and ransoming St Augustine, Florida. He assured his readers that these deeds had been done with great valour but did not consider the strategic objectives of the voyage. Richard Hakluyt noted that Drake sailed on to the struggling colony at Roanoke and brought all but three of the colonists back to England, but Stow curiously chose to overlook the first English attempt to colonize Virginia.[77] His omission cannot have been caused by the unavailability of Hakluyt's book because Stow included a short reference to Sir Thomas Cavendish's voyage 'about the globe of the earth' in 1586–8 with the following recommendation for further reading: of the Cavendish voyage, said Stow, 'ye may read at large in a book entitled, Principal Navigations, Voiages, and Discoueries of the English Nation . . .' by Richard Hakluyt.[78]

Although Stow certainly knew of the existence of a world beyond the Atlantic and the Mediterranean, it mattered less to him than Ireland or Europe. He grew disenchanted with Frobisher and his visionary schemes to find the north-west passage and seems to have been equally unenthusiastic about Sir Francis Drake, whose death in 1596 is not recorded in *Annales of England*. Edmund Howes, perhaps influenced by Christopher Marlowe's popular play, remedied Stow's oversight or deliberate omission and added that Drake 'was as famous in Europe and America, as Tamburlaine in Asia and Africa'.[79] Stow's attitude toward overseas voyages looked to the past when compared with the strident expansionism of Richard Hakluyt, but Kenneth R. Andrews may have exaggerated when he argued that after 1585 Hakluyt's 'message of oceanic imperialism conquered the reading public with such triumphant ease because the public mind was now ready to accept it'.[80] Since Stow's chronicles appeared in more editions and were cheaper than the works of Hakluyt, it is likely that they reached a wider audience, and Stow may have been a more typical spokesman of his age than the professional promoters of overseas expansion. When Stow died in 1605, England was still primarily a European power. It maintained an army in the Netherlands and was still at war with Spain while the colonizing efforts of the Elizabethans had ended in failure.[81] Only in 1607 did the English establish what would be a permanent colony in North America.

John Stow was well informed about the world beyond the British Isles for a citizen historian who never travelled abroad and is often dismissed as merely a London chronicler and antiquarian. He read widely, drawing on continental authorities as well as English writers such as Gorges and Hakluyt. While it would be interesting to know more about Stow's connections with Henry Archer, Robert Glover, and William Segar, his use of their reports from abroad demonstrates his vigorous pursuit of historical information to the very end of his life. Although Stow was incredibly knowledgeable, his chronicles show little historical perspective or understanding of the dynamics of European politics. It is doubtful whether he understood exactly how Spain and France threatened England during the reign of Elizabeth. He recognized dangers to individuals such as London merchants but expressed little concern about the security of the country as a whole or its economic well-being. Stow anticipated modern journalistic influences on historical writing in that dramatic events and pageantry lie at the heart of his work while the broader context tends to be ignored.

Stow is a good example of English cultural insularity since he viewed the outside world exclusively from the vantage point of England. Areas closest to home consistently received the greatest attention. Although he included information about Eastern Europe, North Africa, and overseas exploration, he offered little on Germany and omitted the Italian states altogether. Stow had no understanding of Islam, and his writings suggest complete ignorance of Asian and African cultures. For Stow, the cause of England was always just and received his unequivocal support. The patriotism of the citizen historian was every bit as intense as that of the poets, dramatists, and lawyers who figure prominently in Richard Helgerson's *Forms of Nationhood*.[82]

CHAPTER EIGHT

THE WORLD OF JOHN STOW

This book has focussed on John Stow as a citizen historian writing about his own world, a contemporary world that began at the death of Henry VIII and ended with his own death in 1605. When Stow wrote of ancient and medieval Britain, he relied heavily on established authorities, but as he turned to his own times, he chose from a wide range of sources – pamphlets, broadsides, narratives – and developed his own interpretation of the recent past.[1] While most studies of Tudor historiography have emphasized earlier periods of history and the influence of classical and Renaissance scholars, the popular perception of the sixteenth century has been neglected. Stow, like all historians of the contemporary world, took his own times seriously and was inclined to exaggerate its importance. His world, while unsophisticated compared with that of the intellectuals of his generation, was multi-dimensional and may be defined not only chronologically, but also in its geographical, social, personal, and cultural context.

1. BOUNDARIES OF STOW'S WORLD

Despite Edmund Howes' recollection that Stow travelled on foot visiting cathedrals and 'other chief places of the land',[2] he was not distinguished as a traveller, and it is likely that he spent the bulk of his time in and around London. His chronicles and manuscripts, however, dispel any notion that he was merely a provincial Londoner with no interest in the outside world. Readers of the chronicles learned about a wide variety of historical events that took place across the length and breadth of England, from Kent and Cornwall on the south coast to Durham in the north. The first edition of Stow's abridged chronicle, published in 1566, included 'A Brief Description of England' – seven folios based on Polydore Vergil that placed English history in a British context. By 1605, when the last revision of the quarto *Annales of England* was published, this had grown into a more substantial topographical description of England, Cornwall, Wales, and Scotland where Stow acknowledged that each of the four peoples differed in 'language, conditions, or laws'. By defining geographical parameters, the introduction to the chronicles demonstrated clearly that the citizen historian knew that his subject, the history of England, was part of a larger British environment.

Although best informed about southern England, Stow was able to obtain information about historical events throughout the greater part of the country. But occasionally mistakes identified him as a Londoner whose intimate geographical knowledge did not extend far to the north and west. Such a slip occurred when he described a devastating fire that took place in 1567.

> The 22 of April, by great misfortune of fire in the town of 'Ossestrie' in Wales twelve miles from Shrewsbury, to the number of two hundred houses, that is to say, seven score within the walls, and three score without in the suburbs, besides cloth, corn, cattle, etc. were consumed.

The unfortunate community, Stow noted, had experienced two previous fires as recently as 1542 and 1544. The problem with Stow's otherwise interesting anecdote is that the town would have been Oswestry located not in Wales, but on the Welsh borders of Shropshire.[3]

Never quite able to transcend his own environment, Stow always viewed the outside world through an English lens. Ireland, though only 20 miles from Britain at the closest point, was another world where Stow's compassion for the poor and oppressed was discarded in favour of unequivocal support for the English military presence. Scotland, also an ancient enemy, emerged in a better light only in 1603 when James I was received enthusiastically at Berwick as he made his way southward to claim the throne of Elizabeth.[4] It would be unrealistic to expect an untravelled citizen of London to have extensive knowledge of the world outside the British Isles, yet he was enough of a European to call the English Channel the 'French ocean'.[5] His interests in Europe were closely identified with the national interests of England. Consequently, France, Spain, and the Netherlands loom large in the chronicles because of trade, diplomacy, and war. Germany and the Italian states were practically ignored while Stow's lengthy account of Russia may have been merely fortuitous owing to the availability of sources. In a similar vein, the world outside Europe was also a function of English policy, but Stow's keen eye for unusual events made his narratives compelling reading.

2. A CITIZEN HISTORIAN AND ENGLISH SOCIETY

As a historian Stow considered all sorts and conditions of men but neglected women and children. His character, social status, and personal experiences shaped everything he wrote, and consequently the man and his work cannot be separated. An eyewitness as well as a contemporary chronicler, Stow lived in an early modern society in transition, but changes in population, prices and wages, and patterns of trade were beyond his comprehension. As he was not a court historian, he viewed the Tudor monarchs and aristocracy as an outsider who was respectful of his betters but not fawning for advancement. What mattered for him was popular culture as he drew attention to crime, disease, unemployment and poverty, and war.

Stow's response to rebellions and popular disorder reflected his adherence to the social and political values of the sixteenth century. He clearly understood that the common people throughout a large part of the country suffered under oppressive landlords in 1549 but could offer no practicable remedy for their plight. An enemy of violence, Stow believed passionately in the necessity of maintaining order and denied English subjects the right to take the law into their own hands whatever their grievances might be. The *Annales of England* reveals Stow's increasing sensitivity to religious and social problems, especially human suffering in England during the latter years of Elizabeth's reign. He was ambivalent about the impact of war since he celebrated English victories even as he witnessed its damaging effects on Elizabethan society.

A layman, who was never an apologist for the Church of England, Stow understood the reformed Church as a progressive force for change. At the same time he recognized how Protestant reforms transformed traditional Catholic beliefs and destroyed historic church buildings. Neither his published works nor manuscripts offer convincing evidence that he understood the Reformation as a historical process that was transforming his world. He reminds us that it was quite possible for an intelligent layperson to live through the sixteenth-century Reformation without being consumed by it. Unlike his contemporary and rival, Richard Grafton, Stow felt no call to promote Protestantism through historical writing, and he showed little interest in the evolution of the Church of England, its teachings, liturgy, or ministry. His chronicles include considerable information about the Elizabethan persecution of Roman Catholics as well as fascinating accounts of radical Protestants, who also suffered during the reign, but his own religion was that of the queen.[6]

Despite the traditional format of the chronicles, Tudor monarchs, politicians, and court intrigue did not stand at the centre of Stow's world. His interest in Parliament as well as other institutions of government was surprisingly limited. Stow's agenda clearly differed from that of future generations of political and constitutional historians, who fashioned the English history taught in schools and universities. The citizen historian's understanding of politics may have been unsophisticated, but his patriotism equalled that of Elizabethan intellectuals. While foreign policy was also peripheral to Stow, he wrote extensively about overseas embassies and military campaigns, usually emphasizing ceremony and the heroics of English commanders. The city of London, the real centre of Stow's world, was changing rapidly along lines that he did not wholly approve. Perhaps his interest in the medieval Jewish community was because it was part of a past in which he felt most comfortable.

3. PERSONAL WORLD

While Stow's publications, wide circle of friends, and long life are superficial evidence of worldly success, he was a private man who revealed little of his inner self. He left evidence that he suffered at times from self-pity, and as early as the 1560s he was complaining that he waxed old and decayed in his occupation. Edmund Howes tells us only that Stow was cheerful, sober, and wholly committed to his work, a generalized characterization that would have fitted many contemporary Londoners including Puritan clergy.[7] Toward the end of his life in 1602, Stow spoke with John Manningham, a young Cambridge-educated lawyer, who recalled their conversation in his diary:

> I was with Stowe the Antiquary. He told me that a model of his picture was found in the Recorder Fleetwood's study, with this inscription: *Johannes Stowe, Antiquarius Angliae*, which now is cut in brass and prefixed in print to his *Survey of London*. He sayeth of it as Pilate sayeth, 'What I have written I have written,' and thinks himself worthy of that title for his pains, for he hath no gains by his travail. He gave me this good reason why in his *Survey* he omits many new monuments because those men have been the defacers of the monuments of others, and so thinks them worthy to be deprived of that memory whereof they have injuriously robbed others.[8]

Here we find a more reflective Stow who took pride in his accomplishments and hoped posterity would also have a good opinion of him.

Stow enjoyed a long productive life of eight decades in an age when life was often short and unpleasant. He found time to know London more intimately than any other Elizabethan, to peruse its records in a leisurely fashion, and above all to write. Despite the bitter conflict with his brother over their inheritance, evidence of protracted family conflict is lacking. He once referred to his wife, Elizabeth, as one who could 'neither get nor save', but their marriage proved to be durable. He provided for her and his two married daughters, Julyan Towers and Joan Foster, as well as he was able in his will. Elizabeth Stow showed loving devotion to her husband by erecting at her own expense a monument of Derbyshire marble and alabaster in the parish church of St Anthony's Undershaft where he was buried.[9]

Stow's reputation survived his death and grew as a result of the frequent reprints and enlargements of his work. Howes published new editions of the chronicles in 1607, 1611, 1615, 1618, and 1631 while Anthony Munday with the personal encouragement of Stow and some of his 'best collections' corrected and extended *A Survey of London* in 1618.[10] Another edition appeared in 1633 followed by the two-volume folio edition of John Strype in 1720. Although the chronicles were not reprinted after 1631, nineteenth- and twentieth-century editors of Stow's *Survey* kept his memory alive. Charles L. Kingsford's annotated edition appeared in 1908 (reprinted 1971); four years later the book was first included in Everyman's Library where it passed through many revisions and reprints until 1987, and in 1994 Antonia Fraser edited an edition that remains in print.[11]

Notwithstanding his considerable accomplishments, Stow's personal world also included frustration and failure because he was unable to secure publication of two substantial works. As early as 1590, he began referring to ambitious books that he was writing. Addressing readers of a chronicle, he asked them to support the publication of 'larger volumes, not only of this famous city of London and citizens deserving immortality, but also of this whole Island, princes of the same, and accidents of their times, which I have gathered'.[12] Two years later he had completed a historical work larger than the *Annales of England*. He wrote:

> These labourious collections in so long a time have now at length grown into a large volume, which I was willing to have committed to the press, had not the printer, for some private respects, been more desirous to publish Annales at this present.[13]

William Claxton, who had apparently received a copy of the *Annales* from Stow, wrote to him in 1594 requesting a copy of what he called the 'great volume', which he expected to be published shortly.[14] As late as 1605 Stow still hoped that his work would see the light of day. At the end of his last edition of the *Annales*, he begged God to permit him life either to publish or to leave to posterity a 'far larger' volume that he had undertaken at the request of Archbishop Matthew Parker. He went on to complain that the 'reprinting' of Holinshed's chronicle had prevented his book from being published.[15]

After Stow's death, Edmund Howes noted that he 'purposed if he had lived but one year longer to have put in print Reyne Woolfe's chronicle which he began and finished at the request of [Archbishop John] Whitgift. He left the same in his study orderly written, ready for the press, but it came to nothing. . . .' Charles Kingsford concluded that the manuscript had perished although parts of it may have been included in the *Successions of the History of England* published under Stow's name in 1638.[16] Wolfe, a printer and active Protestant, seems to have envisaged a large history or universal cosmography with maps and illustrations covering western Europe.[17] That Stow was thinking along the same lines is supported by a few manuscript notes recording events in European history, but Kingsford thought Stow's project was a more modest 'history of this island'.[18]

A second large work, referred to as a book of foundations, remained unpublished possibly because Stow never completed it. In recounting the history of this project,

Kingsford traced its existence from a volume found in Stow's study when he was investigated for Catholic tendencies, to the loan of a portion of a manuscript covering four English counties to William Camden, and eventually to William Claxton, who wrote to Stow in 1594 asking to have it copied:

> I perceive also by your letter that you have augmented your book of foundations whereof I am heartily glad and do most earnestly request that you would let me have a copy of the best sort with your new augmentations which truly I would make no small account of and keep as a token of your manifest kindness unto me. And the more earnest I am to have it, as in your letter you said there is no copy of it but your own, which if ought should come unto you but good, might happily be never regarded and spoiled or never come to light and so all your pains frustrated, whereas if I have a copy of it I hope so to use it and dispose of it as it shall be extant to all posterities, and amongst them a never dying fame for you who bestowed such pains in collecting the certainty thereof together. What charge so ever you be at in getting it copied forthwith for me, I will repay unto you with thanks.[19]

After Stow's death Kingsford suggested that the manuscript made its way to Ralph Starkey, Roger Dodsworth, and ultimately to William Dugdale, whose *Monasticon Anglicanum* was in part 'the outcome of Stow's industry'.[20]

Stow probably endured further personal frustration because of his inferior social status as a mere citizen of London. In the best tradition of his era, he deferred to persons of good birth and formal education. A bookish man, who enjoyed solitude and admitted that he was not a 'feast follower', Stow was hardly a social climber, but it is realistic to assume that he would have liked to have had enough worldly success to style himself a gentleman.[21] Contemporaries praised Stow as a record searcher and antiquarian without peer, but younger university-educated scholars belittled him as an anachronism who was out of touch with Renaissance literary fashions.[22] A sense of social inferiority may help explain Stow's commitment to hard work and his sobriety and self-pity. In the future, scholars of higher social status separated themselves from the likes of Stow and strove to control not only the writing but also the teaching of history.

While Stow left no evidence of efforts to improve his social status, financial problems were a persistent source of complaint that continued until his death. Stow's publications and a pension from the Merchant Taylors certainly did not give him the economic security he desired, but it would be unrealistic to conclude that his poverty may be compared with persons deprived of shelter, food, and other basic necessities. The testimony of contemporaries of higher social standing, especially Edmund Howes, who knew him during his later years, and John Strype (b. 1643), a Londoner born less than forty years after Stow's death, support his own complaints. Not surprisingly there is no surviving evidence of a poor person who claimed Stow as one of his own. Howes confirmed Stow's financial difficulties when he wrote in the dedication of a chronicle that 'no man would lend a helping hand unto the late aged painful chronicler'.[23] Strype agreed with Howes' assessment and printed licences issued by James I under the great seal authorizing Stow to 'gather the benevolence of well-disposed people . . . towards his relief now in his old age'. Strype added that Stow died on 4 April 1605 before much could be collected but didn't explain why the king failed to offer a well-deserved pension.[24]

Subsidy assessments offer another index of Stow's personal wealth. In 1582 he was assessed 3s on goods and chattels valued at £3. Of forty-one households assessed in his parish, none had a lower assessment and fifteen were at £3, while the highest assessment was on goods and chattels worth £270. Thomas (presumably his brother) lived in another parish where he was assessed on goods and chattels of £10. While John Stow's assessment placed him at the lowest level, it has been estimated that only 25 per cent of the heads of households were wealthy enough to warrant assessment, and by the end of the sixteenth century 'to be taxed at all for the subsidy was a mark of substance'.[25] Stow's will, signed with a very shaky hand on 30 August 1603, reveals his financial situation at the end of his life. He left bequests of £10 to each of his daughters, Julyan Towers and Joan Foster, and to no other person. 'And for the rest of my goods, household stuff, and apparel,' he wrote, 'I give unto Elizabeth, my wife, as also I give unto her the lease of my house with the residue of the years to come.'[26] That he was not rich is beyond question, but scores of impoverished Londoners and masterless men would have rejoiced to have his wealth.

4. CULTURAL IMPACT

Although John Stow may have thought of himself as a failure, his legacy to posterity was vastly greater than he could have imagined. His contribution proceeds from his books and their effect on early modern cultural life. The growth of printing and the increase in books printed in English had a revolutionary impact on the sixteenth century. It is estimated that if the average edition of an Elizabethan book was about 1,250 copies, some nine million books were published during the queen's reign. The books supplied a growing market created by increased population and literacy. By 1550 most nobles and gentlemen were literate, and as early as the 1580s 60 per cent of the craftsmen and tradesmen in London were able to write. Most yeomen throughout England and about 20 per cent of the husbandmen in the diocese of London were literate in 1603, but the literacy rate for men was higher than for women. Appetites for reading varied and included religious works, practical manuals on hunting and agriculture, as well as poetry and drama, but readers of all social classes shared many of the same interests.[27]

Stow responded to a growing demand for history that is reflected in contemporary writing. Thomas Dekker, the dramatist, exclaimed enthusiastically:

. . . O histories! you sovereign balms to the bodies of the dead that preserve them more fresh than if they were alive, keep the fames of princes from perishing when marble monuments cannot save their bones from being rotten. . . . Hast thou an ambition to be equal to princes! read such books as are the chronicles of ages. . . .

A modern scholar, Louis B. Wright, arguing for the utility of historical study, wrote, 'The Elizabethan citizen shared the belief of his learned and courtly contemporaries that the reading of history was an exercise second only to a study of Holy Writ in its power to induce good morality and shape the individual into a worthy member of society.' He, like Dekker, went on to emphasize the importance of chronicles. 'First in popularity with the citizens were the chronicles of England, particularly those chronicles which emphasized the glory of London and her people,' he added, 'for London citizens had a pride in their own importance not unjustified by the facts of history.' Wright praised the *Annales* of Stow, who 'managed to pack more interesting detail into a briefer compass than any preceding historian'.[28]

Stow provided what the Elizabethan reading public wanted: reliable information about current events, useful knowledge of the past, moralism, patriotism, and amusement. The short chronicles and inexpensive abridgements were ideally suited to supply the growing demand. Stow kept the chronicles current as did Edmund Howes after his death. When Ralph Newbery, the printer, refused Stow's larger work in favour of annals, he spoke as a practical businessman who understood the market for books in London. Stow's chronicles may have looked to the medieval past in the view of Renaissance humanists, but good narrative history was anything but antiquated. His most influencial work, *A Survey of London*, appearing toward the end of his life, successfully promoted the capital and had astonishing success at remaining in print.[29]

The most important Elizabethan chronicler, Stow taught history to readers of his era. The number of editions as well as the variety of his work exceeded that of any other historical writer.[30] Richard Grafton proved an unsuccessful competitor even if his work was better than his critics allow. The famous second edition of Holinshed's chronicle, although more comprehensive than Stow's largest chronicle, did not cover the entire reign of Elizabeth, and its format in three folio volumes probably explains why it was not reprinted during the sixteenth century.[31] Sir John Hayward's history of the early years of Elizabeth was not published in its entirety until the nineteenth century, while John Speed and William Camden were scholars whose historical work informed later generations but not Elizabethans. When Stow's *A Survey of London* is added to his other achievements, the contributions of the citizen historian constitute a rich legacy that had a major impact on the cultural life of early modern England.

NOTES

CHAPTER ONE

1. *Stow's Survey of London* (London: J.M. Dent, 1965), 115, 170–1. Strype, 'The Life of John Stow the Author', in *A Survey of the Cities of London and Westminster*, 2 vols. (London, 1720), 1: i–iv.

2. The most detailed life of Stow may be found in Charles Lethbridge Kingsford, ed., *A Survey of London by John Stow*, 2 vols. (Oxford: Clarendon Press, 1908), 1: vi–xliii. Subsequent references are to this edition unless otherwise indicated. Earlier accounts of Stow's life were written by Edmund Howes and included in his editions of the *Annales or a Generall Chronicle of England* and Strype in *A Survey*, 1: i–xxvii. Stow's account of London schools in *A Survey of London*, 1: 71–6, suggests that he never attended any of the schools described.

3. Charles M. Clode, *The Early History of the Guild of Merchant Taylors*, 2 vols (London, 1888), 2: 298–305. *A Survey of London*, 1: viii, lxii, notes that Stow denied allegations that his wife had two children by another man before she was married.

4. Barrett L. Beer, ed., *The Life and Raigne of King Edward the Sixth by John Hayward* (Kent, OH: Kent State University Press, 1993), 1.

5. British Library, Harl. MS 374, fo. 17r. The letter is dated 3 December, but the year is omitted. *A Survey of London*, 1: lxx has an accurate transcription of Joan's letter, but does not include Stow's notes. For a discussion of women's interest in history, see D.R. Woolf, 'A Feminine Past? Gender, Genre, and Historical Knowledge in England, 1500–1800', *American Historical Review* 102: 3 (June 1997), 645–79.

6. British Library, Harl. MS 367, fos. 6–7.

7. Harl. MS 367, fo. 6v. These comments are crossed out on the manuscript and were deliberately omitted from Kingsford's transcription of the document.

8. Stow's quotation.

9. British Library, Harl. MS 367, fos. 6–7. In *A Survey of London*, 1, Kingsford transcribed the manuscript on pp. liii–lx and the will of Elizabeth Stow on pp. xliv–xlv.

10. For examples see *Annales of England* (London, 1605), 1152, 1201.

11. British Library, Harl. MS 367, fo. 5. Printed in *A Survey of London*, 1: lx–lxii.

12. British Library, Harl. MS 247, fo. 209. Printed in *A Survey of London*, 1: lxii–lxiii. Kingsford suggested that the man might have been Michael Crowche, churchwarden of St Michael, Cornhill, in 1574.

13. Strype, *A Survey*, 1: iii. *A Survey of London*, 1: xxiii, 161–2.

14. Strype, *A Survey*, 1: iv–v. *A Survey of London*, 1: xvi–xviii.

15. Susan Brigden, *London and the Reformation* (Oxford: Clarendon Press, 1991), 417.

16. See Christopher Haigh, *English Reformations: Religion, Politics, and Society under the Tudors* (Oxford: Clarendon Press, 1993) and Robert Whiting, *The Blind Devotion of the People: Popular Religion and the English Reformation* (Cambridge: Cambridge University Press, 1989), 259–61 on the speed at which Protestantism progressed.

17. Strype, *A Survey*, 1: iv–v, xxi. Evidence of Stow's hostility to a radical sect known as the 'Family of Love' may be found in British Library, Harl. MS 247, fo. 211r.; the account in *Annales of England* (London, 1605), 1165, is much more balanced.

18. The *Flores Historiarum* is discussed in May McKisack, *Medieval History in the Tudor Age* (Oxford: Clarendon Press, 1971), 40.

19. *A Survey of London*, 1: xvi–xvii. John Strype, *The History of the Life and Acts of Edmund Grindal* (New

York: Burt Franklin Reprints, 1974), 184, 516–19. Patrick Collinson does not deal with this incident in *Archbishop Grindal, 1519–1583: The Struggle for a Reformed Church* (London: Jonathan Cape, 1979).

20. Strype, *A Survey*, 1: iv; *A Survey of London*, 1: xviii. Charges against Thomas Stow were made in *Annales of England* (London, 1605) under 1556 and *Summarie Abridged* (London, 1587), but omitted from the editions of 1573 and 1604. Strype cited the Register of the Ecclesiastical Commission.

21. See Chapter Five.

22. Reference to Leicester's encouragement is in *Summarie Abridged* (London, 1604), C2r.

23. E.J. Devereux, 'Empty Tuns and Unfruitful Grafts: Richard Grafton's Historical Publications', *Sixteenth Century Journal* 21: 1 (1990), 48–9. Here it is argued that suggesting a raid on Stow's library 'would not have been at all beneath Grafton', but no evidence of his complicity is offered.

24. *A Survey of London*, 1: xlv.

25. Charles M. Clode, *Memorials of the Guild of Merchant Taylors* (London, 1875), 650–2. See also R.B. Wernham, *Before the Armada: The Growth of English Foreign Policy, 1485–1588* (London: Jonathan Cape, 1966), 298.

26. Peter J. French, *John Dee: The World of an Elizabethan Magus* (London: Routledge and Kegan Paul, 1972), 204–7. French dates Dee's letter to Stow as 1592 and includes it in Plate 16. See also *A Survey of London*, 1: lxx where the letter of 4 December is not assigned to a definite year, and William H. Sherman, *John Dee: The Politics of Reading and Writing in the English Renaissance* (Amherst: University of Massachusetts Press, 1995), 119–21.

27. *A Survey of London*, 1: lxxiii.

28. British Library, Harl. MS 551, fos. 63–119. Stow dated his copy June 1576. According to Clode, *The Early History of the Guild of Merchant Taylors*, 2: 303n.1, Stow sold his transcript of Leland to Camden for an annuity of £8.

29. *A Survey of London*, 1: 8; 2: 94.

30. *A Survey of London*, 1: 298. For Lambarde see Retha M. Warnicke, *William Lambarde, English Antiquary, 1536–1601* (London: Phillimore, 1973), 23–35.

31. J.D. Alsop, 'William Fleetwood and Elizabethan Historical Scholarship', *Sixteenth Century Journal* 25: 1 (1994), 155–76.

32. *A Survey of London*, 1: xxv–xxvi.

33. McKisack, *Medieval History in the Tudor Age*, 149.

34. British Library, Harl. MS 374, fo. 21; partially printed in *A Survey of London*, 1: lxxiii–lxxiv.

35. Four of William Claxton's letters from British Library, Harl. MS 374 are printed in *A Survey of London*, 1: lxix–lxx, lxxiii–lxxiv.

36. McKisack, *Medieval History in the Tudor Age*, 63–5.

37. British Library, Harl. MS 374, fo. 24; printed in *A Survey of London*, 1: lxviii. C.L. Kingsford suggested that the letter was written before 1 May 1575 because of what he thought was an allusion to Matthew Parker, Archbishop of Canterbury. It seems more likely that Savile referred to Lord William Howard and that this letter preceded the one discussed below.

38. British Library, Harl. MS 530, fo. 1; printed in *A Survey of London*, 1: lxxii–iii. A book of Savile concerning the Lacy family found its way into Stow's manuscript collection; see British Library, Harl. MS 542. fos. 105–8.

39. *A Survey of London*, 1: lxviii–xix.

40. British Library, Harl. MS 374, fo. 23; partially printed in *A Survey of London*, 1: lxxii.

41. *Calendar of State Papers Foreign, 1585–86*, 20 (London, 1921), 633–4.

42. Edmund Howes, ed., *Annales or a Generall Chronicle of England* (London, 1615), 811.

43. Strype, *A Survey*, 1: x.

44. *Summarie Abridged* (London, 1604), C2r.

45. Franklin B. Williams, Jr., *Index of Dedications and Commendatory Verses in English Books before 1641* (London, 1962). Eleanor Rosenberg, *Leicester: Patron of Letters* (New York: Columbia University Press, 1955), 66–80.

46. *A Survey of London*, 1: xix–xx; McKisack, *Medieval History in the Tudor Age*, 41; Rosenberg, *Leicester: Patron of Letters*, 74.

47. See dedications in *Annales of England* (London, 1592) and *Summarie Abridged* (London, 1604).

48. The 1601 edition of the *Annales of England* [STC 23336 at Folger Library] as well as the 1605 edition were dedicated to Archbishop Whitgift.

49. The 1598 edition of *A Survey of London* was dedicated to the 'lord mayor'.

50. Clode, *Memorials of the Guild of Merchant Taylors*, 16, 184–6, 535; and *The Early History of the Guild of Merchant Taylors*, 2: 298–305.

51. For a fuller discussion of the Stow–Grafton controversy see Devereux, 'Empty Tuns and Unfruitful Grafts', 33–56. British Library, Harl. MS 367. fos. 1–3, 11–12 containing Stow's unpublished attack is partially transcribed by Devereux. The controversy seems more concerned with medieval centuries not recent history where Grafton's account may be more satisfactory.

52. *Annales of England* (London, 1592).

53. Important works on Tudor and early modern historiography include F.J. Levy, *Tudor Historical Thought* (San Marino, CA: Huntington Library, 1967), D.R. Woolf, *The Idea of History in Early Stuart England* (Toronto: University of Toronto Press, 1990), and Orest Ranum, *Artisans of Glory: Writers and Historical Thought in Seventeenth-Century France* (Chapel Hill: University of North Carolina Press, 1980).

54. *Annales of England* (London, 1605), 58–62. In the shorter abridgements Stow omitted source citations.

55. McKisack, *Medieval History in the Tudor Age*, 113–14.

56. McKisack, *Medieval History in the Tudor Age*, 82–5.

57. *A Survey of London*, 1: xcii–xciii. Kingsford augmented his listing of manuscripts in the introduction to the revised edition of 1971. Chronicles and Stow's historical memoranda from Lambeth MS 306 have been edited by James Gairdner, *Three Fifteenth-Century Chronicles with Historical Memoranda by John Stowe, the Antiquary, and Contemporary Notes of Occurrences Written by Him in the Reign of Queen Elizabeth* (London, 1880).

58. Folger Shakespeare Library, MS V.b. 134. Stow's name appears near the end on fo. 25v.

59. McKisack, *Medieval History in the Tudor Age*, 40–1, 58. David Powel also had an interest in Gerald of Wales.

60. Richard Hakluyt, *Divers Voyages Touching the Discouerie of America* (London, 1582), A3; Strype, *Edmund Grindal*, 516–19; *A Survey of London*, 1: xx, lxxxvi–lxxxvii. I find no reason to challenge Kingsford's assertion that 'to make a complete list of extant MSS. which belonged to Stow would be an almost hopeless task'.

61. *A Survey of London*, 1: lxxxvii–xcii.

62. See Edgar B. Graves, ed., *A Bibliography of English History to 1485* (Oxford: Clarendon Press, 1975), 404, 439.

63. British Library, Harl. MS 563.

64. Graves, ed., *A Bibliography of English History*, 430–1.

65. *Henry, Archdeacon of Huntingdon: Historia Anglorum, The History of the English People*, edited and translated by Diana Greenway (Oxford: Clarendon Press, 1996), includes two references to Stow: cxxiv, Oxford, Bodleian Library, MS Bodley 521, marginalia in hand of Stow, presented to Bodley in 1620 by Sir Henry Savile; and cxxxvi, transcript by Stow, British Library, Harley MS 247, fo. 74.

66. Stow copied eighty-two folios of Lambarde in Harl. MS 539. Printed editions appeared in 1576, 1596, 1656 and later.

67. Lucy Toulmin Smith, ed., *The Itinerary of John Leland* (1964 reprint of 1906–8 edn.), 1: xxiv, states that Stow made a copy in 1576 and altered the spelling. Smith based her work on the edition of Thomas Hearne dated 1710, and the editions of 1745 and 1770. The 1745 edition is based on a Bodleian MS but has been collated with Stow's copy. See footnotes 1: 3, 4, 5, 104; 2: 9, 15.

68. R. Ian Jack, *Medieval Wales* (London, 1972), 171.

69. British Library, Harl. MS 544 fo. 2; Harl. MS 551 fos. 3–37. Jack, *Medieval Wales*, 36. See also Thomas Wright, ed., *The Historical Works of Giraldus Cambrensis* (London, 1863; AMS reprint, New York, 1968), which contains translations of his work without reference to Stow; and Michael Richter, *The Growth of the Welsh Nation* (Aberystwyth, 1972) which also does not index Stow. Works of Gerald are also published in Rolls series. McKisack also discusses Gerald but not Stow's copies.

70. British Library, Harl. MS 551, fo. 3r.

71. Harl. MS 551, fos. 38–62, 63–119.

72. The poems of Lydgate are found in Harl. 367, fos. 80–3 and Add. MS 29,729; the copy of 'London Lickpenny' is in Harl. 542, fo. 102. Derek Pearsall, *John Lydgate* (London: Routledge and Kegan Paul, 1970), 74, states that Stow had a collection of John Shirley's manuscripts and, 117, that Add. MS 29,729 is Stow's copy of Trinity R.3.20.

73. In British Library, Stowe MS 942, fos. 303–79 the translation is ascribed to Lydgate. See Bennett, *Chaucer and the Fifteenth Century* (New York: Oxford University Press, 1954), 140, 308.

74. Harl. MS 367, fos. 55–77. Bennett, *Chaucer and the Fifteenth Century*, 103, 126–7, 297; and D.W. Singer, *A Catalogue of Latin and Vernacular Manuscripts in Great Britain and Ireland dating from before the Sixteenth Century*, 3 vols. (Brussels, 1928–31).

75. *A Survey of London*, 1: ix.

76. British Library, Harl. MS 367, fos. 130–43. The text is not in Stow's hand but is very likely to have been among his manuscripts. 'Vox Populi' is printed in R.H. Tawney and E. Power, eds., *Tudor Economic Documents*, 3 vols. (London, 1924), 3: 25–39.

77. The early printed editions of Chaucer are listed in Bennett, *Chaucer and the Fifteenth Century*, 270–1.

78. *A Survey of London*, 2: 110–11. For a corrective to Stow's self-praise see C.S. Lewis, *English Literature in the Sixteenth Century excluding Drama* (New York, 1954), 298 and Alice S. Miskimin, *The Renaissance Chaucer* (New Haven, CT: Yale University Press, 1975), 247–50.

79. *A Survey of London*, 2: 24. For details about John Shirley see Bennett, *Chaucer and the Fifteenth Century*, 116–18, 298.

80. *Pithy Pleasaunt and Profitable Workes* (Menston, Yorks., 1973). [Missing at British Library] C.L. Kingsford did not attribute this work to Stow. See Alexander Dyce, ed., *The Poetical Works of John Skelton*, 2 vols. (New York, 1965), 1: xcvii–xcviii; and Greg Walker, *John Skelton and the Politics of the 1520s* (Cambridge: Cambridge University Press, 1988). According to John N. King, *English Reformation Literature: The Tudor Origins of the Protestant Tradition* (Princeton, NJ: Princeton University Press, 1982), 13, Stow's edition of John Skelton was the last complete edition to appear for 168 years.

81. E.F. Jacob, *The Fifteenth Century 1399–1485* (Oxford: Clarendon Press, 1961), 309–12.

82. British Library, Harl. 542, fos. 125-140. According to Charles Plummer, ed., *The Governance of England* (Oxford, 1885), Stow's text was taken from Yelverton MS 35.

83. British Library, Harl. MS 543, fo. 163v.; Harl. MS 545, fo. 136.

84. For Stow's influence on later scholarship see Plummer, *The Governance of England* and S. B. Chrimes, ed., *De Laudibus Legum Anglia* (Cambridge, 1942).

85. Woolf, *The Idea of History in Early Stuart England*, 65–6.

86. Annabel Patterson, *Reading Holinshed's Chronicles* (Chicago: University of Chicago Press, 1994), 8.

87. Quoted in Charles H. McIlwain and Paul L. Ward, eds., *Archeion or, a Discourse upon the High Courts of Justice in England by William Lambarde* (Cambridge, MA: Harvard University Press, 1957), viii. Thomas Hearne called Stow 'an honest and knowing man', but 'an indifferent scholar'. *A Survey of London*, 1: xxxviii.

88. J.E. Neale, 'John Stow', *Transactions of the London and Middlesex Archaeological Society* 10 (1951), 278.

89. *A Survey of London*, 1: xxxviii. Patterson, *Reading Holinshed's Chronicles*, 3–21, also examines the reputation of Stow and other Tudor chroniclers.

90. McKisack, *Medieval History in the Tudor Age*, 113–14.

91. See A.G. Dickens and John Tonkin, *The Reformation in Historical Thought* (Cambridge, MA: Harvard University Press, 1985).

92. See Claire Cross, *Church and People, 1450–1660: The Triumph of the Laity in the English Church* (Hassocks, Sussex: Harvester Press, 1976); Patrick Collinson, *The Religion of Protestants: The Church in English Society, 1559–1625* (Oxford: Clarendon Press, 1982), and Whiting, *The Blind Devotion of the People*.

93. See Levy, *Tudor Historical Thought*, 195; Arthur B. Ferguson, *Clio Unbound: Perception of the Social and Cultural Past in Renaissance England* (Durham, NC: Duke University Press, 1979), 9; Joseph M.

Levine, *Humanism and History: Origins of Modern English Historiography* (Ithaca, NY: Cornell University Press, 1987); and D.R. Woolf, 'Genre into Artifact: The Decline of the English Chronicle in the Sixteenth Century', *Sixteenth Century Journal* 19: 3 (1988), 321–54.

94. See Chapter Eight for a discussion of editions published after Stow's death.

95. *Summarie Abridged* (London, 1567), sig. ai–iii.

96. See Bernard Capp, *English Almanacs 1500–1800: Astrology and the Popular Press* (Ithaca, NY: Cornell University Press, 1979).

97. *A Survey of London*, 1: xxviii.

98. *Holinshed's Chronicles of England, Scotland, and Ireland*, 6 vols. (London, 1808; reprint New York, 1965).

99. See Patterson, *Reading Holinshed's Chronicles* for a discussion of the authors of the second edition of Holinshed.

100. McKisack, *Medieval History in the Tudor Age*, 131–3.

101. See for example, Margo Todd, 'Puritan Self-Fashioning: The Diary of Samuel Ward', *Journal of British Studies* 31 (July 1992), 236–64, and Paul Seaver, *Wallington's World: A Puritan Artisan in Seventeenth-Century London* (Stanford, CA: Stanford University Press, 1985).

CHAPTER TWO

1. Thomas Fuller, *The History of the Worthies of England* (New York: AMS Press, 1965, reprint of 1840 edition) 2: 380.

2. Joan Evans, *A History of the Society of Antiquaries* (Oxford: Oxford University Press, 1956), 10.

3. D.M. Brodie, ed., *The Tree of Commonwealth: A Treatise Written by Edmund Dudley* (Cambridge: Cambridge University Press, 1948).

4. *A Survey of London*, 1: 16, 108; see also 283, 292; 2: 40-1.

5. Kingsford suggested that the author was James Dalton; see *A Survey of London*, 2: 387. It is likely that Stow knew James Dalton as he identified him as the author of another oration that was included in *Annales of England* (London, 1605), 1218–19 and also *Holinshed's Chronicles*, 4: 902–3.

6. *A Survey of London*, 2: 213.

7. *Stow's Survey of London* (New York: Dutton, 1965), 213–14. Kingsford's edition gives a Latin text.

8. *A Survey of London*, 1: 151. On good lordship see Mervyn James, *Family, Lineage, and Civil Society* (Oxford: Clarendon Press, 1974), and *Society, Politics and Culture: Studies in Early Modern England* (Cambridge: Cambridge University Press, 1986), 270–5.

9. *A Survey of London*, 1: 190, 381–2.

10. *Summarie Abridged* (London, 1604), sig. KK3v.

11. *Annales of England* (London, 1605), 1074, 1095; *A Survey of London*, 1: 331.

12. *A Survey of London*, 1: 104–17. The list included several scholars, Robert Fabyan, John Colet, and Edward Hall. Colet was a benefactor of St Paul's school, but Fabyan and Hall were remembered only for their chronicles.

13. *A Survey of London*, 1: 89.

14. *A Survey of London*, 1: 116. Stow added that the provisions of the will had not been 'performed in more than thirty years after'.

15. *Annales of England* (London, 1605), 1140. Aristocratic hospitality is discussed in Felicity Heal, *Hospitality in Early Modern England* (Oxford: Clarendon Press, 1990), 23–90.

16. *Annales of England* (London, 1605), 1174, 1140, 1162, 1263, 1308.

17. *Annales of England* (London, 1605), 1136.

18. *Annales of England* (London, 1605), 1113–14, 1259.

19. *Annales of England* (London, 1605), 1150. For a study of Parker's medieval scholarship see McKisack, *Medieval History in the Tudor Age*, 26–49.

20. *Annales of England* (London, 1605), 1174–5.

21. *Annales of England* (London, 1605), 1404 (misnumbered page).

22. *Summarie Abridged* (London, 1604), 387. The obituary of Robert Johnson is not included in *Annales of England* (1605).

23. *Annales of England* (London, 1605), 1135. Stow's account is based on his own notes in British Library, Harl. MS 542, fo. 1. See also F.G. Emmison, *Tudor Secretary: Sir William Petre at Court and Home* (London: Longman, 1961), chapter 14.

24. *Annales of England* (London, 1605), 1134, 1160, 1180, 1263.

25. *Annales of England* (London, 1605), 1162–3. Gresham left one part of the Royal Exchange to the mayor and commonalty of London, the other part to the mercers for fifty years; see *A Survey of London*, 1: 76. For a discussion of the value of Gresham's bequests and, more generally, philanthropy in London, see W.K. Jordan, *The Charities of London: 1480–1660* (New York: Russell Sage Foundation, 1960), 253–4.

26. *Annales of England* (London, 1592), 1253–7. Henry Archer supplied Stow's information about the Low Countries.

27. Malcolm William Wallace, *The Life of Sir Philip Sidney* (Cambridge: Cambridge University Press, 1915), 394.

28. Roger Howell, *Sir Philip Sidney: The Shepherd Knight* (London: Hutchinson, 1968), 3–10. See also Arthur F. Kinney and the Editors of *ELR*, *Sidney in Retrospect: Selections from English Literary Renaissance* (Amherst: University of Massachusetts Press, 1988) and Jan Van Dorn et al., eds., *Sir Philip Sidney: 1586 and the Creation of a Legend* (Leiden: J. Brill, 1986).

29. The term is defined in Glanmor Williams, *The General and Common Sort of People, 1540–1640* (Exeter: Exeter University Press, 1977).

30. *A Survey of London*, 1: 198.

31. *A Survey of London*, 1: 128.

32. *A Survey of London*, 2: 60, 24–5.

33. *A Survey of London*, 1: 351.

34. *A Summarye of the Chronicles of England* (London, 1590), 687.

35. *Summarie Abridged* (London, 1604), 428; Howes, ed., *Annales of England* (1615), 791.

36. *Summarie Abridged* (London, 1604), 436; Howes, ed., *Annales of England* (1615), 797. See A.L. Beier, *The Problem of the Poor in Tudor and Early Stuart England* (London: Methuen, 1983) and *Masterless Men: The Vagrancy Problem in England, 1560–1640* (London: Methuen, 1985).

37. *Annales of England* (London, 1605), 1306. The account in the *Summarie Abridged* (London, 1604), 414–15 is quite different and includes details, especially about Twyford, that are missing in the *Annales*. Surprisingly, the abridgement omits the denunciation of the rich. It is unlikely that Stow received new information about a fire that had occurred in 1598 before completing the last edition of the *Annales*; it is more likely that he decided to reinterpret information that he already had.

38. *Annales of England* (London, 1605), 1243; *Summarie Abridged* (London, 1604), 370. The text of the proclamation is printed in Paul L. Hughes and James F. Larkin, eds., *Tudor Royal Proclamations*, 2 vols (New Haven, CT: Yale University Press, 1964–9), 2: 532–4.

39. *Annales of England* (London, 1605), 1132–4. For assessments of social tensions in London, see Steve Rappaport, *Worlds within Worlds: The Structures of Life in Sixteenth-Century London* (Cambridge: Cambridge University Press, 1989), Ian W. Archer, *The Pursuit of Stability: Social Relations in Elizabethan London* (Cambridge: Cambridge University Press, 1991), and Robert Tittler, 'Harmony in the Metropolis: Writings on Medieval and Tudor London and Westminster', *Journal of British Studies* 31:2 (1992), 187–91.

40. *A Survey of London*, 1: 107; 2: 51, 84, 94.

41. *Annales of England* (London, 1605), 1167.

42. *Summarie* (London, 1590), 703. *Holinshed's Chronicles*, 4: 416.

43. *Annales of England* (London, 1605), 1279–81; *Summarie Abridged* (London, 1604), 402.

44. *Annales of England* (London, 1605), 1185, 1281–2.

45. *Annales of England* (London, 1605), 1300.

46. *Annales of England* (London, 1605), 1309.

47. *Annales of England* (London, 1605), 1424.

48. *Annales of England* (London, 1605), 1404, 1417.

49. For an introduction to this topic see J.A. Sharpe, *Crime in Early Modern England: 1550–1750* (London: Longman, 1984) and *Judicial Punishment in England* (London: Faber and Faber, 1990).
50. *Annales of England* (London, 1605), 1063–4.
51. The family controversy is discussed in Chapter One.
52. *A Survey of London*, 1: 100–1.
53. *Annales of England* (London, 1605), 1137.
54. *Annales of England* (London, 1605), 1146–7. *Holinshed's Chronicles*, 4: 324.
55. *Annales of England* (London, 1605), 1153.
56. British Library, Harl. MS 542, fos. 34–7.
57. *Annales of England* (London, 1605), 1020; Raphael Holinshed, *The Laste Volume of the Chronicles of England, Scotlande, and Irelande*, 2 vols. (London, 1577), 2: 1703–8; *Holinshed's Chronicles*, 3: 1024–31. John Lewis, *The History and Antiquities of . . . Faversham in Kent* (n.p., 1727), 52–61, gives the full names of persons who are mentioned by surname only in the manuscript. See also Historical Manuscripts Commission, *6th Report* (London, 1877), App., 500; Louis B. Wright, *Middle-Class Culture in Elizabethan England* (Chapel Hill, NC: University of North Carolina Press, 1935), 632; C.F. Tucker Brooke, *The Shakespeare Apocrypha: Being a Collection of Fourteen Plays Which Have Been Ascribed to Shakespeare* (Oxford: Clarendon Press, 1908, 1967); and Peter Clark, *English Provincial Society from the Reformation to the Revolution: Politics and Society in Kent, 1500–1640* (Hassocks: Harvester Press, 1977), 74, 82–4.
58. North's administrative work is examined in Walter C. Richardson, *History of the Court of Augmentations: 1536–1554* (Baton Rouge: Louisiana State University Press, 1961). Ennobled by Queen Mary, North seems to have accepted the return of Roman Catholicism without difficulty. He was little employed by Elizabeth although his health may have been failing before his death in 1564.
59. Clark, *English Provincial Society*, 74–84 and Lena Cowen Orlin, *Private Matters and Public Culture in Post-Reformation England* (Ithaca, NY: Cornell University Press, 1994), 15–84. According to Historical Manuscripts Commission, *6th Report*, 500, Arden was the king's controller of the customs at the time he was chosen mayor. In 1550 he was disfranchised for opposing the franchise of Faversham.
60. According to Stow, Thomas Arden had obtained a piece of ground on the 'backside of the abbey' from Grene by extortion.
61. *Annales of England* (London, 1605), 1020.
62. For a theoretical discussion of Tudor punishments by a university-educated lawyer see Thomas Smith, *De Republica Anglorum: The Maner of Gouernement or Policie of the Realm of England* (London, 1583), chapter 24. According to Smith, 'When a man is murdered, all be principals and shall die, even he that doth but hold the candle to give light to the murderers.'
63. Orlin, *Private Matters and Public Culture*, 80–1.
64. Brooke, *The Shakespeare Apocrypha*, xiii–xv, 448–55.
65. *Annales of England* (London, 1605), 1140–1; in March 1578 seven other pirates were hanged at Wapping, 1159.
66. *Annales of England* (London, 1605), 1204.
67. Smith, *De Republica Anglorum*, chapters 24 and 25.
68. *Annales of England* (London, 1605), 1168.
69. *Annales of England* (London, 1605), 1271 (June 1592).
70. *Annales of England* (London, 1605), 1204–5.
71. In Stow's account of the execution of Edmund Campion in *Annales of England* (London, 1605), 1169, the reader is advised to 'look more in my continuation of Reine Woolfes chronicle'.
72. *Summarie Abridged* (London, 1604), 327; *Summarye* (London, 1590), 692.
73. Sharpe, *Judicial Punishment in England*, 27–33, suggests that the use of capital punishment increased during the sixteenth century but fell after about 1620.
74. See Jennifer Kermode and Garthine Walker, eds., *Women, Crime and the Courts in Early Modern England* (Chapel Hill: University of North Carolina Press, 1994). The authors of this incompletely indexed book appear to have neglected evidence in Stow and other chronicle accounts. Stow's

prejudices do not fit this volume's definition of 'female' crime, namely witchcraft, infanticide, and scolding.

75. *Annales of England* (London, 1605), 1272; *Summarie Abridged* (1604), 395.

76. *Annales of England* (London, 1605), 1259.

77. *Annales of England* (London, 1605), 1152.

78. *Annales of England* (London, 1605), 1134; the same account appears in *Holinshed's Chronicles*, 4: 262.

79. *Annales of England* (London, 1605), 1173, 1201, 1271. A woman burned in June 1592, like Alice Arden, had a young man as an accomplice, who was also executed. When the husband was not the victim, female murderers were executed on the scaffold in the conventional manner; for example, in April 1583 a man and a woman were hanged for killing an apprentice.

80. See Chapter One for family feuds of the Stow family. The widow's story appears in *Annales of England* (London, 1605), 1152.

81. *Annales of England* (London, 1605), 1148.

82. *A Survey of London*, 2: 54–5.

83. *Annales of England* (London, 1605), 1173. A similar anecdote appears in *Holinshed's Chronicles*, 4: 504. Here the authors offer their own moral: 'Of this lamentable accident people talked diversely, and pamphlets were published to make the same more known; howbeit, to leave the certain means of the event to his knowledge that understandeth and seeth all things, let it be a warning to all ages so to live as that an honest report may attend their death, and shame fly from them as a cloud before the wind.'

84. Paul Slack, *The Impact of Plague in Tudor and Stuart England* (London: Routledge and Kegan Paul, 1985), 22–50 surprisingly overlooks Stow as a witness to the plague but provides an excellent analysis of contemporary attitudes.

85. *Annales of England* (London, 1605), 1004; '. . . one bell at the least by the space of three quarters of an hour'. Slack, *The Impact of Plague in Tudor and Stuart England*, 148.

86. Slack, *The Impact of Plague in Tudor and Stuart England*, 70 and references cited on 360 n.40.

87. *Annales of England* (London, 1605), 1021.

88. *Annales of England* (London, 1605), 1063.

89. *Annales of England* (London, 1605), 1073. The deaths of Queen Mary and Cardinal Pole are discussed in D.M. Loades, *The Reign of Mary Tudor* (New York: St Martin's Press, 1979), 390. Slack, *The Impact of Plague in Tudor and Stuart England*, 71.

90. *Annales of England* (London, 1605), 1154. Slack, *The Impact of Plague in Tudor and Stuart England*, 207 regards this as an outbreak of 'jail fever' that caused only a few deaths, but he apparently did not consider the higher number of fatalities mentioned in Stow's account.

91. *Annales of England* (London, 1605), 1202. According to A.L. Rowse, *The Expansion of Elizabethan England* (New York, 1955), 261 n.1, Sir Bernard Drake was a prominent local man not directly related to Francis Drake.

92. *Annales of England* (London, 1605), 1020.

93. *Annales of England* (London, 1605), 1111–12, 1425.

94. Howes, ed., *Annales of England* (1615), 766. Page numbers have been cut from 1605 edition. For a discussion of the social distribution of the plague see Slack, *The Impact of Plague in Tudor and Stuart England*, 151–69.

95. *Annales of England* (London, 1605), 1425. In *Summarie Abridged* (London, 1604), 455, Stow noted that the wealthy citizens 'voided the city' and that there was no feast for the mayor at Guildhall.

96. See Slack, *The Impact of the Plague in Tudor and Stuart England*, Table 6.1, p. 151 and authorities cited in nn. 18–20, pp. 375–6.

97 This literature is examined in Tessa Watt, *Cheap Print and Popular Piety, 1550–1640* (Cambridge: Cambridge University Press, 1991) and the work of Margaret Spufford, especially, *Small Books and Pleasant Histories* (Athens: University of Georgia Press, 1982).

98. Neale, 'John Stow', 278.

99. Watt, *Cheap Print*, 258, 311.

100. Watt, *Cheap Print*, 1–8; see also Peter Burke, *Popular Culture in Early Modern Europe* (New York:

Harper and Row, 1978), 23–64 and Anthony Fletcher and John Stevenson, *Order and Disorder in Early Modern England* (Cambridge: Cambridge University Press, 1985), 1–15.

101. *Annales of England* (London, 1605), 1176.

102. *Annales of England* (London, 1605), 1166. *Summarie Abridged* (London, 1604), 336.

103. See Watt, *Cheap Print*, 165–6.

104. *Summarie Abridged* (London, 1604), 335.

105. *Annales of England* (London, 1605), 1173.

106. *Annales of England* (London, 1605), 1026; Beer, ed., *The Life and Raigne of King Edward*, 170–1. See also Katharine Park and Lorraine J. Daston, 'Unnatural Conceptions: The Study of Monsters in Sixteenth-Century and Seventeenth-Century France and England', *Past and Present* 92 (1981), 20–54.

107. *A Survey of London*, 1: 59.

108. Charles Nicholl, *The Reckoning: The Murder of Christopher Marlowe* (New York: Harcourt Brace, 1994), 225–33.

109. British Library, Harl. MS 247, fos. 204–5.

110. *Annales of England* (London, 1605), 1275–7; Edmund Howes, ed., *Annales or a Generall Chronicle of England* (London, 1631), 767–8.

111. *Annales of England* (London, 1605), 1275. Howes' edition of 1631, 767, adds the latter observation that Stow had difficulty obtaining accurate information.

112. *Annales of England* (London, 1605), 1168; *Summarie Abridged* (London, 1604), 338–9.

113. *Annales of England* (London, 1605), 1202–3.

114. *Annales of England* (London, 1605), 1299.

115. Howes, ed., *Annales of England* (1631), 782–3.

116. Christopher Hill, 'The Many-Headed Monster in Late Tudor and Early Stuart Political Thinking', in Charles H. Carter, ed., *From the Renaissance to the Counter-Reformation: Essays in Honor of Garrett Mattingly* (New York: Random House, 1965), 296–324.

117. See Christopher Hill, 'The Poor and the People', in *The Collected Essays of Christopher Hill*, 3 vols. (Amherst: University of Massachusetts Press, 1986), 3: 247–73.

CHAPTER THREE

1.   The best introduction to this topic is Anthony Fletcher, *Tudor Rebellions*, 3rd edn. (Harlow, Essex: Longman, 1983). See also Roger B. Manning, *Village Revolts: Social Protest and Popular Disturbances in England, 1509–1640* (Oxford: Clarendon Press, 1988); David Underdown, *Revel, Riot, and Rebellion: Popular Politics and Culture in England, 1603–1660* (Oxford: Clarendon Press, 1985); Perez Zagorin, *Rebels and Rulers, 1500–1660*, 2 vols. (Cambridge: Cambridge University Press, 1982); and Buchanan Sharp, *In Contempt of All Authority: Rural Artisans and Riot in the West of England, 1586–1660* (Berkeley, CA: University of California Press, 1980).

2.   Hughes and Larkin, eds., *Tudor Royal Proclamations*. For a study of the government response to the Pilgrimage of Grace, see David Sandler Berkowitz, *Humanist Scholarship and Public Order* (Washington, DC: Folger Shakespeare Library, 1984). The Parker Society publications include examples of sermons preached against Tudor rebellions. Also important is the homily 'Against Disobedience and Wilful Rebellion', *Certain Sermons or Homilies Appointed to Be Read in Churches* (London, 1843), 587–642.

3.   John Proctor, *The History of Wyates Rebellion* (London, 1554) represents the view of the queen's government, while Alexander Neville, *Alexandri Neuylli Angli de Fororibus Norfolciensium Ketto Duce* (London, 1575) not only appeared long after the event but was not translated into English until 1615.

4.   For this research I have used the copy of Carion in the Kent State University Library, STC 4626.

5.   See STC 9968–9976 for information about the editions of this chronicle that appeared between 1552 and 1561.

6.   Robert Fabyan, *The Chronicles of Fabyan* (London, 1559); Richard Grafton, *An Abridgement of the Chronicles of England* (London, 1562).

7. Barrett L. Beer, ' "The Commoyson in Norfolk, 1549": A Narrative of Popular Rebellion in Sixteenth-Century England', *Journal of Medieval and Renaissance Studies* 6:1 (1976), 73–99.

8. *A Survey of London*, 1: 144–5.

9. Stow, *A Summarie of Englyshe Chronicles* (London, 1565), fo. 211r; *Coopers Chronicle* (London, 1560), fo. 345r.

10. British Library, Harl. MS 540, fo. 10v. The manuscript differs from the version published in the *Annales of England* (London, 1605). Stow's assessment may be compared with *Coopers Chronicle* (London 1560), fo. 345r., '. . . the common people in all parts of the realm . . . '.

11. Stow, *Summarie* (London, 1565), fo. 211r; *The Chronicles of England* (London, 1580), 1042.

12. Rosenberg, *Leicester, Patron of Letters*, 124–30.

13. There is a brief reference to the bailiff in *Annales of England* (London, 1605), 1005.

14. *Coopers Chronicle* (London, 1560), fo. 345r.

15. *Summarie* (London, 1565), fo. 221v. In 1570 Richard Grafton criticized authors who '. . . by their fond writing have opened [gaps] to the hateful spoil and wiste of rebellion', criticism that may have been directed against Stow. Another possibility is Thomas Cooper, whose chronicles appeared in two editions plus a partially reset reissue during the 1560s. See Patterson, *Reading Holinshed's Chronicles*, 24 and especially Devereux, 'Empty Tuns and Unfruitful Grafts', 33–56. I want to thank Andrea Manchester for focussing my attention on this issue and making a strong case for the accuracy of Grafton's complaint.

16. British Library, Harl. MS 247, fo. 198.

17. The above is based on William H. Wiatt, 'The Lost History of Wyatt's Rebellion', *Renaissance News* 15 (1962), 128–33. John Mychell, *A Breuiat Cronicle Contaynynge All the Kings from Brute to This Day* (Canterbury, 1553 [1553/4]). [STC 9970]

18. The best account of Proctor may be found in the *Dictionary of National Biography*. Dr Lillian Hromiko has begun a study of Proctor's writings and has tentatively identified the unnamed heretic mentioned in *The Fal of the Late Arrian* (London, 1549), STC 20,406, as John Assheton, the Antitrinitarian who appeared before Archbishop Cranmer and recanted his beliefs.

19. These chronicles are discussed in Levy, *Tudor Historical Thought*, 177–83; and F. Smith Fussner, *The Historical Revolution: English Historical Writing and Thought, 1580–1640* (London: Routledge and Kegan Paul, 1962), 230. For a study of Robert Crowley, see King, *English Reformation Literature*, 319–57.

20. J.G. Nichols, ed., *The Chronicle of Queen Jane and of Two Years of Queen Mary* (London: Camden Society, 1850), v–viii. I have examined the *Calendar of Patent Rolls*, which was published after 1850, and other printed sources but have not been able to add anything to Nichols' comments regarding the author of this chronicle.

21. Barrett L. Beer, 'John Stow and the English Reformation, 1547–1559', *Sixteenth Century Journal* 16:2 (1985), 258.

22. 'Underhill's Narrative', in A.F. Pollard, ed., *Tudor Tracts, 1532–1588* (New York, 1903).

23. Stow, *Summarie* (London, 1565), fo. 227r.

24. Stow, *Summarie* (London, 1565), fo. 228v; *Coopers Chronicle* (London, 1560), fo. 362v.

25. *Coopers Chronicle* (London, 1560), fo. 363v; Stow, *Summarie* (London, 1565), fo. 229r.

26. *Annales of England* (London, 1605), 1054.

27. *Annales of England* (London, 1605), 1055; Nichols, ed., *Chronicle of Queen Jane*, 73–4.

28. Compare Charles Wriothesley, *A Chronicle of England*, ed. W.D. Hamilton, 2 vols. (London: Camden Society, 1877), vol. 2, entries for 22, 25, 26, 27 and 29 January 1554. Neither Stow nor Wriothesley have entries for 28 January. In the entry for 6 February 1554, Stow has many details not in Wriothesley, but the latter places more emphasis on Wyatt, the rebel and traitor. J.G. Nichols, ed., *Chronicle of the Grey Friars of London* (London: Camden Society, 1852), viii.

29. D.M. Loades, *Two Tudor Conspiracies* (Bangor, Gwynedd: Headstart History, 1992), 16. The revised second edition modifies arguments found in the 1965 edition of this work.

30. Stow, *Summarie* (London, 1565), fo. 227r and v.

31. *Annales of England* (London, 1605), 1046.

32. Stow, *Summarie* (London, 1565), fo. 228v; *A Summarye of the Chronicles of England* (London, 1570), fo. 377r; *Chronicles* (London, 1580), 1081; *Annales* (London, 1605), 1047.

33. The looting at Winchester Place is mentioned by John Proctor, 'History of Wyatt's Rebellion', 241–3; but Stow gives a better account in the *Annales of England*.

34. Winthrop S. Hudson, *John Ponet (1516?–1556): Advocate of Limited Monarchy* (Chicago: University of Chicago Press, 1942), 63–5, 97; Clark, *English Provincial Society*, 92; Barrett L. Beer, 'John Ponet's *Shorte Treatise of Politike Power* Reassessed', *Sixteenth Century Journal* 21:3 (1990): 373–83.

35. Hudson's source, 63, was the 1600 edition of the *Annales of England*, 1048; see also *Annales* (London, 1605), 1048.

36. Nichols, ed., *Chronicle of Queen Jane*, 49; *Annales of England* (London, 1605), 1049-50.

37. 'Underhill's Narrative', in Pollard, ed., *Tudor Tracts*, 190.

38. Loades, *Two Tudor Conspiracies* (1965), 27–8. See also Loades, *The Reign of Mary Tudor*, 125.

39. Stow, *Summarie* (London, 1565), fo. 227v.

40. Stow, *Summarie* (London, 1570), fo. 376r. In the *Annales of England* (London, 1605), 1046, Stow inserted 'etc'.

41. Loades, *Two Tudor Conspiracies*, 27, 115.

42. Stow, *Summarie* (London, 1565), fo. 229r, *Chronicles* (London, 1580), 1089, *Annales of England* (London, 1605), 1052.

43. *Summarie* (London, 1565), fo. 229v.

44. *Holinshed's Chronicles*, 4: 25.

45. British Library, Harl. MS 537, fo. 109; *Holinshed's Chronicles*, 4: 85; *Annales of England* (London, 1605), 1063. The *Annales'* account is one paragraph in length and identical to Holinshed.

46. Wallace T. MacCaffrey, *The Shaping of the Elizabethan Regime* (Princeton, NJ: Princeton University Press, 1968), 367–71, and Norman L. Jones, *The Birth of the Elizabethan Age: England in the 1560s* (Oxford: Blackwell, 1995), 81–4.

47. John Stow, *The Summary of the Chronicles of England Lately Collected, Newly Corrected and Continued vnto This Present Yeare of Christ 1573* (London, 1573), British Library shelf-mark 570 a.9., 229–34; *Summary* (London, 1574), fo. 413v.; *Chronicles* (London, 1580), 1138; *Annales of England* (London, 1605), 1124. Another version, shorter and different from the edition of 1574, may be found in *Summarie Abridged* (London, 1579), STC 23,325.7. For dating purposes Stow was compared with Sir Cuthbert Sharp, *Memorials of the Rebellion of 1569* (London, 1840). For a study of the literary responses to the rebellion, see James K. Lowers, *Mirrors for Rebels: A Study of the Polemical Literature relating to the Northern Rebellion, 1569* (Berkeley, CA: University of California Press, 1953).

48. *Annales of England* (London, 1605), 1125. This reference does not appear in *Chronicles* (London, 1580).

49. Sharp, *Memorials*, 14, 21.

50. Sharp, *Memorials*, 37, 56n.

51. Sharp, *Memorials*, 45.

52. Sharp, *Memorials*, 78–82.

53. Sharp, *Memorials*, 96.

54. Stow, *Summary* (London, 1574), fo. 414v.

55. *Annales of England* (London, 1605), 1124. The same account appears in *Chronicles* (London, 1580).

56. Sharp, *Memorials*, 45.

57. Fletcher, *Tudor Rebellions*, 88.

58. *Annales of England* (London, 1605), 1124.

59. Stow, *Summary* (London, 1574), fo. 414v, *Chronicles* (London, 1580), 1138.

60. Stow, *Summary* (London, 1574), fo. 414v, *Annales of England* (London, 1605), 1124. The same account appears in *Chronicles* (London, 1580).

61. The text is printed in Sharp, *Memorials*, 189–213.

62. Raphael Holinshed, *The Third Volume of Chronicles* (London, 1587), British Library shelf-mark LR 400 b. 23., 1212–13.

63. William Camden, *The History of the Most Renowned and Victorious Princess Elizabeth Late Queen of England*, ed. Wallace T. MacCaffrey (Chicago: University of Chicago Press, 1970), 120–2.

64. Neville Williams, *Thomas Howard Fourth Duke of Norfolk* (London: Barrie and Rockliff, 1964), 179–88. *Annales of England* (London, 1605), 1129–30. *Holinshed's Chronicles*, 4: 253–4 has a similar account.

65. *Annales of England* (London, 1605), 1138.

66. British Library, Harl. MS 247, fo. 82v.

67. Carole Levin, 'Throckmorton Plot (1583)', in R.H. Fritze *et al.*, *Historical Dictionary of Tudor England, 1485–1603* (New York: Greenwood Press, 1991), 501–2.

68. *Annales of England* (London, 1605), 1177.

69. John Guy, *Tudor England* (Oxford: Oxford University Press, 1990), 332; *Annales of England* (London, 1605), 1180; *Holinshed's Chronicles*, 4: 561–87. This is the last official account of the Parry plot.

70. *Annales of England* (London, 1605), 1217–20; *Holinshed's Chronicles*, 4: 909–20. The account in Holinshed is more exuberant and patriotic and the descriptions of the executions appear to be those of an unidentified eyewitness, who may have been Stow. The festivities, which were censored from the original printing, have been characterized as a 'sociopolitical eucharist'. See Patterson, *Reading Holinshed's Chronicles*, 211–14, 257–63.

71. Guy, *Tudor England*, 449–52; Lacey Baldwin Smith, *Treason in Tudor England: Politics and Paranoia* (Princeton NJ: Princeton University Press, 1986), 192–255.

72. *Annales of England* (London, 1605), 1405–6. Robert Lacey, *Robert Earl of Essex, An Elizabethan Icarus* (London: Weidenfeld and Nicolson, 1971), 2.

73. *Annales of England* (London, 1605), 1402.

74. *Annales of England* (London, 1605), 1408. The official source to which Stow referred was most likely [Francis Bacon] *A Declaration of the Practices and Treasons . . .* (London, 1601). [STC 1133]

75. William Camden, *Annales Rerum Anglicarum et Hibernicarum* (London, 1615). Part IV, which covers the period from 1589 to the end of the reign, was published in 1627 and is bound with Parts I–III in a single volume.

76. William Camden, *The History of the Most Renowned and Victorious Princess Elizabeth . . .*, 4th edn. (London, 1688), 609.

77. Camden, *The History of the Most Renowned and Victorious Princess Elizabeth . . .* , 622–3.

78. Smith, *Treason in Tudor England*, 254; Lacey, *Robert Earl of Essex*, 109–10; Alison Wall, 'An Account of the Essex Revolt, February 1601', *BIHR* 54 (1981), 131–3. *Annales of England* (London, 1605), 1408. The Latin edition of Camden, 180, gives the full name of Henry Cuffe. It is unlikely that Stow had access to the documents in *Calendar of State Papers Domestic, 1598–1601*, ed. M.A.E. Green (London, 1869), 547–53.

79. British Library, Harl. MS 367, fos. 130–43; not in Stow's hand but bound in a volume including other documents copied by him or belonging to him. Printed in Tawney and Power, eds., *Tudor Economic Documents*, 3: 25–39.

80. *A Survey of London*, 2: 206.

81. Annabel Patterson, *Censorship and Interpretation: The Conditions of Writing in Early Modern England* (Madison, WI: University of Wisconsin Press, 1984), 11.

82. Frances Rose-Troup, *The Western Rebellion of 1549* (London, 1913), 399–403.

83. Loades, *Two Tudor Conspiracies*, 271; Clark, *English Provincial Society*, 98.

84. R.R. Reid, 'The Rebellion of the Earls, 1569', *Transactions of the Royal Historical Society*, n.s., 20 (1906), 171; James, *Society, Politics and Culture: Studies in Early Modern England*, 297.

85. *A Survey of London*, 1: xxviii, xxxviii–xxxix.

CHAPTER FOUR

1. *Annales of England* (London, 1605), 816, 831, 876. *A Survey of London*, 2: 44. Stow carefully avoided the legal issues surrounding the marriage of Henry VIII and Catherine of Aragon and referred his readers to Edward Hall. In a manuscript note, British Library, Harl. MS 247, fo. 190, he mentioned the birth of 'Lady Mary, King Henry's daughter'.

2. Miriam U. Chrisman, 'Lay Response to the Protestant Reformation in Germany, 1520–1528', in Peter N. Brooks, ed., *Reformation Principle and Practice* (London: Scolar Press, 1980), 35.

3. Woolf, *The Idea of History in Early Stuart England*, 121. For the authors of the second edition of Holinshed, see Patterson, *Reading Holinshed's Chronicles*, 128–53.

4. William Haller, *Foxe's Book of Martyrs and the Elect Nation* (London: Jonathan Cape, 1967), 224–6.

5. Smith Fussner, *The Historical Revolution*, 219–20. In 1569 Stow's house was searched for Catholic books. A list of the unlawful books in his possession is printed in Strype, *Edmund Grindal*, 516–19. See also *A Survey of London*, 1: xviii.

6. British Library, Harl. MS 530, fo. 76; William Camden asked Stow about foundations of abbeys. See also Harl. MS 247, fos. 184, 220v, 222; and Harl. MS 551, fos. 1–2.

7. *A Survey of London*, 1: 300, 335f.

8. J.G. Nichols, ed., *Diary of Henry Machyn* (London: Camden Society, 1847). On the questions of censorship see Fredrick S. Siebert, *Freedom of the Press in England, 1476–1776* (Urbana: University of Illinois Press, 1965), 21–104 and H.S. Bennett, *English Books and Readers, 1558 to 1603* (Cambridge: Cambridge University Press, 1965), 56–86.

9. The most detailed general studies of the Reformation during the reign of Edward VI are A.G. Dickens, *The English Reformation*, 2nd edn., (University Park, PA: Pennsylvania State University Press, 1991), and W.K. Jordan, *Edward VI: The Young King* (London: George Allen and Unwin, 1968) and *Edward VI: The Threshold of Power* (London: George Allen and Unwin, 1970).

10. *A Summarie of Englyshe Chronicles* (London, 1565), fo. 209, 209v.

11. *Annales of England* (London, 1605), 1000–2.

12. *Annales of England* (London, 1605), 1004.

13. Somerset's construction of Somerset House, located in the Strand, London, is discussed in W.K. Jordan, *Edward VI: The Young King*, 498–9 and M.L. Bush, *The Government Policy of Protector Somerset* (Montreal: McGill-Queen's University Press, 1974), 57.

14. *Chronicles of England* (London, 1580), 1037, *Annales of England* (London, 1605), 1004. The *Summarie* mentions the feud between the Duchess of Somerset and the Dowager Queen, wife of Thomas, Lord Seymour, but the *Chronicles* and *Annales* omit this.

15. *Annales of England* (London, 1605), 1003–4.

16. *Annales of England* (London, 1605), 1001.

17. *Annales of England* (London, 1605), 1002, 1004.

18. *Annales of England* (London, 1605), 1002.

19. *Annales of England* (London, 1605), 1001, 1005. Stow also heard Sir Stephen preach against idols, see *A Survey of London*, 1: 143–4.

20. Barrett L. Beer, *Rebellion and Riot: Popular Disorder during the Reign of Edward VI* (Kent, OH: Kent State University Press, 1985), 24–5.

21. A.F. Pollard, *England under Protector Somerset* (London, 1900), 261–2; Jordan, *Edward VI: The Young King*, 308–9; *Edward VI: The Threshold of Power*, 240–1. Although generally critical of Jordan, D.E. Hoak, *The King's Council in the Reign of Edward VI* (Cambridge: Cambridge University Press, 1976), 174, accepts his view that Somerset's religious moderation contrasted with Northumberland's extremism. More recent studies include Beer, 'London Parish Clergy and the Protestant Reformation, 1547–1553', *Albion* 18 (1986), 375–93, 'Philip Melanchthon and the Cambridge Professorship', *Notes and Queries* 34 (June 1987), 185 and 'Episcopacy and Reform in Mid-Tudor England', *Albion* 23 (1991), 231–52; and Haigh, *English Reformations*, 176–81 where older views have been challenged.

22. British Library, Harl. MS 247, fo. 198; this unpublished note refers to the restoration of mass in Shrewsbury churches in 1550.

23. *Annales of England* (London, 1605), 1011–3. See also *The Letters of Stephen Gardiner*, ed. James A. Muller (Westport, CT: Greenwood Press, 1970), 443–5 and Glyn Redworth, *In Defence of the Church Catholic: The Life of Stephen Gardiner* (Oxford: Blackwell, 1990), 286–9.

24. *Summarie* (London, 1565), fo. 214v.

25. *Chronicles of England* (London, 1580), 1048; *Annales of England* (London, 1605), 1020.

26. *Annales of England* (London, 1605), 1019, 1027.

27. *Annales of England* (London, 1605), 1027.

28. Introductions to the extensive literature on the *Book of Common Prayer* include Dickens, *The English Reformation*, chapters 10 and 11; Philip Hughes, *The Reformation in England*, 2 vols. (New York: Macmillan, 1963), 2, chapters 2 and 4; and Haigh, *English Reformations*, 241–2.

29. *Annales of England* (London, 1605), 1029; *Coopers Chronicle* (London, 1560), fo. 358v.

30. *Summarie* (London, 1565), fo. 223; *Coopers Chronicle* (London, 1560), fo. 359v.

31. *Summarie* (London, 1565), fo. 224–4v.; *Coopers Chronicle* (London, 1560), fos. 359–60.

32. *Summarie* (London, 1565), fo. 226v.

33. Stow's attitude may be compared with the revisionist accounts of Haigh, *English Reformations*, 203–34, and Eamon Duffy, *The Stripping of the Altars: Traditional Religion in England c.1400–c.1580* (New Haven, CT: Yale University Press, 1992), 524–64.

34. Loades, *The Reign of Mary Tudor*, 155.

35. Smith, *De Republica Anglorum*, 35. See Michael A.R. Graves, *The Tudor Parliaments: Crown, Lords and Commons, 1485–1603* (London: Longman, 1985), 108–9 and Jennifer Loach, *Parliament and the Crown in the Reign of Mary Tudor* (Oxford: Clarendon Press, 1986), 99.

36. *Summarie* (London, 1565), fo. 226–6v.

37. *Annales of England* (London, 1605), 1043, 1058.

38. *Summarie* (London, 1565), fo. 232; *Chronicles of England* (London, 1580), 1093–4; *Annales of England* (London, 1605), 1058.

39. *Summarie* (London, 1565), fo. 232v; *Annales of England* (London, 1605), 1058.

40. *Summarie* (London, 1565), fo. 233; *Chronicles of England* (London, 1580), 1097.

41. *Annales of England* (London, 1605), 1060. That Stow did not always avoid giving a detailed account of heretical teachings is indicated by his description of the execution of Matthew Hamon at Norwich. The fullest account of Nicholas Ridley occurs in *A Survey of London*, 2: 135–6.

42. *Annales of England* (London, 1605), 1019, 1021.

43. *Annales of England* (London, 1605), 1063.

44. British Library, Harl. MS 247, fo. 200. See also Harl. MS 537, fo. 112 for the same text in a different hand (not Stow's).

45. British Library, Harl. MS. 530, fo. 109v.

46. *A Survey of London*, 1: xiii, n. 1.

47. From the extensive literature on Foxe see, for example, J.F. Mozley, *John Foxe and His Book* (New York: Macmillan, 1940), Haller, *Foxe's Book of Martyrs and the Elect Nation*, and D.R. Woolf, 'The Rhetoric of Martyrdom: Generic Contradiction and Narrative Strategy in John Foxe's *Acts and Monuments*', in Thomas F. Mayer and D.R. Woolf, eds., *The Rhetorics of Life-Writing in Early Modern Europe* (Ann Arbor: University of Michigan Press, 1995), 243–73. Stow's association with Matthew Parker is discussed in *A Survey of London*, 1: xix–xxi, and Levy, *Tudor Historical Thought*, 188. It is surprising to find that *A Survey of London* also has very little information about the Marian martyrs especially in view of the fact that sixty-seven burnings took place in the city and another eleven in Middlesex.

48. Stow refers to Foxe in *A Survey of London*, 1: 300 only as 'the learned John Foxe writer of the Actes and Monuments of the English Church'.

49. There is an account of the Protestant underground in Dickens, *The English Reformation*, 301–7. See also C.H. Garrett, *The Marian Exiles* (Cambridge: Cambridge University Press, 1938), Andrew Pettegree, *Foreign Protestant Communities in Sixteenth-Century London* (Oxford: Clarendon Press, 1986), 124–31, and Kenneth R. Bartlett, 'The English Exile Community in Italy and the Political Opposition to Queen Mary I', *Albion* 13 (1981), 223–41.

50. *Annales of England* (London, 1605), 1037, 1054, 1056.

51. *Annales of England* (London, 1605), 1056.

52. *Annales of England* (London, 1605), 1077.

53. For a discussion of the 'Troubles at Frankfurt', see Collinson, *Archbishop Grindal*, 73–7 and the authorities cited in the notes.

54. *Summarie* (London, 1565), fo. 239v; *Chronicles of England* (London, 1580), 1108; *Annales of England* (London, 1605), 1074.

55. *Summarie* (London, 1565), fo. 240.

56. *Chronicles of England* (London, 1580), 1111; *Annales of England* (London, 1605), 1075. William P. Haugaard, *Elizabeth and the English Reformation* (Cambridge: Cambridge University Press, 1968), 96–100 and J.E. Neale, *Elizabeth I and Her Parliaments, 1559–1581* (New York: W.W. Norton, 1966), 71–2, examine the work of the disputation at Westminster that was held between 31 March and 3 April 1559.

57. Neale, *Elizabeth I and Her Parliaments*, 29, 51, 83.

58. Winthrop S. Hudson, *The Cambridge Connection and the Elizabethan Settlement of 1559* (Durham, NC: Duke University Press, 1980), 93, 147. See also Norman L. Jones, *Faith by Statute: Parliament and the Settlement of Religion 1559* (London: Royal Historical Society, 1982) and T.E. Hartley, *Elizabeth's Parliaments: Queen, Lords and Commons, 1559–1601* (Manchester: Manchester University Press, 1992).

59. Neale, *Elizabeth I and Her Parliaments*, 77–9; Hudson, *The Cambridge Connection*, 94–9; and Haugaard, *Elizabeth and the English Reformation*, 104–27.

60. *Annales of England* (London, 1605), 1082. Here we find another chronological error, as Whitsunday was 14 May. According to Charles Wriothesley, *A Chronicle of England*, 2: 142, whose account is very similar to that of Stow, the new service was first used on 14 May. The error in *Annales* may be the result of a printer's error, or perhaps Stow knew of London churches where the new service was actually introduced on 8 May, because it was on that date that Parliament ended its session. See Neale, *Elizabeth I and Her Parliaments*, 80–1.

61. See Jones, *The Birth of the Elizabethan Age*, 25–7.

62. *Annales of England* (London, 1605), 1075, 1082, 1083.

63. *Annales of England* (London, 1605), 1149–50, 51. *Holinshed's Chronicles*, 4: 326–8 offer a slightly more detailed account. The shorter *Summarie Abridged* (London, 1604), 315–16, gives the same account of the banished Anabaptists as *Annales* but omits the roaring and crying of those burned at Smithfield.

64. W.K. Jordan, *The Development of Religious Toleration in England* (Cambridge, MA: Harvard University Press, 1932), 1: 181. Pettegree, *Foreign Protestant Communities in Sixteenth-Century London*, 288, does not cite chronicle accounts that offer more information than the sources that he consulted.

65. *Annales of England* (London, 1605), 1151, 1165. The complete text of the proclamation is printed in Hughes and Larkin, eds., *Tudor Royal Proclamations*, 1: 474–5.

66. British Library, Harl. MS 247, fo. 211.

67. Alastair Hamilton, *The Family of Love* (Cambridge: J. Clarke, 1981), 123; Christopher W. Marsh, *The Family of Love in English Society* (Cambridge: Cambridge University Press, 1994), 34–5, 82; and J.W. Martin, *Religious Radicals in Tudor England* (London: Hambleton Press, 1989), 194–5.

68. The seventeen articles of Leonard Romsye are found in British Library, Harl. MS 367, fo. 17.

69. For the articles against the preachers see British Library, Harl. MS 530, fo. 122. Hamon's surname is also spelled Hamont.

70. *Annales of England* (London, 1605), 1161.

71. Marsh, *The Family of Love in English Society*, 249–53. See also a further reference to the Family of Love in British Library, Harl. MS 537, fo. 110.

72. *Annales of England* (London, 1605), 1174.

73. Jordan, *The Development of Religious Toleration in England*, 1: 182, Diarmaid MacCulloch, *Suffolk and the Tudors* (Oxford: Clarendon Press, 1986), 204, 206. Henry Martyn Dexter, *The Congregationalism of the Last Three Hundred Years*, 2 vols. (New York: Burt Franklin, 1970), 1: 208–10.

74. British Library, Harl. MS 247, fo. 217.

75. See Dexter, *The Congregationalism of the Last Three Hundred Years*, 1: 246–51; B.R. White, *The English Separatist Tradition* (Oxford: Clarendon Press, 1971) 89; Donald J. McGinn, *John Penry and the Marprelate Controversy* (New Brunswick, NJ: Rutgers University Press, 1966), v, 182; and *Apologie, or Defence of such trve Christians as are commonly but vniustly called Brovvnists . . .* (London, 1604). The last words of Barrow and Greenwood are not included in *The Writings of John Greenwood and Henry Barrow, 1591–1593*, ed. L.H. Carlson (London: Allen and Unwin, 1970).

76. *Annales of England* (London, 1605), 1272.

77. See 'The Examinations of Henry Barrowe, John Greenewood, & John Penrie . . .', *Harleian Miscellany*, 12 vols. (London, 1809), 2: 10–41; and Dexter, *The Congregationalism of the Last Three Hundred Years*, 1: 244–5.

78. British Library, Harl. MS 537, fo. 113. A Matheus Harman, worsted weaver, appeared in the mayor's court in 1554 charged with devising unfitting songs. See David Galloway, ed., *Norwich, 1540–1642* [Records of Early English Drama] (Toronto, 1984), 33–4 and Robert Wallace, *Antitrinitarian Biography*, 3 vols. (London, 1850), 2: 364–6.

79. *Chronicles of England* (London, 1580), 1194–5; *Annales of England* (London, 1605), 1161. The incident appears in *Holinshed's Chronicles*, 4: 405–6, where it is included with the events of 1579. -

80. Patterson, *Reading Holinshed's Chronicles*, 128–9.

81. *Annales of England* (London, 1605), 1175. *Holinshed's Chronicles*, 4: 507 offers the same account.

82. *Annales of England* (London, 1605), 1261.

83. Kett wrote *Glorious and Beautiful Garland* (London, 1585), STC 14945 and *An Epistle sent to divers Papists* (London, 1585), STC 14944.5.

84. See *The Life and Complete Works in Prose and Verse of Robert Greene* (London, 1881), which includes a biography by Nikolai Storojenko [Storozhenko] that examines Kett's heresies and his possible influence on Greene, 1: 42-45, 259-60. An appendix includes excerpts from the charges against Kett from British Library, Lansd. MS 982, fo. 102 and the Public Record Office.

85. *Annales of England* (1605), 1094–5. See also *Holinshed's Chronicles*, 4: 202. Neither man is indexed in *A Survey of London*.

86. *Holinshed's Chronicles*, 4: 202, gives the same account with marginal note, 'a false Christ whipped till he changed his song'.

87. *Annales of England* (London, 1605), 1265. The latter phrase is a quotation from Richard Cosin, *Conspiracie for Pretended Reformation: viz. Presbyteriall Discipline. A Treatise discouering the late designments and courses held for aduancement thereof by William Hacket, Yeoman, Edmund Coppinger, and Henry Arthington, Gent out of others despositions and their own letters, writings, and confessions vpon Examination* (London, 1592), 59.

88. *Annales of England* (London, 1605), 1266.

89. *Annales of England* (London, 1605), 1264–6; *Summarie Abridged* (London, 1604), 389. Cosin, *Conspiracie for Pretended Reformation*, 59, 67, 71, 96. Stow speaks of a conspiracy against the queen but not a plot to murder her, but Cosin's account offers additional details.

90. W.J. Sheils, *The Puritans in the Diocese of Peterborough, 1558–1610* (Northampton: Northamptonshire Record Society, 1979), 136–8. Patrick Collinson, *The Elizabethan Puritan Movement* (London: Jonathan Cape, 1967), 424–5 wrote that Coppinger and Arthington proclaimed William Hacket the new messiah and king of Europe at the cross in Cheapside and claimed that the queen had forfeited her crown. Collinson portrays Hacket as a psychopath.

91. *Annales of England* (London, 1605), 1177. The first book, consisting of only six pages, *A Declaration of the Favorable Dealing of Her Majesty's Commissioners* (1583) [British Library shelf-mark, C.33.b.6.] was a defence of the queen's religious policies against 'slanderous reports spread abroad'. Stow wrote that he 'caused [the book] to be set down in the continuation of the chronicle first collected by Reigne Wolfe and finished by Raphaell Hollenshed'. Written by Lord Burghley, it is essentially a defence of the English use of torture, but Stow's account in the *Annales* gave no indication of its contents. The second book was *A True and Perfect Declaration of the Treasons Practised and Attempted by Francis Throckmorton*.

92. The execution of Campion is covered in only about a third of a page in *Annales of England* (London, 1605), 1169; execution of Southwell, 1279. See *Holinshed's Chronicles*, 4: 417f, Patterson, *Reading Holinshed's Chronicles*, 130, and Richard Simpson, *Edmund Campion: A Biography* (London, 1867).

93. British Library, Harl. MS 247, fo. 220v. *A Survey of London*, 2: 135–7.

94. *Annales of England* (London, 1605), 1146.

95. *Annales of England* (London, 1605), 1147–8.

96. *Annales of England* (London, 1605), 1176–7.

97. For Margaret Ward see *Annales of England* (London, 1605), 1259; this incident is also mentioned in *Summarie Abridged* (London, 1604). Ann Line's execution is mentioned in *Annales*, 1408.

98. See Maria Dowling and Joy Shakespeare, 'Religion and Politics in Mid-Tudor England through the Eyes of an English Protestant Woman: the Recollections of Rose Hickman', *BIHR* 55 (1982), 94–102, for an example of a lay person who was acutely aware of the religious changes through which she had lived.

99. *A Survey of London*, 1: 275. See Ian Archer, 'The Nostalgia of John Stow', in D.L. Smith, R. Strier and D. Bevington, eds., *The Theatrical City: Culture, Theatre and Politics in London, 1576–1649* (Cambridge: Cambridge University Press, 1995), 17–34.

100. A good example of Stow's compassion for the suffering may be found in his discussion of the mistreatment of prisoners; see *A Survey of London*, 1: 350–1.

101. See, for example, *A Survey of London*, 1: 309.

102. *A Survey of London*, 2: 54.

CHAPTER FIVE

1. *Hall's Chronicle* (London, 1809, New York: AMS Press, 1965), 505, 868. Richard Grafton, 'imprinter of this work', noted in the 1548 edition, vii, that Edward Hall completed the work only to the 24th year of reign of Henry VIII leaving the rest only in pamphlets and papers which he gathered together and 'have in suchwise compiled them' without any additions of his own. *Annales of England* (London, 1605), 813–14, 999. Stow's account of the death of Henry VIII remained unamended in Edmund Howes' edition; see *Annales of England* (1631), 593.

2. *A Summarie of Englyshe Chronicles* (London, 1565); *Coopers Chronicle* [Thomas Lanquet's chronicle] (London, 1560); and Grafton, *An Abridgement* . . . (London, 1563) offer accounts of the reign of Edward VI which have many similarities. A handwritten note by Thomas Grenville in the later work refers to an earlier edition of Stow, but Grenville seems to have confused this non-existent work with another chronicle, *Breuiate Chronicle* (London, 1561), a copy of which in the Grenville collection at the British Library (G. 5896) is bound in a cover with the title *Stowe's Summary*. Robert Crowley's continuation of Thomas Lanquet's chronicle, *An Epitome of Chronicles* (London, 1559), gives a more Protestant interpretation of Edward's reign than Stow, Cooper, or Grafton.

3. *Summarie Abridged* (London, 1604), 229–47.

4. *Annales of England* (London, 1605), 1008.

5. *Annales of England* (London, 1605), 1028.

6. The charitable work of the reign of Edward VI is discussed in Jordan, *Edward VI: The Threshold of Power*, 204–39.

7. *Annales of England* (London, 1605), 1029. A similar assessment may be found in Grafton, *An Abridgement* . . . (London, 1563); Stow's *Summarie* (1565); and Edmund Howes' continuation, *Annales of England* (1631).

8. Barrett L. Beer, 'Northumberland: The Myth of the Wicked Duke and the Historical John Dudley', *Albion* 11 (1979), 1–14; Beer, ed., *The Life and Raigne of King Edward*.

9. Both the *Summarie Abridged* (London, 1604) and *Annales of England* (London, 1605) state that Edward Seymour was elected lord protector.

10. *Annales of England* (London, 1605), 1004.

11. *Annales of England* (London, 1605), 1024. The same narrative appears in Stow's earliest chronicle, *Summarie* (London, 1565), fo. 215v.

12. British Library, Harl. MS 247, fo. 198v.

13. *Annales of England* (London, 1605), 1030.

14. *Annales of England* (London, 1605), 1031.

15. John Gough Nichols, ed., *The Chronicle of Queen Jane and of Two Years of Queen Mary and Especially of the Rebellion of Sir Thomas Wyat Written by a Resident in the Tower of London* (London, 1850, reprint New York: AMS Press, 1968).

16. Stow also allowed Northumberland to speak for himself at his trial although his guilt is not brought into question. At the execution Stow side-stepped the question of Northumberland's conversion and only quoted these words, '. . . I die in the true Catholic faith'. See *Annales of England* (London, 1605), 1037–9. These events are discussed more fully in Barrett L. Beer, *Northumberland: The Political Career of John Dudley, Earl of Warwick and Duke of Northumberland* (Kent, OH: Kent State University Press, 1973) and David Loades, *John Dudley, Duke of Northumberland, 1504–1553* (Oxford: Clarendon Press, 1996).

17. See Watt, *Cheap Print*, 284; and Carole Levin, 'Lady Jane Grey: Protestant Queen and Martyr', in Margaret P. Hannay, ed., *Silent But for the Word: Tudor Women as Patrons, Translators, and Writers of Religious Works* (Kent, OH: Kent State University Press, 1985), 92–106.

18. *Summarie Abridged* (London, 1604), 247. *Annales* (London, 1605), 1035 and Howes, ed., *Annales of England* (1631), 612, add, 'And thus was the matter ended without bloodshed, which men feared would have brought the death of many thousands.'

19. According to Stow, George Ferrers (1500–79) collected the whole history of Queen Mary 'as the same is set down under the name of Richard Grafton'; see *Annales of England* (London, 1605), 1070. Ferrers wrote 'The Winning of Calais by the French, January 1558 AD', in Pollard, ed., *Tudor Tracts* and other works.

20. British Library, Harl. MS 530 fo. 109v contains the following entry: 'In the time of the reign of this queen [Mary] there were burned and some also that died in prison for religion little under or over 2000–2040 men and women.'

21. *Annales of England* (London, 1605), 1073; Howes, ed., *Annales of England* (1631), 634.

22. *Holinshed's Chronicles*, 4: 140–1, 155. Note the hostile, pro-Protestant approach where the authors state that more English blood had been shed during Queen Mary's reign than in any of her predecessors' and contrast 'a calm and quiet season' under Elizabeth with the stormy, tempestuous, and blustering windy weather of Mary. Howes, ed., *Annales of England* (1631), 635.

23. *Annales of England* (London, 1605), 1057, 1044.

24. *Annales of England* (London, 1605), 1058.

25. For the growth of celebrations of Elizabeth's accession and coronation see David Cressy, *Bonfires and Bells: National Memory and the Protestant Calendar in Elizabethan and Stuart England* (Berkeley, CA: University of California Press, 1989), 50–7.

26. *Annales of England* (London, 1605), 1162. The queen's comforting words are omitted from *Holinshed's Chronicle*, 4: 425. Like Stow's *Annales*, Holinshed offers nothing about the unfortunate boatman who was shot.

27. *Annales of England* (London, 1605), 1299, 1401.

28. *Summarie Abridged* (London, 1604), 439, 444–5; *Annales of England* (London, 1605), misnumbered pages, 1425, 1427.

29. *Annales of England* (London, 1605), 1425. Edmund Howes' edition of the *Annales of England* (1631) retained Stow's observation on the significance of Thursday to the Tudor dynasty.

30. Edmund Howes' first continuation of Stow's work, *The Abridgement or Summarie of the English Chronicles* (London, 1607), retained Stow's version of the death of Elizabeth. Howes added a 'Commemoration of Queen Elizabeth' to his first edition of *Annales of England* (1615), 813–15, and it was retained in the edition of 1631, 815.

31. Paul Johnson, *Elizabeth I: A Study in Power and Intellect* (London: Weidenfeld and Nicholson, 1974), 441 attributes Howes' assessment of public grief at the death of the queen to Stow.

32. *Summarie Abridged* (London, 1604), 440–1; *Annales of England* (London, 1605), 1426 [misnumbered], 1427.

33. *Annales of England* (London, 1605), 1416 [misnumbered page].

34. See Carole Levin, *'The Heart and Stomach of a King': Elizabeth I and the Politics of Sex and Power* (Philadelphia: University of Pennsylvania Press 1994), 168–9 and the authorities cited in note 62.

35. J.E. Neale, *Queen Elizabeth I* (New York: Doubleday, 1957), 54.

36. *Summarie Abridged* (London, 1604), 416; *Annales of England* (London, 1605), 1308.

37. Smith, *De Republica Anglorum*, 35.

38. *Summarie Abridged* (London, 1604), 258; *Annales of England* (London, 1605), 1058.
39. *Annales of England* (London, 1605), 1132–4.
40. See Chapter Two for details.
41. *Chronicles of England* (London, 1580), 1.
42. *Chronicles of England* (London, 1580), 10–13.
43. See Hugh Kearney, *The British Isles: A History of Four Nations* (Cambridge: Cambridge University Press, 1989) and Geraint D. Owen, *Wales in the Reign of James I* (Woodbridge: Boydell Press, 1988).
44. *Annales of England* (London, 1605), 3–6.
45. *Annales of England* (London, 1605), 1001. William Patten, 'The Expedition into Scotland . . .', in Pollard, ed., *Tudor Tracts*. Stow's manuscript narrative, which is different from Patten, is British Library, Harl. MS 540 fo. 70f and has the title 'Two War-like Voyages into Scotland 1547 and 1560'.
46. *Annales of England* (London, 1605), 1085.
47. See John Guy, *Tudor England* (Oxford: Oxford University Press, 1990), 264–7 and authorities cited in n. 32.
48. *Annales of England* (London, 1605), 1122.
49. *Annales of England* (London, 1605), 1126–7.
50. Wernham, *Before the Armada*, 326.
51. *Annales of England* (London, 1605), 1143–5. The printed account lists only the highest ranking prisoners taken at Edinburgh Castle, but Stow had a manuscript listing over 160 men, women, and boys. British Library, Harl. MS 367, fo. 17b [a separate folio].
52. *Annales of England* (London, 1605), 1118.
53. *Annales of England* (London, 1605), 1241. The same account of Queen Mary's execution survived in Howes' edition of 1631, 742.
54. For a discussion of various interpretive approaches to early modern Ireland, see Nicholas Canny, *Kingdom and Colony: Ireland in the Atlantic World 1560–1800* (Baltimore, MD: Johns Hopkins University Press, 1988), 6–13.
55. *Annales of England* (London, 1605), 1119.
56. *Summarie Abridged* (London, 1604), 302 and *Annales of England* (London, 1605), 1139 contain almost identical accounts.
57. Mary Dewar, *Sir Thomas Smith: A Tudor Intellectual in Office* (London: Athlone Press, 1964), 156–170; Steven G. Ellis, *Tudor Ireland: Crown, Community and Conflict of Cultures, 1470–1603* (London: Longman, 1985), 266–7; Canny, *Kingdom and Colony*, 1–2.
58. *Annales of England* (London, 1605), 1165; Ellis, *Tudor Ireland*, 278–80, some sixty men; Guy, *Tudor England*, 362–3.
59. *Annales of England* (London, 1605), 1176.
60. For Bingham's career see Ellis, *Tudor Ireland*, 288f and T.W. Moody, F.X. Martin, F.J. Byrne, eds., *A New History of Ireland, III, Early Modern Ireland 1534–1691* (Oxford: Clarendon Press, 1991), 112. See also *Calendar of State Papers Ireland 1586–1588 July*, ed. H.C. Hamilton (London, 1877), 162–3. On 29 September 1586 Geoffrey Fenton wrote to Walsingham praising Bingham who had slain 1,300 to 1,400 Scots; in Fenton's opinion this was the 'only piece of service, next to Smerwick, that hath been done in this land in many years'.
61. *Annales of England* (London, 1605), 1204.
62. British Library, Harl. MS 247, fos. 215–16, 'Good government of Sir Richard Byngham in province of Connaught'. There is no entry in the Harleian catalogue for these folios. The narrative is not included in *Holinshed's Chronicle*, 6, where Bingham is only briefly mentioned. Sir Henry Docwra's account has been published in J. O'Donovan, ed., 'Docwra's Tracts', *Miscellany of the Celtic Society* (Dublin, 1849), 187–213. According to the editor, the manuscript may be found in Harl. MS 357, fo. 235, but this reference is incorrect. A search of the British Library *Index of Manuscripts* did not yield any reference to the text cited.
63. *Annales of England* (London, 1605), 1204–5.
64. The account of Sir Richard Bingham's campaign in *Annales of England* (London, 1605) ends on p. 1217.
65. *Annales of England* (London, 1605), 1216.

66. See Ellis, *Tudor Ireland*, 285, 288–91 and Moody *et al.*, eds., *A New History of Ireland*, 3: 112.

67. *Annales of England* (London, 1605), 1267–9. Ellis, *Tudor Ireland*, 297–8; Cyril Falls, *Elizabeth's Irish Wars* (New York: Barnes and Noble, 1970), 171.

68. *Annales of England* (London, 1605), 1309–10. A detailed account of Essex's Irish campaign may be found in Falls, *Elizabeth's Irish Wars*; see also Penry Williams, *The Later Tudors: England 1547–1603* (Oxford: Clarendon Press, 1995), 369–72.

69. *Annales of England* (London, 1605), 1412–21. No marginal notations. Nicholas Canny, 'Early Modern Ireland, c.1500–1700', in R.F. Foster, ed., *The Oxford History of Ireland* (Oxford: Oxford University Press, 1989), 113.

70. *Annales of England* (London, 1605), 1412 [misnumbered page]. This account is not based on Docwra in *Celtic Miscellany*. Sir William Drury, lord president of Munster, who died September/October 1579 and was buried in Dublin, is one possible author. For a eulogy on Drury see John Hooker in *Holinshed's Chronicles*, 6: 415, 418–19.

71. *Annales of England* (London, 1605), 1506, 1417 [consecutive misnumbered pages], 1418. Stow also included the terms of the treaty whereby the Spanish were permitted to withdraw, 1421–3.

72. *Annales of England* (London, 1605), 1424.

73. John S. Nolan, 'The Militarization of the Elizabethan State', *The Journal of Military History* 58:3 (1994), 391–420.

CHAPTER SIX

1. In addition to the editions of 1598 and 1603, the British Library, shelf-mark 5972, has a reprint of the first edition in the original binding, dated 1599; this may have been specially printed for Stow's wife, Elizabeth, as her name is printed on the back of the title page and her arms with the initials of her name are on the binding.

2. *A Survey of London*, 1: xxviii. Kingsford added, xxix, that *A Survey* 'is at once the summary of sixty observant years, and a vivid picture of London as he saw it'.

3. A.L. Rowse, *The England of Elizabeth: The Structure of Society* (New York: Collier Books, 1966), 191; Rappaport, *Worlds within Worlds*, 18.

4. Archer, *The Pursuit of Stability*, 16; 'The Nostalgia of John Stow', in Smith *et al.*, eds., *The Theatrical City*, 17–34. M.J. Power, 'John Stow and his London', *Journal of Historical Geography* 11 (1985), 1–20. See also H.R. Trevor-Roper, 'John Stow', *Transactions of the London and Middlesex Archaeological Society* 26 (1975), 337–42, who used *A Survey* as a source to confirm his own views about Tudor politics and the destructive aspects of the Reformation.

5. D.R. Woolf, 'Historical Thought', in R.H. Fritze *et al.*, *Historical Dictionary of Tudor England, 1485–1603*, 240–4.

6. Levy, *Tudor Historical Thought*, 163.

7. See Hans Baron, *In Search of Florentine Civic Humanism*, 2 vols. (Princeton, NJ: Princeton University Press, 1988), 1: 13f. Italian humanists believed that individuals could grow through participation in the life of the polis and respublica. Baron shows that an aloof humanism of the fourteenth century was transformed into civic humanism of the fifteenth century. Bruni stressed the importance of an active political life. Cicero and Dante are seen as examples of politically active intellectuals. While Stow was closer to the older tradition in that he had reclusive tendencies and avoided political issues and an active political life, *A Survey of London* shows devotion to an urban area.

8. *A Survey of London*, 1: xcvii–xcviii.

9. The 1598 edition, sig. a1, is more effusive claiming that 'as Rome the chief city of the world to glorify itself drew her original from the Gods . . . by the Trojan progeny so this famous city of London for greater glory and in emulation of Rome derives itself from the very same original. . . .'

10. *A Survey of London*, 1: 195, 201.

11. A.L. Beier and Roger Finlay, eds., *London 1500–1700: The Making of the Metropolis* (London: Longman, 1986).

12. *A Survey of London*, 1: xxx–xxxvi.

13. *A Survey of London*, 1: xxxvii.

14. British Library, Harl. MS 544, fos. 96–9.

15. A draft – not the copy sent to the printer in 1598 – Harl. MS 544 is heavily corrected with lines crossed out and corrections added between the lines. In the 1603 edition the account of Westminster follows Southwark; in Harl. MS 544 Stow wrote, 'now leaving the city of Westminster the farthest part of . . .' and then turned to Southwark.

16. *A Survey of London*, 1: 196, 2: 244. Stow heard about this from his father and noted that he actually saw marks.

17. *A Survey of London*, 1: xxxvii–xxxviii, 2: 187.

18. *A Survey of London*, 1: 278–82, 2: 252. Kingsford's notes give variant readings in 1598 edn., 219.

19. *A Survey of London*, 1: xxxvii–xxxviii, 231, 239–42, 2: 247. *A Survey of London* (London, 1598), 192. The conflict with the vintners reveals Stow's hard work in collecting information and the frustration he felt when assistance was not forthcoming. Stow approached the company two years earlier, but they refused to assist him.

20. *A Survey of London*, 1: 44–5.

21. *A Survey of London*, 1: 66, 70.

22. *Norman London by William Fitz Stephen*, introduction by F. Donald Logan (New York: Italica Press, 1990), 61–3. Kingsford printed a different text of Fitz Stephen; see *A Survey of London*, 1: 387–8.

23. *A Survey of London*, 1: 89, 20. See also Archer, 'The Nostalgia of John Stow', in Smith *et al.*, eds., *The Theatrical City*, 17–21.

24. *A Survey of London*, 1: 126.

25. *A Survey of London*, 1: 184.

26. *A Survey of London*, 1: 83, 72.

27. *A Survey of London*, 1: xxix–xxx.

28. *A Survey of London*, 1: 133.

29. *A Survey of London*, 1: 151–2.

30. *A Survey of London*, 2: 45.

31. *A Survey of London*, 2: 33, 197–8.

32. *A Survey of London*, 1: 105.

33. Cecil Roth, *A History of the Jews in England*, 3rd edn. (Oxford: Clarendon Press, 1964), 133, but this author does not consider any of Stow's writings.

34. *Annales of England* (London, 1605), 1274.

35. David S. Katz, *The Jews in the History of England, 1485–1850* (Oxford: Clarendon Press, 1994), 1–14, 49–106. See also Lucien Wolf, 'Jews in Elizabethan England', *Transactions of the Jewish Historical Society of England* 11 (1928), 1–91, C.J. Sisson, 'A Colony of Jews in Shakespeare's London', *Essays and Studies by Members of the English Association* 23 (1938), 38–51, and Charles Meyers, 'Lawsuits in Elizabethan Courts of Law: The Adventures of Dr. Hector Nunez, 1566–1591: A Precis', *The Journal of European Economic History* 25: 1 (1996), 157–68.

36. *A Survey of London*, 1: 9, British Library, Harl. MS 538, fo. 4r; the story is repeated 1: 38 and 1: 279 with more details. Jonathan I. Israel, *European Jewry in the Age of Mercantilism: 1550–1750*, 2nd edn. (Oxford, 1989) has virtually nothing on the Elizabethan period and no references to Stow.

37. *A Survey of London*, 1: 278–84.

38. *A Survey of London*, 1: 279.

39. *A Survey of London*, 1: 277, 280–1; *Annales of England* (London, 1605), 293, states that the synagogue was attacked because 'one Jew would have forced a Christian to have paid more than 2d. for the loan of 20s. a week'. Roth, *A History of the Jews in England*, 76, dates the destruction of the synagogue as 1272.

40. *A Survey of London*, 1: 279. See Roth, *A History of the Jews in England*, 22–4.

41. *A Survey of London*, 2: 42–3.

42. *A Survey of London*, 1: 36 from Matthew Paris; see 1: 280 for another incident from Paris dated 20 Henry III.

43. *A Survey of London*, 1: 280. 40 Henry III.

44. *A Survey of London*, 1: 280, 2: 335n. *Annales of England* (London, 1605), 291.
45. *A Survey of London*, 1: 281. See Roth, *A History of the Jews in England*, 274–5.
46. *A Survey of London*, 1: 283–4.
47. *A Survey of London*, 1: 276–8.
48. *A Survey of London*, 1: 286–7.
49. *A Survey of London*, 1: 76–7.
50. *A Survey of London*, 1: 75–6.
51. *A Survey of London*, 1: 318, 328.
52. *A Survey of London*, 1: 274–5.
53. *A Survey of London*, 1: 91.
54. *A Survey of London*, 1: 93.
55. *A Survey of London*, 1: 95.
56. *A Survey of London*, 1: 94, 104.
57. *A Survey of London*, 1: 95.
58. *A Survey of London*, 2: 55.
59. *A Survey of London*, 1: 95, 97.
60. *A Survey of London*, 1: 99. Ronald Hutton, *The Rise and Fall of Merry England: The Ritual Year 1400–1700* (Oxford: Clarendon Press, 1994), 28, 37–8.
61. British Library, Harl. MS 540, fo. 123r. Valerie Pearl, 'John Stow', *Transactions of the London and Middlesex Archaeological Society* 30 (1979), 130–4; and 'Introduction', in Valerie Pearl, *Stow, A Survey of London* (London, 1987), x–xi.
62. *A Survey of London*, 1: 264.
63. *A Survey of London*, 1: 316, 2: 34.
64. *A Survey of London*, 1: 188.
65. *A Survey of London*, 2: 11.
66. See 'Water Supply', in Ben Weinreb and Christopher Hibbert, eds., *The London Encyclopaedia*, 2nd edn. (London: Papermac, 1993), 953–9.
67. *A Survey of London*, 1: 12.
68. *A Survey of London*, 1: 19.
69. *A Survey of London*, 1: 20.
70. *A Survey of London*, 1: xl; 213 refers to Drake as 'that famous mariner'. Stow's manuscripts and the *Annales of England* include references to Drake and other Elizabethan seamen.
71. *A Survey of London*, 1: 93.
72. See Williams, *The Later Tudors*, 408–9 and sources listed in footnotes.
73. *A Survey of London*, 1: 44.
74. *A Survey of London*, 1: 326, 345, 2: 104–8.
75. *A Survey of London* (London, 1598), 449.
76. *A Survey of London*, 2: 186-7.
77. See, for example, Archer, *The Pursuit of Stability*, Frank Freeman Foster, *The Politics of Stability: A Portrait of the Rulers in Elizabethan London* (London: Royal Historical Society, 1977), and Rappaport, *Worlds within Worlds*.
78. *A Survey of London*, 2: 190.
79. *A Survey of London*, 2: 218. Stow's vision of London as an international city is reflected in a fragmented and anecdotal account that recognized trade with the outside world but failed to focus on the subject so that an outsider would be able to comprehend London's growing importance in the world economy.
80. *A Survey of London*, 2: 102.
81. David Starkey *et al.*, *The English Court: From the Wars of the Roses to the Civil War* (London: Longman, 1987), 19.
82. *A Survey of London*, 2: 112, 117.
83. *A Survey of London*, 2: 119–20.
84. Power, 'John Stow and his London', *Journal of Historical Geography* 11 (1985), 1–20.

85. Rappaport, *Worlds within Worlds*, 16.

86. Rappaport, *Worlds within Worlds*, 11. Although Rappaport used a wide range of sources, he curiously neglected the *Annales of England*, which contain Stow's strongest statements about social instability.

87. Archer, *The Pursuit of Stability*, 1–17, 257–60; 'The Nostalgia of John Stow', in Smith *et al.*, eds., *The Theatrical City*, 25–7.

88. See, for example, Peter Clark, ed., *The European Crisis of the 1590s* (London: Allen and Unwin, 1985), 44–66.

89. Manning, *Village Revolts*, 208.

90. Rappaport, *Worlds within Worlds*, 377–8.

91. Manning, *Village Revolts*, 190.

92. Richard Helgerson, *Forms of Nationhood: The Elizabethan Writing of England* (Chicago: University of Chicago Press, 1992), 301.

93. *A Survey of London* (London, 1598), sig. a2r.

94. Helgerson, *Forms of Nationhood*, 131–47, 297; and Lawrence Manley, 'Of Sites and Rites', in Smith *et al.*, eds., *The Theatrical City*, 35–54.

CHAPTER SEVEN

1. *Annales of England* (London, 1605), 1044.

2. *Annales of England* (London, 1605), 1048.

3. *Annales of England* (London, 1605), 1068.

4. *Annales of England* (London, 1605), 1070. Taking a swipe at his rival, Stow added that the history of Queen Mary had been written by Master George Ferrers and 'set down under the name of Richard Grafton'. *Summarie Abridged* (London, 1604), 266. Modern studies of this episode include, E.H. Harbison, *Rival Ambassadors at the Court of Queen Mary* (Princeton: Princeton University Press, 1940), 333–5; David Loades, *The Reign of Mary Tudor* (New York: St Martin's, 1979); and C.S.L. Davies, 'England and the French War, 1557–9', in Robert Tittler and Jennifer Loach, eds., *The Mid-Tudor Polity c. 1540–1560* (Totowa, NJ: Rowman and Littlefield, 1980), 159–85.

5. *Annales of England* (London, 1605), 1155–9. R.B. Wernham, *The Making of Elizabethan Foreign Policy, 1558–1603* (Berkeley, CA: University of California Press, 1980), 48–53. See also Wallace T. MacCaffrey, *Queen Elizabeth and the Making of Policy, 1572–1588* (Princeton, NJ: Princeton University Press, 1981), 227–8.

6. Modern works on the Armada include Garrett Mattingly, *The Armada* (Boston, 1959) and Colin Martin and Geoffrey Parker, *The Spanish Armada* (New York: Norton, 1988), but the latter work does little with historiography and chronicle accounts. See also R.B. Wernham, *After the Armada: Elizabethan England and the Struggle for Western Europe, 1588–1595* (Oxford: Clarendon Press, 1984) and Wallace T. MacCaffrey, *Elizabeth I: War and Politics, 1588–1603* (Princeton, NJ: Princeton University Press, 1992).

7. The copy, an octavo volume of 760 pages, at the Folger Shakespeare Library has no title page or preface. The title in the Folger catalogue has been taken from the British Library catalogue.

8. *Summarie* (London, 1590), 751.

9. *Summarie* (London, 1590), 751. See Cressy, *Bonfires and Bells*, 115n.14 for comments on the historicity of the queen's speech at Tilbury.

10. *Summarie* (London, 1590), 751–5.

11. Adams used the signature 'A. Ryther'. The best discussion of authorities for the Armada is Julian S. Corbett, *Drake and the Tudor Navy*, 2 vols. (London, 1912), 2: 412–21. See also Eugene L. Rasor, *The Spanish Armada of 1588: Historiography and Annotated Bibliography* (Westport, CT: Greenwood, 1993).

12. *Annales of England* (London, 1592), 1263–4.

13. *Annales of England* (London, 1592), 1280.

14. *Annales of England* (London, 1605), 1282–3. MacCaffrey, *Elizabeth I: War and Politics*, 114–15.

15. See William Slingsby, 'Relation of the Voyage to Cadiz, 1596', ed. J.S. Corbett, *Navy Records Society*

Miscellany 1 (1902), 23–92. The fullest discussion of the various accounts of the expedition may be found in Julian S. Corbett, *Successors to Drake* (London, 1900), 25–6.

16. *Annales of England* (London, 1605), 1293 (1) misnumbered page. See R.B. Wernham, *The Return of the Armadas: The Last Years of the Elizabethan War Against Spain, 1598–1603* (Oxford: Clarendon Press, 1994), 93–129.

17. *Annales of England* (London, 1605), 1300–2.

18. Samuel Purchas, *Purchas His Pilgrimage* (London, 1625), IV, 1935–8.

19. *Summarie Abridged* (London, 1604), 411. This edition curiously neglected to inform the reader that the expedition went to the Azores. A modern account of the expedition may be found in Wernham, *The Return of the Armadas*, 159–90.

20. See Raphael Maffeius (Volanterranus), *Historia de vita quattuor Maxi. Ponti . . .* (1518) [British Library shelf-mark, 4855.h.3.] which includes lives of Sixtus IV, Innocent VIII, Alexander VI, and Pius III.

21. *Annales of England* (London, 1605), 1402–3.

22. *Annales of England* (London, 1605), 1430–1.

23. *Annales of England* (London, 1605), 1067–8.

24. MacCaffrey, *The Shaping of the Elizabethan Regime*, 117–41. See also Conyers Read, *Mr. Secretary Cecil and Queen Elizabeth* (London: Jonathan Cape, 1962), 239–60.

25. *Annales of England* (London, 1605), 1096. See *Calendar of State Papers Foreign 1562* (London, 1867), nos. 667–74 for several drafts of 'Why the Queen Puts Her Subjects in Arms' written by Sir William Cecil.

26. MacCaffrey, *The Shaping of the Elizabethan Regime*, 127f.; Guy, *Tudor England*, 267–8.

27. *Annales of England* (London, 1605), 1102.

28. *Annales of England* (London, 1605), 1111.

29. Stow's account in *Annales of England* (1605) may be compared with the *Chronicles of England* (1580), 1122ff. and the lengthy account in the second edition of *Holinshed's Chronicles*, 4: 204–23. Although the *Annales* and Holinshed both give great prominence to Ambrose Dudley, Holinshed is more enthusiastic and offers a better discussion of policy issues. In marginal notes, 4: 221, 223, Holinshed refers to 'additions of Lanquet'. Since Lanquet died in 1545, this is probably a reference to Cooper's chronicle of 1565. On page 223 'John Stow' is cited without indicating what work the Holinshed editors used.

30. See STC 22241. This reference is not mentioned in *Holinshed's Chronicles* under '1573'.

31. *Annales of England* (London, 1605), 1141, 1148. See also MacCaffrey, *Queen Elizabeth and the Making of Policy*, 177.

32. *Annales of England* (London, 1605), 1137–8. MacCaffrey, *The Shaping of the Elizabethan Regime*, 440–3; *Queen Elizabeth and the Making of Policy*, 164–7; Guy, *Tudor England*, 278.

33. *Annales of England* (London, 1605), 1167; *Holinshed's Chronicles*, 4: 435–45.

34. *Annales of England* (London, 1605), 1168-9. For an account of the courtship, see Neale, *Queen Elizabeth I*, 260–3; Charles Wilson, *Queen Elizabeth and the Revolt of the Netherlands* (London: Macmillan, 1970), 74–5; and Williams, *The Later Tudors*, 284–5.

35. *Annales of England* (London, 1605) 1290–8.

36. *Annales of England* (London, 1605), 1264, 1264 (2), 1266. For a detailed account of these military operations see MacCaffrey, *Elizabeth I: War and Politics*, 140–2.

37. See Wilson, *Queen Elizabeth and the Revolt of the Netherlands* and MacCaffrey, *Queen Elizabeth and the Making of Policy*

38. British Library, Harl. MS 247, fos. 202–3. *Annales of England* (London, 1605), 1112.

39. *Annales of England* (London, 1605), 1122.

40. *Annales of England* (London, 1605), 1171. MacCaffrey, *Queen Elizabeth and the Making of Policy*, 243–4, 279.

41. *Annales of England* (London, 1605), 1173. Stow gives an incorrect date for Anjou's death, but several modern historians have also got it wrong. See Neale, *Queen Elizabeth I*, 263; Wilson, *Queen Elizabeth and the Revolt of the Netherlands*, 77; and Wernham, *The Making of Elizabethan Foreign Policy*, 55.

42. *Annales of England* (London, 1605), 1184–6 and *Holinshed's Chronicles*, 4: 616–30. The two accounts

are very similar at the beginning, but Holinshed gives the deputies' oration in French and English and what appears to be a full text of the queen's declaration, *A Declaration of the Causes Moouing the Queene . . .* Dated at Richmond 1 October, 1585.

43. *Annales of England* (London, 1605), 1188–9.

44. *Annales of England* (London, 1605), 1201, 1239. Arms were granted to Henry Archer of Theydon Gernon, Essex on 2 April 1575. *Calendar of State Papers Domestic: 1547–1580* (London, 1850), 495. Archer sent letters from the Netherlands with military news for his master, Sir Thomas Heneage on 16 May 1586 [*Calendar of State Papers, Foreign, 1585-86*, vol. 20 (London, 1921), 633–4] and 23 October 1586 [John Bruce, ed., *Correspondence of Robert Dudley, Earl of Leycester during His Government of the Low Countries* (London, 1844), 478–80]. There is a reference to 'a book penned' by Henry Archer, one of the guards to Leicester, in *Holinshed's Chronicle*, 4: 660. For Leicester's campaign in the Netherlands see R.C. Strong and J.A. Van Dorsten, *Leicester's Triumph* (Leiden: Sir Thomas Browne Institute, 1964) and Alan Haynes, *The White Bear: Robert Dudley, The Elizabethan Earl of Leicester* (London: P. Owen, 1987).

45. *Annales of England* (London, 1605), 1221–31.

46. *Annales of England* (London, 1605), 1233.

47. *Annales of England* (London, 1605), 1243.

48. Wilson, *Queen Elizabeth and the Revolt of the Netherlands*, 101; MacCaffrey, *Queen Elizabeth and the Making of Policy*, 387–90; Haynes, *The White Bear*, 200; Guy, *Tudor England*, 286–9, 338.

49. James Gairdner, ed., *Three Fifteenth-Century Chronicles*, i–iv, 129–30. This volume prints long extracts from Lambeth MS 306. *Annales of England* (London, 1605), 1114. The emperor died while the queen was negotiating a possible marriage treaty with Charles, Archduke of Austria. For further information see Neale, *Queen Elizabeth I*, 142–3.

50. *Annales of England* (London, 1605), 1264. See also Lawrence Stone, *An Elizabethan: Sir Horatio Palavicino* (Oxford: Clarendon Press, 1956), 167–74; Wernham, *After the Armada*, 264–301.

51. *Annales of England* (London, 1605), 1174–5.

52. British Library, Harl. MS 247, fo. 218 is very similar to the printed accounts in *Annales of England* (London, 1605), 1302–4 and Howes, ed., *Annales of England* (1631), 784–5. See Wernham, *The Return of the Armadas*, 199–201 and the authorities cited.

53. *Annales of England* (London, 1605), 1029. See also T.S. Willan, *The Early History of the Russia Company, 1553–1603* (Manchester: Manchester University Press, 1956), 1–18 and D.M. Palliser, *The Age of Elizabeth: England under the Later Tudors 1547–1603*, 2nd edn., (London: Longman, 1992), 334–5.

54. *Annales of England* (London, 1605), 1064–7.

55. British Library, Harl. MS 247, fo. 208. The author of the first narrative wrote, 'In one house perished Thomas Sowtham and Thomas Field' and adds that twenty-five persons died 'in our house'. According to the second narrative thirty died. See Willan, *The Early History of the Russia Company*, 130–1, which states that company servants who escaped were William Rowley, chief agent, Thomas Glover, and Ralph Rutter. 'The company estimated its material losses in the fire at more than 10,000 roubles, that is more than 6600 pounds, and for this loss the Tsar refused to accept any responsibility.'

56. E. Delmar Morgan and C. H. Coote, eds., *Early Voyages and Travels to Russian and Persia*, 2 vols. (London: Hakluyt Society, 1886), 2: 338–40.

57. *Calendar of State Papers Foreign Series of the Reign of Elizabeth, 1569–71*, ed. A.J. Crosby (London, 1874) 2 July 1571, no. 1842. Public Record Office, SP70/119, fo. 3.

58. Further information about the fire at Moscow may be found in Edward A. Bond, ed., *Russia at the Close of the Sixteenth Century* (London: Hakluyt Society, 1856) and Lloyd E. Berry and Robert O. Crummey, eds., *Rude and Barbarous Kingdom: Russia in the Accounts of Sixteenth-Century English Voyages* (Madison, WI: University of Wisconsin Press, 1968).

59. *Annales of England* (London, 1605), 1404–5.

60. Howes, ed., *Annales of England* (1631), 791–2. None of Howes' account appears in the edition of 1605. Neither author showed any knowledge or understanding of the issues affecting Anglo-Russian relations. For a discussion of these see Willan, *The Early History of the Russia Company*, 236–8.

61. For diplomatic relations between the two countries, see Walther Kirchner, 'England and Denmark, 1558–1588', *Journal of Modern History* 17 (1945), 1–15 and Arthur J. Slavin, 'Daniel Rogers in Copenhagen, 1588: Mission and Memory', in Malcolm R. Thorp and A.J. Slavin, eds., *Politics, Religion, and Diplomacy in Early Modern Europe: Essays in Honor of De Lamar Jensen*, (Kirksville, MO: Sixteenth Century Journal Publishers, 1994), 245–66.

62. *Annales of England* (London, 1605), 1170; *Holinshed's Chronicles*, 4: 495.

63. See Edward P. Cheyney, 'England and Denmark in the Later Days of Queen Elizabeth', *Journal of Modern History* 1 (1929), 9–39.

64. *Annales of England* (London, 1605), 1304–5.

65. *Annales of England* (London, 1605), 1307.

66. When Christian IV visited Theobalds in 1606, the English reciprocated with similar entertainment and drunken revelry. See D.H. Willson, *King James VI and I* (New York: Oxford University Press, 1967), 192–3.

67. *Annales of England* (London, 1605), 1433–7 [misnumbered pages].

68. *Annales of England* (London, 1605), 1084. See also Joannis Levenclavii, *De Moscovitarum Bellis Commentarius* in A. Starczewski, *Historiae Ruthenicae Scriptores Exteri Saeculi XVI* (Berolini et Petropoli, 1841), vol. 1.

69. *Annales of England* (London, 1605), 1134–5; *Summarie Abridged* (London, 1604), 298–9.

70. *Annales of England* (London, 1605), 1403–4; Howes, ed., *Annales of England* (1631), 791.

71. Hakluyt, *Divers Voyages*, sig. A3. A similar reference may be found in Richard Hakluyt, *The Principall Navigations of the English Nation*, Imprinted at London, 1589, 2 vols. (London, 1589: reprint Cambridge: Cambridge University Press, 1965), 2: 515.

72. Frobisher, who had been implicated in the unsuccessful attempt to transfer the crown to Lady Jane following the death of Edward VI, had close ties with the Dudley family.

73. *Annales of England* (London, 1605), 1152. Each of the three Frobisher voyages is mentioned in *Chronicles of England* (1580), which was published before the first edition of Hakluyt, *Principall Navigations*. Stow's narrative in *Annales* appears to be based on the account of the first voyage written by George Best, *A True Discourse of the Late Voyages of Discoverie, for the Finding of a Passage to Cathaya* (London, 1578), reprinted in *The Three Voyages of Martin Frobisher* (New York: Burt Franklin, *c.* 1963). Best's discourse was incorporated only in the second edition of *Principall Navigations* (1598). An excellent modern account of Frobisher's first voyage may be found in Kenneth R. Andrews, *Trade, Plunder, and Settlement: Maritime Enterprise and the Genesis of the British Empire, 1480–1630* (Cambridge: Cambridge University Press, 1984), 167–74.

74. *Annales of England* (London, 1605), 1154.

75. *Chronicles of England* (London, 1580), 1193. This chronicle was published before the first edition of Hakluyt's *Principall Navigations*. *Annales of England* (London, 1605), 1160. Stow also included a lengthy account of the three Frobisher voyages to 'Cathay' in *Summarie Abridged* (London, 1604), 317–26. George Best wrote *A True Discourse . . . .* Dedicated to Sir Christopher Hatton, it contains no references to Stow. See also Andrews, *Trade, Plunder and Settlement, 167–79* and A L. Rowse, *The Expansion of Elizabethan England, 190–4.*

76. British Library, Harl. MS 247, fo. 194; *Annales of England* (London, 1605), 1164–5. G.B. Parks, *Richard Hakluyt and the English Voyages*, 2nd edn. (New York: F. Ungar, 1961) and Andrews, *Trade, Plunder and Settlement*, 144–62.

77. *Annales of England* (London, 1605), 1187. Hakluyt, *Principall Navigations . . . ,* 2: 747–8. Andrews, *Trade, Plunder and Settlement*, 209–11.

78. *Annales of England* (London, 1605), 1204.

79. Howes, ed., *Annales of England* (1631), 808.

80. Andrews, *Trade, Plunder and Settlement*, 248.

81. For a different perspective on the achievements of the Elizabethans see Wernham, *The Return of the Armadas*, 411–15.

82. Helgerson, *Forms of Nationhood*.

CHAPTER EIGHT

1. For a discussion of pamphlets and broadsides see Bennett, *English Books and Readers*, 220f.
2. See Chapter One, p. 12.
3. *Annales of England* (London, 1592), 1126–7. The error was not corrected in the *Annales of England* (London, 1605), 1119. While Stow located the town 12 miles from Shrewsbury, modern authorities place it 18 miles to the north-west.
4. *Annales of England* (London, 1605), 4, 1428.
5. *The Summarie of Englyshe Chronicles . . . Abridged* (London, 1566), fo. 2v. [STC 23325.4]
6. Cf. Watt, *Cheap Print*, 328–32.
7. See Chapter One, p. 12.
8. Robert Parker Sorlien, ed., *The Diary of John Manningham of the Middle Temple 1602–1603* (Hanover, NH: University Press of New England, 1976), 154–5.
9. *A Survey of London*, 1: xxvii, lviii.
10. A.M., 'The Epistle Dedicatorie', *The Survey of London* (London, 1618). Munday wrote, 'I have (to my great cost, care, and no mean labour, both of body and mind, and for the space of above twelve years) done my diligent endeavour, to effect the full scope of that which I had set down to myself. . . .'
11. *A Survey of London Written in the Year 1598*, introduction by Antonia Fraser (Stroud: Sutton, 1994).
12. *Summarye* (London, 1590), 760.
13. *Annales of England* (London, 1592), sig. A2r.
14. British Library, Harl. MS 374, fo. 21.
15. *Annales of England* (London, 1605), 1438.
16. Howes, ed., *Annales of England* (1615), 811. *A Survey of England*, 1: xxi. *Successions of the History of England* no longer exists.
17. Pettegree, *Foreign Protestant Communities in Sixteenth-Century London*, 93.
18. British Library, Harl. MS 247, fos. 198, 199, 218; *A Survey of London*, 1: xxi.
19. British Library, Harl. MS 374, fo. 21; printed in *A Survey of London*, 1: lxxiii.
20. *A Survey of London*, 1: xxi–xxii.
21. Chapter Six, p. 143 n.78.
22. Lawrence Manley, *Literature and Culture in Early Modern London* (Cambridge: Cambridge University Press, 1995), 158, describes Stow as 'essentially an old-fashioned annalist'. See also Woolf, 'Genre into Artifact', *Sixteenth Century Journal* 19:3 (1988), 321–54.
23. Howes, ed., *The Abridgement* (London, 1607), sig. A4.
24. Strype, *A Survey*, 1: xii–xiii. See also E.H. Miller, *The Professional Writer in Elizabethan England* (Cambridge, MA: Harvard University Press, 1959), 244.
25. R.G. Lang, ed., *Two Tudor Subsidy Assessment Rolls for the City of London: 1541 and 1582* (London: HMSO, 1993). Stow was not assessed in 1541 and is not listed in the assessments at Guildhall.
26. *A Survey of London*, 1: xlv.
27. Palliser, *The Age of Elizabeth*, 412–20 and authorities cited; Keith Thomas, 'The Meaning of Literacy in Early Modern England', in Gerd Baumann, ed., *The Written Word: Literacy in Transition* (Oxford: Clarendon Press, 1986), 97–131.
28. Wright, *Middle-Class Culture in Elizabethan England*, 297–337. He also praised Stow's abridged chronicles, 'Certainly so much history had never before been packed into so convenient a pocket manual' (309).
29. Patterson, *Reading Holinshed's Chronicles*, 264–7.
30. Bennett, *English Books and Readers*, 217. 'Stow was obviously a most important figure in the story of Elizabethan historical publishing, and the continued reprints of his works reflect this.'
31. Patterson, *Reading Holinshed's Chronicles*, 266–76, argues that Holinshed was read by a select group of influential persons into the seventeenth century and beyond; Stow's chronicles were sufficiently popular to justify seventeenth-century editions while *A Survey of London* enjoyed even greater popularity.

BIBLIOGRAPHY

MANUSCRIPTS

British Library
  Egerton Manuscripts
  Harleian Manuscripts
  Stowe Manuscripts

Corporation of London Records Office

Folger Shakespeare Library, Washington, DC
  Manuscript V.b. 134

Guildhall Library, London

Public Record Office
  Court of Requests
  State Papers Domestic
  State Papers Foreign

PRINTED SOURCES

Beer, Barrett L. '"The Commoyson in Norfolk, 1549": A Narrative of Popular Rebellion in Sixteenth-Century England', *Journal of Medieval and Renaissance Studies* 6: 1 (1976): 73–99

Beer, Barrett L., ed. *The Life and Raigne of King Edward the Sixth by John Hayward*, Kent, OH and London: Kent State University Press, 1993

Berry, Lloyd E., and Crummey, Robert O., eds., *Rude and Barbarous Kingdom: Russia in the Accounts of Sixteenth-Century English Voyages*, Madison: University of Wisconsin Press, 1968

Bond, Edward A. *Russia at the Close of the Sixteenth Century*, London: Hakluyt Society, 1856

Breuiate Chronicle, London, 1561

Brodie, D.M., ed. *The Tree of Commonwealth: A Treatise Written by Edmund Dudley*, Cambridge: Cambridge University Press, 1948

Calendar of State Papers Foreign Series, 23 vols., London, 1863–1950

Calendar of State Papers Domestic Series of the Reigns of Edward VI, Mary, and Elizabeth, 12 vols., London, 1856–72

Calendar of State Papers Domestic Series 1547–1553, London, 1992

Calendar of State Papers Ireland 1586–1588 July, ed. H.C. Hamilton, London, 1877

Camden, William. *Annales Rerum Anglicarum et Hibernicarum*, London, 1615

——. *The History of the Most Renowned and Victorious Princess Elizabeth Late Queen of England*, 4th edn., London, 1688

——. *The History of the Most Renowned and Victorious Princess Elizabeth Late Queen of England*, ed. Wallace T. MacCaffrey, Chicago: University of Chicago Press, 1970

Cooper, Thomas. *Coopers Chronicle*, London, 1560

Cosin, Richard. *Conspiracie for Pretended Reformation . . .*, London, 1592

Crowley, Robert. *An Epitome of Chronicles*, London, 1559

Fabyan, Robert. *The Chronicles of Fabyan*, London, 1559

Foxe, John. *Acts and Monuments*, 3 vols., London, 1684

Gairdner, James, ed. *Three Fifteenth-Century Chronicles with Historical Memoranda by John Stowe*, London: Camden Society, 1880

Grafton, Richard. *An Abridgement of the Chronicles of England*, London, 1563

——. *A Chronicle at Large*, 2 vols., London, 1569

Hakluyt, Richard. *Divers Voyages Touching the Discouerie of America*, London, 1582

——. *The Principall Navigations of the English Nation, Imprinted at London, 1589*, 2 vols., London, 1589; reprint Cambridge: Cambridge University Press, 1965

Hall's Chronicle, London, 1809; reprint New York: AMS Press, 1965

Holinshed, Raphael. *The Firste Volume of the Chronicles of England, Scotlande, and Irelande*, 3 vols., London, 1577

——. *First and Second Volumes of Chronicles*, 3 vols. London, 1587

Holinshed's Chronicles of England, Scotland and Ireland, 6 vols., London, 1808; reprint New York: AMS Press, 1965

Hughes, Paul L., and Larkin, James F., eds. *Tudor Royal Proclamations*, 2 vols., New Haven, CT: Yale University Press, 1964–9

Kingsford, Charles Lethbridge, ed. *A Survey of London by John Stow*, 2 vols., Oxford: Clarendon Press, 1908 (reprinted 1971)

Lang, R.G., ed. *Two Tudor Subsidy Assessment Rolls for the City of London: 1541 and 1582*, London: HMSO, 1993

Miscellany of the Celtic Society, ed. J. O'Donovan, Dublin, 1849

Morgan, E. Delmar, and Coote, C.H. *Early Travels to Russia and Persia*, 2 vols., London: Hakluyt Society, 1866

Mychell, John. *A Breuiat Cronicle Contaynynge All the Kings from Brute to This Day*, Canterbury, 1553 [1553/4]

Neville, Alexander. *Alexandri Neuylli Angli de Furoribus Norfolciensium Ketto Duce*, London, 1575

Nichols, J.G., ed. *Diary of Henry Machyn*, London: Camden Society, 1847

——. *Chronicles of Queen Jane and Two Years of Queen Mary*, London: Camden Society, 1850

——. *Chronicle of the Grey Friars of London*, London: Camden Society, 1852

Pollard, A.F. *Tudor Tracts, 1532–1588*, New York, 1903

Proctor, John. *The History of Wyates Rebellion*, London, 1554

Purchas, Samuel. *Purchas His Pilgrimage*, London, 1625

Smith, Thomas. *De Republica Anglorum*, London, 1583

Sorlien, R.P., ed. *The Diary of John Manningham of the Middle Temple 1602–1603*, Hanover, NH: University Press of New England, 1976

Stow, John: chronicles in order of publication:

A Summarie of Englyshe Chronicles, London, 1565

The Summarie of Englyshe Chronicles . . . Nowe Abridged . . ., London, 1566

The Summarie of Englyshe Chronicles . . . Nowe Abridged . . ., London, 1567

The Summary of the Chronicles of England Lately Collected, Newly Corrected and Continued vnto This Present Yeare of Christ 1573, London, 1573

The Summarie of the Chronicles of Englande . . . Abridged . . . , London, 1579

The Chronicles of England, London, 1580

A Summarie of the Chronicles of England [abridgement], London, 1587

Annales of England, London, 1592

Annales of England, London, 1601

A Summarie of the Chronicles of England [abridgement], London, 1604

Annales of England, London, 1605

The Abridgement or Summarie of the English Chronicles, ed. Edmund Howes, London, 1607

Annales or a Generall Chronicle of England, ed. Edmund Howes, London, 1615

Annales or a Generall Chronicle of England, ed. Edmund Howes, London, 1631

Stow, John: other works:

Certaine Worthye Manuscript Poems of Great Antiquitie Reserued Long in the Studie of a Northfolke Gentleman, London, 1597

Pithy Pleasaunt and Profitable Workes of Maister Skelton, London, 1568

A Recital of Stow's Collection concerning the Rise of the Court of Requests, London, ?1640 [Library of Congress 23346]

The Worke of Geffrey Chaucer Newly Printed with Diuers Additions, London, 1561

A Suruay of London, London, 1598

A Suruay of London, London, 1599 [British Library G. 5972]

A Suruay of London, London, 1603

Stow's Survey of London. Introduction by H.B. Wheatley. London: Dent, 1965

Strype, John, ed. *A Survey of the Cities of London and Westminster*, 2 vols., London, 1720

Tawney, R.H., and Power, Eileen, eds. *Tudor Economic Documents*, 3 vols., London: Longmans, 1924

Wriothesley, Charles. *A Chronicle of England*, ed. W.D. Hamilton, 2 vols., London: Camden Society, 1877

SECONDARY WORKS

Andrews, Kenneth R. *Trade, Plunder, and Settlement: Maritime Enterprise and the Genesis of the British Empire, 1480–1630*, Cambridge: Cambridge University Press, 1984

Archer, Ian W. *The Pursuit of Stability: Social Relations in Elizabethan London*, Cambridge: Cambridge University Press, 1991

——. 'The Nostalgia of John Stow', in D.L. Smith, R. Strier, and D. Bevington, eds., *The Theatrical City: Culture, Theatre and Politics in London, 1576–1649*, Cambridge: Cambridge University Press, 1995

Baron, Hans. *In Search of Florentine Civic Humanism*, 2 vols., Princeton, NJ: Princeton University Press, 1988

Bartlett, Kenneth R. 'The English Exile Community in Italy and the Political Opposition to Queen Mary I', *Albion* 13 (1981): 223–41

Baumann, Gerd, ed. *The Written Word: Literacy in Transition*, Oxford: Clarendon Press, 1986

Beer, Barrett L. *Northumberland: The Political Career of John Dudley, Duke of Northumberland and Earl of Warwick*, Kent, OH: Kent State University Press, 1973

——. 'Northumberland: The Myth of the Wicked Duke and the Historical John Dudley', *Albion* 11 (1979): 1–14

——. *Rebellion and Riot: Popular Disorder during the Reign of Edward VI*, Kent, OH: Kent State University Press, 1985

——. 'Episcopacy and Reform in Mid-Tudor England', *Albion* 23 (1991): 231–52

Beier, A.L. *The Problem of the Poor in Tudor and Early Stuart England*, London: Methuen, 1983

——. *Masterless Men: The Vagrancy Problem in England, 1560–1640*, London: Methuen, 1985

Beier, A.L., and Finlay, Roger, eds. *London 1500–1700: The Making of the Metropolis*, London: Longman, 1986

Bennett, H.S. *English Books and Readers 1558 to 1603*, Cambridge: Cambridge University Press, 1965

Berkowitz, David Sandler. *Humanist Scholarship and Public Order*, Washington, DC: Folger Shakespeare Library, 1984

Brigden, Susan. *London and the Reformation*, Oxford: Clarendon Press, 1991

Brooke, C.F. Tucker. *The Shakespeare Apocrypha: Being a Collection of Fourteen Plays Which Have Been Ascribed to Shakespeare*, Oxford: Clarendon Press, 1908, 1967

Burke, Peter. *Popular Culture in Early Modern Europe*, New York: Harper and Row, 1978

Bush, M.L. *The Government Policy of Protector Somerset*, Montreal: McGill-Queen's University Press, 1974

Canny, Nicholas. *Kingdom and Colony: Ireland in the Atlantic World 1560–1800*, Baltimore, MD: Johns Hopkins University Press, 1988

Capp, Bernard. *English Almanacs 1500–1800: Astrology and the Popular Press*, Ithaca, NY: Cornell University Press, 1979

Carlson, L.H., ed. *The Writings of John Greenwood and Henry Barrow, 1591–1593*, London: Allen and Unwin, 1970

Cheyney, Edward P. 'England and Denmark in the Later Days of Queen Elizabeth', *Journal of Modern History* 1 (1929): 9–39

Chrisman, Miriam U. 'Lay Response to the Protestant Reformation in Germany, 1520–1528', in Peter N. Brooks, ed. *Reformation Principle and Practice*, London: Scolar Press, 1980

Clark, Peter. *English Provincial Society from the Reformation to the Revolution: Politics and Society in Kent, 1500–1640*, Hassocks: Harvester Press, 1977

———, ed. *The European Crisis of the 1590s*, London: Allen and Unwin, 1985

Clode, Charles M. *Memorials of the Guild of Merchant Taylors*, London, 1875

———. *The Early History of the Guild of Merchant Taylors*, 2 vols., London, 1888

Collinson, Patrick. *The Elizabethan Puritan Movement*, London: Jonathan Cape, 1967

———. *Archbishop Grindal, 1519–1583: The Struggle for a Reformed Church*, London: Jonathan Cape, 1979

Corbett, Julian S. *Successors to Drake*, London, 1900

———. *Drake and the Tudor Navy*, 2 vols., London, 1912

Cressy, David. *Bonfires and Bells: National Memory and the Protestant Calendar in Elizabethan and Stuart England*, Berkeley, CA: University of California Press, 1989

Devereux, E.J. 'Empty Tuns and Unfruitful Grafts: Richard Grafton's Historical Publications', *Sixteenth Century Journal* 21: 1 (1990): 33–56

Dewar, Mary. *Sir Thomas Smith: A Tudor Intellectual in Office*, London: Athlone Press, 1964

Dexter, Henry Martyn. *The Congregationalism of the Last Three Hundred Years*, 2 vols., New York: Burt Franklin, 1970

Dickens, A.G. *The English Reformation*, 2nd edn., University Park, PA: Pennsylvania State University Press, 1991

Dickens, A.G., and Tonkin, John. *The Reformation in Historical Thought*, Cambridge, MA: Harvard University Press, 1985

Dowling, Maria and Shakespeare, Joy. 'Religion and Politics in Mid-Tudor England through the Eyes of an English Protestant Woman: the Recollections of Rose Hickman', *Bulletin of the Institute of Historical Research* 55 (1982): 94–102

Duffy, Eamon. *The Stripping of the Altars: Traditional Religion in England c. 1400– c. 1580*, New Haven, CT: Yale University Press, 1992

Ellis, Steven G. *Tudor Ireland: Crown, Community and Conflict of Cultures, 1470–1603*, London: Longman, 1985

Elton, G.R. *England 1200–1640*, London: The Sources of History Ltd, 1969

Emmison, F.G. *Tudor Secretary: Sir William Petre at Court and Home*, London: Longmans, 1961

Evans, Joan. *A History of the Society of Antiquaries*, Oxford: Oxford University Press, 1956

Falls, Cyril. *Elizabeth's Irish Wars*, New York: Barnes and Noble, 1970

Fideler, Paul A., and Mayer, T. F., eds. *Political Thought and the Tudor Commonwealth*, London: Routledge, 1992

Fletcher, Anthony. *Tudor Rebellions*, 3rd edn., Harlow, Essex: Longman, 1983

Fletcher, Anthony, and Stevenson, John. *Order and Disorder in Early Modern England*, Cambridge: Cambridge University Press, 1985

Foster, Frank Freeman. *The Politics of Stability: A Portrait of the Rulers in Elizabethan London*, London: Royal Historical Society, 1977

Foster, R.F., ed. *The Oxford History of Ireland*, Oxford: Oxford University Press, 1989

French, Peter J. *John Dee: The World of an Elizabethan Magus*, London: Routledge and Kegan Paul, 1972

Fuller, Thomas. *The History of the Worthies of England*, New York: AMS Press, 1965

Fussner, F. Smith. *The Historical Revolution: English Historical Writing and Thought, 1580–1640*, London: Routledge and Kegan Paul, 1962

Garrett, C.H. *The Marian Exiles*, Cambridge: Cambridge University Press, 1938

Graves, Michael A.R. *The Tudor Parliaments: Crown, Lords and Commons, 1485–1603*, London: Longman, 1985

Guy, John. *Tudor England*, Oxford: Oxford University Press, 1990

Haigh, Christopher. *English Reformations: Religion, Politics, and Society under the Tudors*, Oxford: Clarendon Press, 1993

Haller, William. *Foxe's Book of Martyrs and the Elect Nation*, London: Jonathan Cape, 1967

Hamilton, Alastair. *The Family of Love*, Cambridge: J. Clarke, 1981

Hartley, T.E. *Elizabeth's Parliaments: Queen, Lords and Commons, 1559–1601*, Manchester: Manchester University Press, 1992

Haugaard, William P. *Elizabeth and the English Reformation*, Cambridge: Cambridge University Press, 1968

Haynes, Alan. *The White Bear: Robert Dudley, The Elizabethan Earl of Leicester*, London: P. Owen, 1987

Heal, Felicity. *Hospitality in Early Modern England*, Oxford: Clarendon Press, 1990

Helgerson, Richard. *Forms of Nationhood: The Elizabethan Writing of England*, Chicago: University of Chicago Press, 1992

Hill, Christopher. 'The Many-Headed Monster in Late Tudor and Early Stuart Political Thinking', in Charles H. Carter, ed., *From the Renaissance to the Counter-Reformation: Essays in Honor of Garrett Mattingly*, New York: Random House, 1965

——. *The Collected Essays of Christopher Hill*, 3 vols., Amherst: University of Massachusetts Press, 1986

Hoak, D.E. *The King's Council in the Reign of Edward VI*, Cambridge: Cambridge University Press, 1976

Howell, Roger. *Sir Philip Sidney: Shepherd Knight*, London: Hutchinson, 1968

Hudson, Winthrop S. *John Ponet (1516?–1556): Advocate of Limited Monarchy*, Chicago: University of Chicago Press, 1942

——. *The Cambridge Connection and the Elizabethan Settlement of 1559*, Durham, NC: Duke University Press, 1980

Hutton, Ronald. *The Rise and Fall of Merry England: The Ritual Year 1400–1700*, Oxford: Clarendon Press, 1994

James, Mervyn. *Family, Lineage, and Civil Society*, Oxford: Clarendon Press, 1974

——. *Society, Politics and Culture: Studies in Early Modern England*, Cambridge: Cambridge University Press, 1986

Johnson, Francis R. 'Notes on English Retail Book-Prices, 1550–1640', *The Library*, 5th series, 5: 2 (1950): 83–112

Johnson, Paul. *Elizabeth I: A Study in Power and Intellect*, London: Weidenfeld and Nicholson, 1974

Jones, Norman L. *Faith by Statute: Parliament and the Settlement of Religion 1559*, London: Royal Historical Society, 1982

——. *The Birth of the Elizabethan Age: England in the 1560s*, Oxford: Blackwell, 1995

Jordan, W.K. *The Development of Religious Toleration in England*, 4 vols., Cambridge, MA: Harvard University Press, 1932–40

——. *The Charities of London: 1480–1660*, New York: Russell Sage Foundation, 1960

——. *Edward VI: The Young King*, London: George Allen and Unwin, 1968

——. *Edward VI: The Threshold of Power*, London: George Allen and Unwin, 1970

Katz, David S. *The Jews in the History of England, 1485–1850*, Oxford: Clarendon Press, 1994

Kearney, Hugh. *The British Isles: A History of Four Nations*, Cambridge: Cambridge University Press, 1989

Kermode, Jennifer, and Walker, Garthine, eds. *Women, Crime and the Courts in Early Modern England*, Chapel Hill: University of North Carolina Press, 1994

King, John N. *English Reformation Literature*, Princeton, NJ: Princeton University Press, 1982

Kinney, Arthur F., and the Editors of *ELR*. *Sidney In Retrospect: Selections from English Literary Renaissance*, Amherst: University of Massachusetts Press, 1988

Kirchner, Walther. 'England and Denmark, 1558–1588', *Journal of Modern History* 17 (1945): 1–15

LaCapra, Dominick. *History and Criticism*, Ithaca, NY: Cornell University Press, 1985

Lacey, Robert. *Robert Earl of Essex, An Elizabethan Icarus*, London: Weidenfeld and Nicolson, 1971

Levin, Carole. *Tudor Historical Thought,* San Marino, CA: Huntington Library, 1967

——. '*The Heart and Stomach of a King*': *Elizabeth I and the Politics of Sex and Power*, Philadelphia: University of Pennsylvania Press, 1994

Levy, F.J. 'Lady Jane Grey: Protestant Queen and Martyr', in Margaret P. Hannay, ed., *Silent But for the Word: Tudor Women as Patrons, Translators, and Writers of Religious Works*, Kent, OH: Kent State University Press, 1985

Lewis, John. *The History and Antiquities of . . . Faversham in Kent*, n.p., 1727

Loach, Jennifer. *Parliament and the Crown in the Reign of Mary Tudor*, Oxford: Clarendon Press, 1986

Loades, D.M. *The Reign of Mary Tudor*, New York: St. Martin's Press, 1979

——. *Two Tudor Conspiracies*, Bangor, Gwynedd: Headstart History, 1992

——. *Tudor Government: Structures of Authority in the Sixteenth Century*, Oxford: Blackwell, 1997

Logan, F. Donald. *Norman London by William Fitz Stephen*, New York: Italica Press, 1990

Lowers, James K. *Mirrors for Rebels: A Study of the Polemical Literature relating to the Northern Rebellions*, 1569, Berkeley, CA: University of California Press, 1953

MacCaffrey, Wallace T *The Shaping of the Elizabethan Regime*, Princeton, NJ: Princeton University Press, 1968

——. *Queen Elizabeth and the Making of Policy, 1572–1588*, Princeton, NJ: Princeton University Press, 1981

——. *Elizabeth I: War and Politics 1588–1603*, Princeton, NJ: Princeton University Press, 1992

MacCulloch, Diarmaid. *Suffolk and the Tudors*, Oxford: Clarendon Press, 1986

McGinn, Donald J. *John Penry and the Marprelate Controversy*, New Brunswick, NJ: Rutgers University Press, 1966

McKisack, May. *Medieval History in the Tudor Age*, Oxford: Clarendon Press, 1971

Manley, Lawrence. *Literature and Culture in Early Modern London*, Cambridge: Cambridge University Press, 1995

Manning, Roger B. *Village Revolts: Social Protest and Popular Disturbances in England, 1509–1640*, Oxford: Clarendon Press, 1988

Marsh, Christopher W. *The Family of Love in English Society*, Cambridge: Cambridge University Press, 1994

Martin, Colin, and Parker, Geoffrey. *The Spanish Armada*, New York: Norton, 1988

Martin, J.W. *Religious Radicals in Tudor England*, London: Hambleton Press, 1989

Mattingly, Garrett. *The Armada*, Boston: Houghton Mifflin, 1959

Mayer, Thomas F., and Woolf, D.R., eds. *The Rhetorics of Life-Writing in Early Modern Europe*, Ann Arbor: University of Michigan Press, 1995

Meyers, Charles. 'Lawsuits in Elizabethan Courts of Law: The Adventures of Dr. Hector Nunez, 1566–1591: A Precis', *The Journal of European Economic History* 25: 1 (1996), 157–68

Miller, E.H. *The Professional Writer in Elizabethan England*, Cambridge, MA: Harvard University Press, 1959

Miskimin, Alice S. *The Renaissance Chaucer*, New Haven, CT: Yale University Press, 1975

Moody, T.W., Martin, F.X. and Byrne, F.J., eds. A New History of Ireland, III, *Early Modern Ireland 1534–1691*, Oxford: Clarendon Press, 1991

Mozley, J.F. *John Foxe and His Book*, New York: Macmillan, 1940

Neale, J.E. 'John Stow', *Transactions of the London and Middlesex Archaeological Society* 10 (1951): 276–9

——. *Queen Elizabeth I*, New York: Doubleday, 1957

——. *Elizabeth I and Her Parliaments, 1559–1581*, New York: W.W. Norton, 1966

Nicholl, Charles. *The Reckoning: The Murder of Christopher Marlowe*, New York: Harcourt Brace, 1992

Nolan, John S. 'The Militarization of the Elizabethan State', *The Journal of Military History* 58: 3 (1994): 391–420

Orlin, Lena Cowen. *Private Matters and Public Culture in Post-Reformation England*, Ithaca, NY: Cornell University Press, 1994

Owen, Geraint D. *Wales in the Reign of James I*, Woodbridge: Boydell Press, 1988

Palliser, D.M. *The Age of Elizabeth: England under the Later Tudors 1547–1603*, 2nd edn., London: Longman, 1992

Park, Katherine, and Daston, Lorraine J. 'Unnatural Conceptions: The Study of Monsters in Sixteenth-Century and Seventeenth-Century France and England', *Past and Present* 92 (1981): 20–54

Patterson, Annabel. *Censorship and Interpretation: The Conditions of Writing in Early Modern England*, Madison: University of Wisconsin Press, 1984

——. *Reading Holinshed's Chronicles*, Chicago: University of Chicago Press, 1994

Pearl, Valerie. 'John Stow', *Transactions of the London and Middlesex Archaeological Society* 30 (1979), 130–4

Pettegree, Andrew. *Foreign Protestant Communities in Sixteenth-Century London*, Oxford: Clarendon Press, 1986

Pollard, A.F. *England under Protector Somerset*, London, 1900

Power, M.J. 'John Stow and his London', *Journal of Historical Geography* 11 (1985), 1–20

Rappaport, Steve. *Worlds within Worlds: The Structures of Life in Sixteenth-Century London*, Cambridge: Cambridge University Press, 1989

Rasor, Eugene L. *The Spanish Armada of 1588: Historiography and Annotated Bibliography*, Westport, CT: Greenwood, 1993

Read, Conyers. *Mr. Secretary Cecil and Queen Elizabeth*, London: Jonathan Cape, 1962

Redworth, Glyn. *In Defence of the Church Catholic: The Life of Stephen Gardiner*, Oxford: Blackwell, 1990

Reid, R.R. 'The Rebellions of the Earls, 1569', *Transactions of the Royal Historical Society*, n.s., 20 (1906)

Richardson, Walter C. *History of the Court of Augmentations: 1536–1554*, Baton Rouge: Louisiana State University Press, 1961

Rose-Troup. Frances. *The Western Rebellion of 1549*, London, 1913

Rosenberg, Eleanor. *Leicester: Patron of Letters*, New York: Columbia University Press, 1955

Roth, Cecil. *A History of the Jews in England*, 3rd edn., Oxford: Clarendon Press, 1964

Rowse, A.L. *The Expansion of Elizabethan England*, New York: Harper and Row, 1955

——. *The England of Elizabeth: The Structure of Society*, New York: Collier Books, 1966

Sessions, William K. *John Mychell, Canterbury's First Printer*, York: Ebor Press, 1983

Sharp, Buchanan. *In Contempt of All Authority: Rural Artisans and Riot in the West of England, 1586–1660*, Berkeley, CA: University of California Press, 1980

Sharp, Sir Cuthbert. *Memorials of the Rebellion of 1569*, London, 1840

Sharpe, J.A. *Crime In Early Modern England: 1550–1750*, London: Longman, 1984

——. *Judicial Punishment in England*, London: Faber and Faber, 1990

Sheils, W.J. *The Puritans in the Diocese of Peterborough, 1558–1610*, Northampton: Northamptonshire Record Society, 1979

Sherman, William H. *John Dee: The Politics of Reading and Writing in the English Renaissance*, Amherst: University of Massachusetts Press, 1995

Siebert, Fredrick S. *Freedom of the Press in England, 1476–1776*, Urbana: University of Illinois Press, 1965

Sisson, C.J. 'A Colony of Jews in Shakespeare's London', *Essays and Studies by Members of the English Association* 23 (1938), 38–51

Slack, Paul. *The Impact of Plague in Tudor and Stuart England*, London: Routledge and Kegan Paul, 1985

Slavin, A.J. 'Daniel Rogers in Copenhagen, 1588', in *Politics, Religion, and Diplomacy in Early Modern Europe: Essays in Honor of De Lamar Jensen*, Kirksville, MO: Sixteenth Century Journal Publishers, 1994

Smith, Lacey Baldwin. *Treason in Tudor England: Politics and Paranoia*, Princeton, NJ: Princeton University Press, 1986

Spufford, Margaret. *Small Books and Pleasant Histories*, Athens: University of Georgia Press, 1982

Starkey, David, et al. *The English Court: From the Wars of the Roses to the Civil War*, London: Longman, 1987

Stone, Lawrence. *An Elizabethan: Sir Horatio Palavicino*, Oxford: Clarendon Press, 1956

Strong, Roy, and Van Dorsten, J.A. *Leicester's Triumph*, Leiden: Sir Thomas Browne Institute, 1964

Strype, John. *The History of the Life and Acts of Edmund Grindal*, New York: Burt Franklin, 1974

Tittler, Robert. 'Harmony in the Metropolis: Writings on Medieval and Tudor London and Westminster', *Journal of British Studies* 31: 2 (1992): 187–91

Trevor-Roper, H.R. 'John Stow', *Transactions of the London and Middlesex Archaeological Society* 26 (1975): 337–42

Underdown, David. *Revel, Riot and Rebellion: Popular Politics and Culture in England, 1603–1660*, Oxford: Clarendon Press, 1985

Van Dorsten, Jan, et al., eds. *Sir Philip Sidney: 1586 and the Creation of a Legend*, Leiden: J. Brill, 1986

Wall, Alison. 'An Account of the Essex Revolt, February 1601', *Bulletin of the Institute of Historical Research* 54 (1981): 131–3

Wallace, Malcolm William. *The Life of Sir Philip Sidney*, Cambridge: Cambridge University Press, 1915

Wallace, Robert. *Antitrinitarian Biography*, 3 vols., London, 1850

Watt, Tessa. *Cheap Print and Popular Piety, 1550–1640*, Cambridge: Cambridge University Press, 1991

Weinreb, Ben, and Hibbert, Christopher. *The London Encyclopaedia*, 2nd edn., London: Papermac, 1993

Wernham, R.B. *Before the Armada: The Growth of English Foreign Policy, 1485–1588*, London: Jonathan Cape, 1966

——. *The Making of Elizabethan Foreign Policy, 1558–1603*, Berkeley, CA: University of California Press, 1980

——. *After the Armada: Elizabethan England and the Struggle for Western Europe, 1588–1595*, Oxford: Clarendon Press, 1984

——. *The Return of the Armadas: The Last Years of the Elizabethan War against Spain, 1598–1603*, Oxford: Clarendon Press, 1994

White, B.R. *The English Separatist Tradition*, Oxford: Clarendon Press, 1971

Whiting, Robert. *The Blind Devotion of the People: Popular Religion and the English Reformation*, Cambridge: Cambridge University Press, 1989

Wiatt, William H. 'The Lost History of Wyatt's Rebellion', *Renaissance News* 15 (1962): 128–33

Willan, T.S. *The Early History of the Russia Company, 1553-1603*, Manchester: Manchester University Press, 1956

Williams, Glanmor. *The General and Common Sort of People, 1540–1640*, Exeter: Exeter University, 1977

Williams, Neville. *Thomas Howard Fourth Duke of Norfolk*, London: Barrie and Rockliff, 1964

Williams, Penry. *The Later Tudors: England 1547–1603*, Oxford: Clarendon Press, 1995

Willson, D.H. *King James VI and I*, New York: Oxford University Press, 1967

Wilson, Charles. *Queen Elizabeth and the Revolt of the Netherlands*, London: Macmillan, 1970

Wolf, Lucien. 'Jews in Elizabethan England', *Transactions of the Jewish Historical Association* 11 (1928): 1–91

Woolf, D.R. 'Genre into Artifact: The Decline of the English Chronicle in the Sixteenth Century', *Sixteenth Century Journal* 19:3 (1988): 321–54

——. *The Idea of History in Early Stuart England*, Toronto: University of Toronto Press, 1990

——. 'Historical Thought', in R.H. Fritze et al., eds., *Historical Dictionary of Tudor England, 1485–1603*, New York: Greenwood Press, 1991: 240–4

——. 'A Feminine Past? Gender, Genre, and Historical Knowledge in England, 1500–1800', *American Historical Review* 102: 3 (June 1997): 645–79

Wright, C.J., ed. *Sir Robert Cotton as Collector*, London: British Library, 1997

Wright, Louis B. *Middle-Class Culture in Elizabethan England*, Chapel Hill: University of North Carolina Press, 1935

Zagorin, Perez. *Rebels and Rulers, 1500–1660*, 2 vols., Cambridge: Cambridge University Press, 1982

INDEX